FLOYD CLYMER'S MOTORCYCLIST'S LIBRARY

The Book of the
A.J.S.

A RELIABLE GUIDE FOR OWNERS OF A.J.S. MOTOR-CYCLES (COVERS SINGLE- AND TWIN-CYLINDER MODELS FROM 1932 ONWARDS)

BY

W. C. HAYCRAFT, F.R.S.A.

ANNOUNCEMENT

By special arrangement with the original publishers of this book, Sir Isaac Pitman & Son, Ltd., of London, England, we have secured the exclusive publishing rights for this book, as well as all others in THE MOTORCYCLIST'S LIBRARY.

Included in THE MOTORCYCLIST'S LIBRARY are complete instruction manuals covering the care and operation of respective motorcycles and engines; valuable data on speed tuning, and thrilling accounts of motorcycle race events. See listing of available titles elsewhere in this edition.

We consider it a privilege to be able to offer so many fine titles to our customers.

FLOYD CLYMER
Publisher of Books Pertaining to Automobiles and Motorcycles

2125 W. PICO ST.   LOS ANGELES 6, CALIF.

INTRODUCTION

Welcome to the world of digital publishing ~ the book you now hold in your hand, while unchanged from the original edition, was printed using the latest state of the art digital technology. The advent of print-on-demand has forever changed the publishing process, never has information been so accessible and it is our hope that this book serves your informational needs for years to come. If this is your first exposure to digital publishing, we hope that you are pleased with the results. Many more titles of interest to the classic automobile and motorcycle enthusiast, collector and restorer are available via our website at www.VelocePress.com. We hope that you find this title as interesting as we do.

NOTE FROM THE PUBLISHER

The information presented is true and complete to the best of our knowledge. All recommendations are made without any guarantees on the part of the author or the publisher, who also disclaim all liability incurred with the use of this information.

TRADEMARKS

We recognize that some words, model names and designations, for example, mentioned herein are the property of the trademark holder. We use them for identification purposes only. This is not an official publication.

INFORMATION ON THE USE OF THIS PUBLICATION

This manual is an invaluable resource for the classic motorcycle enthusiast and a "must have" for owners interested in performing their own maintenance. However, in today's information age we are constantly subject to changes in common practice, new technology, availability of improved materials and increased awareness of chemical toxicity. As such, it is advised that the user consult with an experienced professional prior to undertaking any procedure described herein. While every care has been taken to ensure correctness of information, it is obviously not possible to guarantee complete freedom from errors or omissions or to accept liability arising from such errors or omissions. Therefore, any individual that uses the information contained within, or elects to perform or participate in do-it-yourself repairs or modifications acknowledges that there is a risk factor involved and that the publisher or its associates cannot be held responsible for personal injury or property damage resulting from the use of the information or the outcome of such procedures.

WARNING!

One final word of advice, this publication is intended to be used as a reference guide, and when in doubt the reader should consult with a qualified technician.

PREFACE
TO THE SIXTH EDITION

THIS completely new edition of *The Book of the A.J.S.* covers *fully* the range of post-war A.J.S. models, and it also retains complete instructions applicable to the maintenance and overhaul of 1932-9 machines. To avoid unnecessarily confusing the reader, Chapters VI and VII have been added, dealing with the lubrication and overhaul respectively of the 1945-8 range. This range, though small in quantity, is of the very highest quality. Later on, the range may be appreciably enlarged. At present it comprises two O.H.V. singles, Models 16M and 18, of 350 c.c. and 500 c.c. respectively. These machines are the product of a steady process of evolution dating back to 1909, when A.J.S. machines were first introduced to the public.

It has been the consistent policy of the A.J.S. Co. to develop their machines and engines gradually, and to perfect their technical improvements through participation in racing *and* trials events.

The post-war models have a very lively push-rod type O.H.V. engine which responds to the twist-grip in a fascinating manner. The "Teledraulic" front forks (developed during the war and appreciated by thousands of Service riders) ensure comfort and safety at all speeds.

The A.J.S. range of models undoubtedly merits most careful consideration by all intending purchasers. Those who want snappy performance plus good looks should write to A.J.S. Motor Cycles, of Plumstead Road, London, S.E.18, for a copy of their latest catalogue. A.J.S. prices are reasonable, and every machine has electric lighting and compensated voltage control.

The A.J.S. factory is the largest in the world devoted exclusively to the production of motor-cycles. Standards of acceptance in the inspection department are very high and rigidly insisted upon. A visit to the factory is quite an education. As hitherto, the primary object of this handbook is to assist the A.J.S. rider in maintaining his investment at the highest efficiency and market value.

In this connection I would thank A.J.S. Motor Cycles for their invaluable assistance in supplying data and for kindly permitting numerous illustrations to be reproduced.

W. C. H.

CONTENTS

CHAP.		PAGE
I.	1945–8 A.J.S. MODELS	1
II.	THE AMAL CARBURETTOR	10
III.	ALL ABOUT LUBRICATION (1932–9)	21
IV.	OVERHAULING (1932–9)	37
V.	CARE OF LIGHTING EQUIPMENT	86
VI.	ALL ABOUT LUBRICATION (1945–8)	104
VII.	OVERHAULING (1945–8)	117
	INDEX	159

CHAPTER I

1945–8 A.J.S. MODELS

BOTH the attractive and sporty 1945–8 A.J.S. Models 16M and 18 (see Fig. 2) have an identical specification, except that the cubic capacity of the Model 16M engine is 347 c.c., whereas on Model 18 it is 498 c.c. The 1947 models remain unchanged except for some detail improvements (see also page 9).

1948 Improvements. Further attention has been given by Associated Motor Cycles, Ltd., to cleaning up their fast standard models and to perfecting their road holding qualities and stability. A steering damper is *not* provided as camouflage! Since 1947, slight, but important, alterations have been made to the steering head angle, the rake, and the trail, the cumulative effect of which is most beneficial. The "Teledraulic" front forks have been simplified internally.

Other improvements incorporated on A.J.S. models include: a more robust oil pump plunger and guide screw; a neater petrol

FIG. 1. NEAT DESIGN—MOUNTING OF HANDLEBARS, HEADLAMP, AND SPEEDOMETER
On both 1948 models an aluminium alloy head lug is provided. This includes a four-stud fixing for the adjustable handlebars.

pipe; an improved exhaust pipe (500 c.c.); larger chromidium brake drums with new shoe adjustment, and a twin-screw anchorage for the front brake cover plate; larger section (3·50 × 19) rear tyres; an improved prop stand; a saddle spring mounting with vertically disposed screws, providing an adjustment for angle; and last, but not least, a new type of steering head lug and fixing for the handlebars. Below is an outline of the general specification.

GENERAL SPECIFICATION (MODELS 16M AND 18)

The Push-rod O.H.V. Engine. The bore and stroke are 69 mm. (82·5 mm. on Model 18) and 93 mm. respectively. A compression ratio of 6·3 to 1, or 5·97 to 1 (Model 18) is used. With the compression plate removed, the C.R. of 5·97 to 1 can be increased to 7·24 to 1. The lubrication system is of the full dry sump type, incorporating a duplex plunger pump of large capacity, which pressure feeds engine oil to the cylinder walls, big-end bearing, main shaft and camshaft bearings, and the rocker-box. The oil

FIG. 2. FAST AND CLEAN-LOOKING—THE 1948 A.J.S.
The 350 c.c. and 500 c.c. Models 16M and 18 are of identical appearance. Two special competition models (350 c.c. and 500 c.c.) are also available. These have a short wheel base and high ground clearance.

is kept clean by a large fabric type filter incorporated in the oil tank.

A well-protected chain-driven Lucas magneto (in front of the engine) supplies the current for the sparking plug, and a two-lever semi-automatic down-draught Amal carburettor is responsible for carburation. Other prominent features of a robust engine include: a triple-row roller big-end bearing; a large diameter two-piece crankpin; a "Lo-ex" alloy piston, with three rings; and a double camshaft timing gear which is flood-lubricated.

Transmission Details. Four carefully chosen gear ratios are provided by a pivot-mounted heavyweight Burman gearbox. The gearbox has foot control and a multi-plate clutch. An engine shaft shock-absorber eliminates snatch. An oil-bath chain case encloses the clutch, shock-absorber, and primary chain. The secondary chain is protected by a chain guard. Primary and secondary chain dimensions are $\frac{1}{2}$ in. × ·305 in. and $\frac{5}{8}$ in. × ·308 in. respectively.

Frame and Forks. The A.J.S. engine is neatly installed in a tough cradle frame of the duplex type. Good road holding and extreme comfort are ensured by the combination of this frame and the patented "Teledraulic" front forks, which have hydraulic damping and require negligible attention. The 1948 "Teledraulic" forks are simpler than the 1947 type, and a light alloy shuttle is provided above the piston in each fork leg.

Fuel and Oil Tanks. Separate tanks are provided. The capacity of the fuel and oil tanks is 3 gal. and 3 pt. respectively.

Miscellaneous Features. Included in a luxury specification are: a Lycett spring-seat saddle (adjustable); semi-sports adjustable handlebars; smooth but very powerful internal expanding brakes having finger adjustment; 3·25 × 19 tyres (3·5 × 19, rear, 1948); mudguards adequate for riding in dirty weather, with the rear portion of the rear guard detachable; Lucas dynamo lighting equipment, with compensated voltage control; an illuminated trip type speedometer (extra); toe-operated prop stand, in addition to an easy-lift spring-up rear stand and tubular front stand. All machines are stove-enamelled (three coats) in durable glossy black (with gold lining) on bonderizing. Extras: speedometer, mudguard pillion seat, folding pillion footrests, luggage carrier.

THE A.J.S. CONTROLS

Lay-out on Models 16M and 18. A plan view of the control lay-out on the 1945–8 350 c.c. and 500 c.c. A.J.S. models is shown in Fig. 3. It is assumed that the reader is familiar with the function of motor-cycle controls and has at least an elementary knowledge of the four-stroke engine, including carburation and ignition. An understanding of basic principles is essential to the intelligent handling of any motor-cycle, but basic principles are beyond the scope of this handbook.

Attention is drawn to a few important points concerning the A.J.S. controls. All controls operate by *inward* movement (i.e. movement towards the rider). The air lever and ignition control should normally be kept fully open and fully advanced respectively, except for starting up. It is, however, permissible to retard the ignition control slightly when the engine tends to pink under severe load, such as is imposed during a stiff hill climb. But such retarding should only be temporary, and at all times full use must be made of the very efficient four-speed gearbox provided.

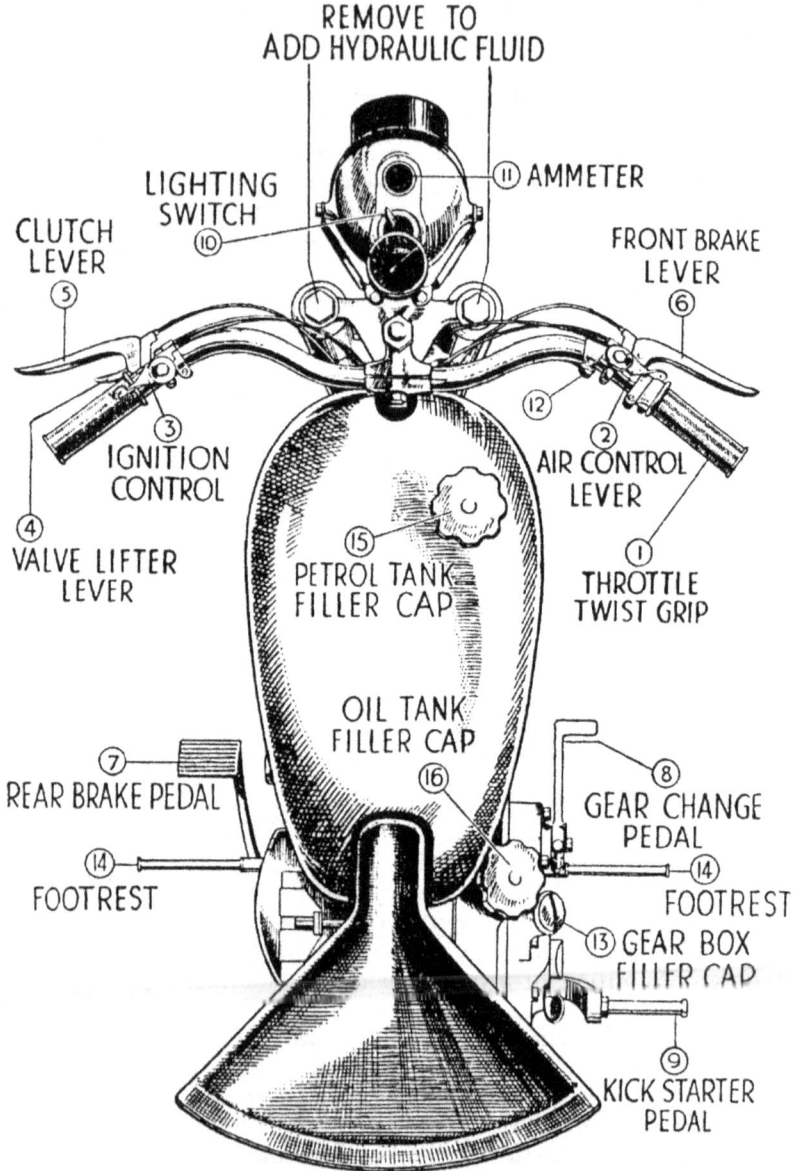

Fig. 3. Arrangement of Controls on All 1945–8 A.J.S. Models
This plan view shows all controls except the dipping switch, used to obtain a "dipped" beam when the lighting switch at the back of the headlamp is in the "H" position. The dipping switch is adjacent to the ignition control.

The exhaust valve lifter must be used solely for starting up and for stopping (where the throttle stop is adjusted to give a tickover with the throttle closed).

Gear changing is effected by means of a gear-change pedal on the off-side, and a "neutral" indicator is provided. The indicator shows at a glance the position of the foot control, as one pointer is attached to the spindle of the gear-change pedal and the other is rigidly fixed to the cover of the kick-starter casing. This will be clearly understood by reference to Fig. 4. The two pointers are in alignment only when the gear-change pedal is in the "neutral" position. It should be particularly noted that *the pedal always returns to the horizontal position* after a gear change has been made. To make an upward gear change, the pedal is pressed downwards with the toe, and to make a downward change (i.e. to a lower gear) the pedal is raised with the instep of the foot. All A.J.S. controls are adjustable for operation and position. As regards position, it is unlikely that any adjustment will be called for, except perhaps in the case of the rear brake pedal and the gear-change pedal.

If you are inexperienced with the A.J.S. control lay-out and have just acquired an A.J.S., you are advised before doing anything else to sit astride the saddle, "twiddle" the levers, and obtain a clear mental picture of the exact operation of all the controls, paying special regard to the procedure for gear changing and stopping. Failure to do this on the part of a novice can have the most serious consequences due to "panicking" in an emergency on the first solo trip.

Starting Up. Check that the oil and fuel tanks are properly replenished. The former is dealt with on page 106. With regard to fuel replenishment, the author advises the use of a No. 1 grade of petrol. Anti-knocking fuels containing "Lead" have their merits, but tend to make the rider lazy in respect of the gearbox, a habit which is, to say the least, detrimental to the engine and transmission.

Turn on the petrol by pushing the hexagon knob marked "PUSH ON" towards the body of the petrol tap. Two petrol taps are provided beneath the rear end of the fuel tank, and when an A.J.S. is left standing for more than a few minutes, *both* taps must be shut. It is advisable to use only the petrol tap situated on the off-side, as this enables the other tap to be used for obtaining a reserve supply. If the reserve tap has to be opened, replenish the fuel tank immediately afterwards and close the reserve tap.

Check that the gear-change pedal is in "Neutral" (see Fig. 4) and proceed to adjust the engine controls for starting. Open the throttle slightly by turning the twist-grip inwards about one-sixth of its total movement. Close the air lever completely. Advance the ignition control fully and then retard it about two-fifths of its maximum movement by pushing it outwards. Fill the float chamber of the carburettor completely by momentarily depressing the plunger on the top of the chamber.

If the engine is *cold*, turn it over several times with the kick-starter pedal, so as to free the engine. While this is being done, the exhaust valve lifter should be kept raised. Normally it should be sufficient to operate the kick-starter pedal *three* times.

Turn the engine over with the kick-starter until compression is felt. Next raise the exhaust valve lifter to ease the piston just over compression. Permit the kick-starter pedal to return almost to its normal position, and (with the exhaust valve closed) give it a long swinging kick.

As soon as the engine starts up, advance the ignition lever and open the air lever to give a nice steady tick-over. There should be no "hunting" or unevenness. Now adjust the throttle until the engine is running at a moderate speed, and warm up the engine so as to circulate the oil and heat it to an efficient running temperature. Be careful not to race the engine from cold or to allow it to tick-over too slowly. Both are bad for it. Also never forget that the engine is of the air-cooled type. Check the oil circulation (see page 107) before moving off.

Hints on Use of Kick-starter. It is important never to employ much force on the kick-starter until the ratchet pinion and quadrant are in full engagement. Failure to observe this precaution causes rapid wear of the quadrant teeth, and may result in damage being caused. Initial operation of the kick-starter from its normal position should be gentle and gradual until full engagement of the gear and quadrant teeth is actually *felt*. Thereafter more, but not excessive, force may be used.

" Flooding " the Carburettor. It is quite unnecessary and inadvisable to "flood" the carburettor to such an extent that petrol drips from the base of the mixing chamber and/or float chamber. With a down-draught carburettor, this entails a risk of neat petrol entering the cylinder and breaking down the vital oil film. An appreciable risk of fire is also incurred in the event of the engine back-firing at a critical moment.

Should ignition of the petrol in the carburettor accidentally occur, immediately turn off the petrol tap, open the throttle wide, and kick the engine over quickly with the exhaust valve lifter raised. Fuel in the carburettor will then be quickly sucked into the engine combustion chamber and discharged into the exhaust system.

Advice on Gear Changing. On a new A.J.S. slight difficulty is sometimes experienced in engaging first gear, but this trouble soon disappears automatically. If proper engagement is not obtained at the first attempt, wait a few seconds before making another attempt by operating the clutch lever and raising the gear-change pedal with the instep from "neutral" into first gear position. (See Fig. 4.)

To move off after engaging first gear, gradually release the clutch lever and, as the machine gathers momentum, progressively increase the throttle opening so as to take up the load and

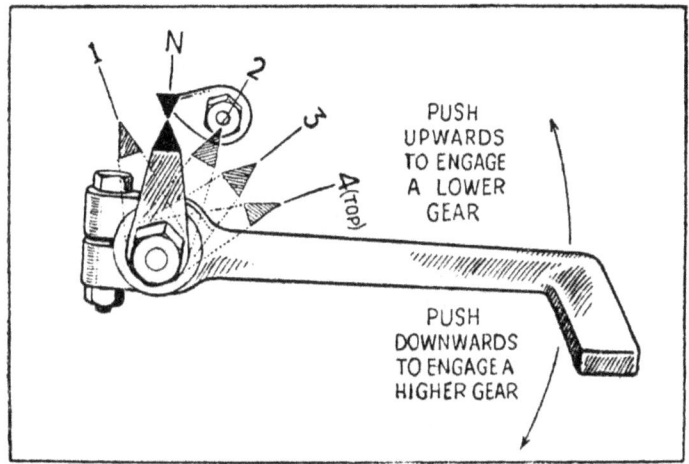

FIG. 4. POSITIONS OF FOOT GEAR-CHANGE INDICATOR.
This diagram clearly shows the five positions of the indicator attached to the spindle of the gear-change pedal. To verify that the gear is in "neutral," it is only necessary to check that the moving indicator is in alignment with the fixed indicator shown at N.

still further increase the speed. When sufficient speed has been attained, again raise the clutch lever, close the throttle slightly (to compensate for the smaller gear ratio), depress the foot gear-change pedal with the toe into second gear position (see Fig. 4), and then throttle up to take up the load and increase the speed of the machine. The pedal must always be depressed to the full extent of its travel, and all movement must be decisive and firm, but never vicious. As soon as a gear change has been effected, remove the foot from the pedal, otherwise it will not return to its original position to enable another gear to be engaged. Third and fourth gears can be engaged in a similar manner to second gear.

When changing down into a lower gear, it is necessary to raise the clutch and open the throttle slightly (to compensate for the bigger gear ratio), and then raise the foot gear-change pedal with the instep fully to obtain the desired gear. To obtain silent gear changing, it is important to operate the clutch, throttle, and gear-change pedal in one simultaneous action. Experienced riders ease the clutch only *slightly* when making a gear change, but full raising of the clutch is advised until a rider becomes proficient through experience. Always remember that a rider is largely judged by others by the manner in which he changes gear. Good gear changing is, in fact, the hall-mark of a good rider.

Stopping the Machine. For the benefit of novices, the following instructions are included. To make a normal stop on the road, close the throttle, raise the clutch lever, progressively and simultaneously apply the front and rear brakes, place the foot gear-change pedal in "neutral," and stop the engine by raising the exhaust valve lifter. If you stop for a cup of coffee at a snack bar, park your A.J.S. where you can *see* it, and turn off the petrol to avoid the consequences of the carburettor "flooding." (See page 6.)

In connection with braking, it should be noted that it is the best procedure always to use *both* brakes, though many riders insist on reserving the rear brake for use only in emergencies. By using both brakes, wear is minimized and there is less tendency for skidding to occur. Cultivate the habit of driving on the throttle and using the brakes as little and seldom as possible. Bad riders can always be seen jumping on the brakes, and this accounts for rapid wear of the tyres and transmission, and nerves!

If it is desired to stop the engine, as apart from the machine, close the throttle, raise the exhaust valve lifter, and keep the valve lifter raised until life is extinct! Never use the valve lifter for slowing up on the road, and this applies with emphasis to slipping the clutch. Only those of low grade mentality drive in this manner!

Checking Oil Circulation. Check the oil circulation as described on page 107 whenever you are about to set forth on a run.

Running-in is Vital. If you are the proud owner of a new A.J.S., and wish for continuous good performance plus long life, you *must* obey certain recognized running-in instructions which are absolutely vital. The running-in period proper lasts for about 500 miles. During this period, observe the following points—

(*a*) On no account use *full* throttle.

(*b*) *Never* allow the engine to labour, but change to a lower gear in good time.

(*c*) Be content with very moderate throttle openings both on the road and when idling.

(*d*) Do not permit the engine to stand running idle without proper air-cooling for more than a few minutes.

(*e*) Avoid running the engine fast in the lower gears.

(*f*) In first gear, do not exceed about 10 m.p.h.; in second, about 15 m.p.h.; in third, about 25 m.p.h.; and in fourth, about 30 m.p.h.

(g) Pay special regard to lubrication. (See Chapter VI.)

(h) After covering 100-150 miles (by which time some bedding-down occurs), check the adjustment of the tappets, contact-breaker, brakes, wheel bearings, chain, and steering head, as described in the appropriate paragraphs of Chapter VII.

When the running-in period proper has been exceeded, it is permissible to step up the speed gradually, but it is advisable to refrain from opening the throttle fully either on the level or

(*From* "*The Motor Cycle*")
Fig. 5. A.J.S. Fitted with Siddaway Spring Heel

on gradients until approximately 2000 miles have been covered.

A Super 350 c.c. Racing A.J.S. The A.M.C. factory have recently designed and put into limited production a genuine racing job for private owners. This fast and most accessible machine has a chain-driven overhead-camshaft engine, and (thanks to extensive use of light alloys) has a very high power/weight ratio. It looks a real winner!

Interesting Spring Heel Conversion Set. For only £15 you can (with only a few spanners and no frame alteration) convert your Model 16M or Model 18 into a machine with rear wheel springing. Fig. 5 shows the Siddaway spring heel with hydraulic damping. The conversion set is obtainable from the Grantham Motor Cycle Depot, of 5 Chapel Street, Grantham.

CHAPTER II

THE AMAL CARBURETTOR

SATISFACTORY engine performance naturally depends to a great extent on correct carburation. All A.J.S. models are sent out from the works with the carburettors carefully tuned.

How It Works. The carburettor fitted to all except the earlier O.H.C. engines is of the two-lever needle jet type, the mixture at slow or idling speeds being controlled by a readily adjustable pilot jet, whilst at higher speeds the mixture is controlled by means of a needle attached to the throttle slide and working in a restriction jet. The two-lever control must not be confused with the type of control that was used a considerable time ago on the two-lever carburettor, in which it was necessary constantly to adjust the air lever in accordance with the conditions under which the machine was running. This carburettor is for all practical purposes automatic, the air lever being closed only to facilitate starting. At all other times it should be fully opened. The carburettor slides are chromium plated to provide hard wearing surfaces. The air slide is operated by a trigger or lever type handlebar control and the throttle by a twist-grip.

In connection with the float chamber of the Amal it should be pointed out that alteration in the float position can only have detrimental results.

Referring to the sectional view (Fig. 6) illustrating the construction, A is the carburettor body or mixing chamber, the upper part of which has a throttle valve B, with taper needle C attached by the needle clip. The throttle valve regulates the quantity of mixture supplied to the engine. Passing through the throttle valve is the air valve D, independently operated and serving the purpose of obstructing the main air passage for starting and mixture regulation. Fixed to the underside of the mixing chamber by the union nut E is the jet block F, and interposed between them is a fibre washer to ensure a petrol-tight joint. On the upper part of the block is the jet block barrel H, forming a clean through-way. Integral with the jet block is the pilot jet J, supplied through the passage K. The adjustable pilot air intake L communicates with a chamber, from which issues the pilot outlet M and the by-pass N. A throttle stop (see Fig. 6A) is provided on the mixing chamber, by which the position of the throttle valve for tick-over is regulated independently of the cable adjustment. The needle jet O is screwed in the underside of the jet block, and carries at its bottom end the main jet P. Both these jets are removable when the jet plug Q, which bolts the mixing chamber and the float chamber together, is removed. The float chamber, which has bottom feed, consists of a cup R

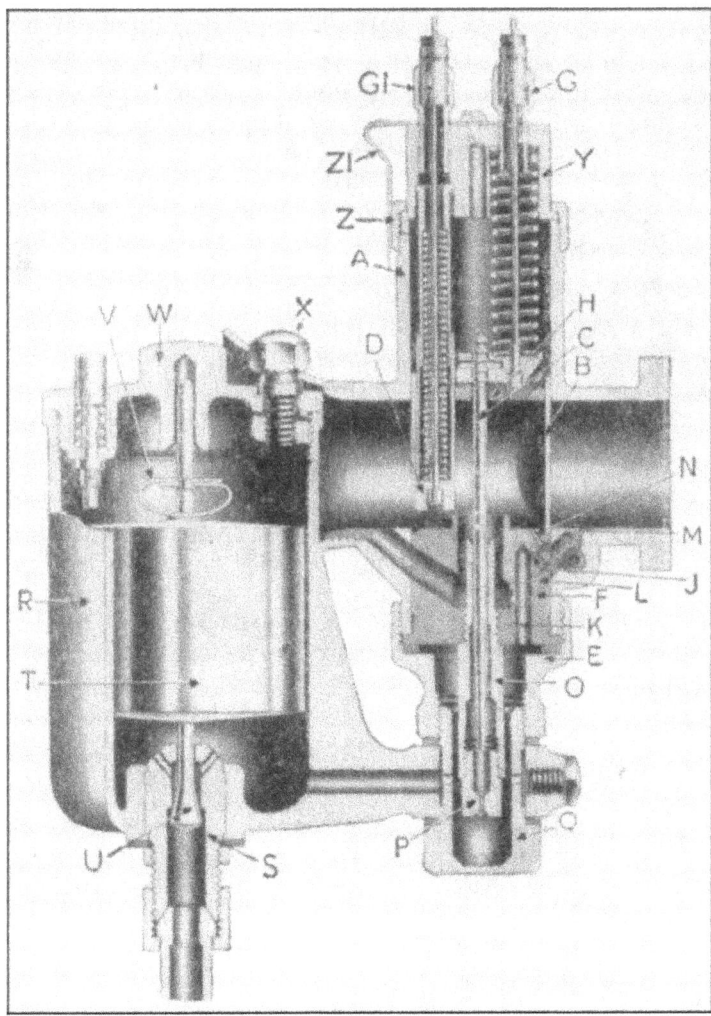

Fig. 6. Sectional View of Amal Needle-jet Two-lever Carburettor

supplied with petrol by union S. It contains the float T and the needle valve U attached by the clip V. The float chamber cover W has a lock screw X for security.

The petrol tap having been turned on, petrol will flow past the needle valve U until the quantity of petrol in the chamber R is sufficient to raise the float *T*, when the needle valve *U* will prevent a further supply entering the float chamber until some in the chamber has already been used up by the engine. The float chamber having filled to its correct level, the fuel passes along the passages through the diagonal holes in the jet plug *Q*, when it will be in communication with the main jet *P* and the pilot feed hole *K*; the level in these jets being, obviously, the same as that maintained in the float chamber.

Imagine the throttle valve *B* very slightly open. As the piston descends, a partial vacuum is created in the carburettor, causing a rush of air through the pilot air hole *L* and drawing fuel from the pilot jet *J*. The mixture of air and fuel is admitted to the engine through the pilot outlet *M*. The quantity of mixture capable of being passed by the pilot outlet *M* is insufficient to run the engine. This mixture also carries excess of fuel. Consequently, before a combustible mixture is admitted, throttle valve *B* must be slightly raised, admitting a further supply of air from the main air intake. The farther the throttle valve is opened, the less will be the depression on the outlet *M*, but, in turn, a higher depression will be created on the by-pass *N*, and the pilot mixture will flow from this passage as well as from the outlet *M*. The mixture supplied by the pilot and by-pass system is supplemented at about one-eighth throttle by fuel from the main jet *P*, the throttle valve cut-away determining the mixture strength from here to one-quarter throttle. Proceeding up the throttle range, mixture control by the needle position occurs from one-quarter to three-quarters throttle, and from this point the main jet is the only regulation.

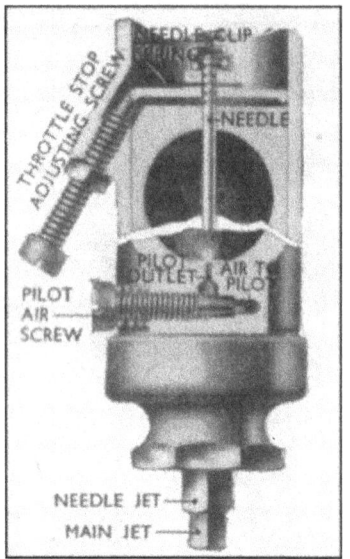

FIG. 6A. THROTTLE STOP AND PILOT AIR SCREW

The air valve *D*, which is cable-operated on the two-lever carburettor, has the effect of obstructing the main through-way and, in consequence, increasing the depression on the main jet, enriching the mixture. Two cable adjusters, *G*, *G1*, are provided.

The Throttle Stop Screw. The throttle stop adjusting screw (shown in Fig. 6A) is normally adjusted so as to prop the throttle slide open sufficiently to enable the engine to tick-over when the throttle twist-grip is completely closed.

The Pilot Air Screw. This controls the suction imposed on the pilot jet by metering the volume of air which mixes with the fuel. It controls the strength of the mixture for "idling" and also for initial throttle openings. On A.J.S. machines the air for the pilot jet is admitted externally.

The Main Jet. This regulates the fuel supply at throttle openings exceeding three-quarters full open. At smaller openings of the throttle, the fuel supplied passes through the main jet, but the amount is decreased due to the needle in the needle jet having a metering effect. The main jet is screwed into the needle jet and can readily be detached after removing the jet plug shown at Q in Fig. 6. Referring to Fig. 6A, to remove the main jet, hold the needle jet with one spanner, and with another unscrew the main jet.

Each Amal main jet is numbered and calibrated so that its precise discharge is known. It thus follows that any two main jets having the same number are identical in all respects. The larger the jet, the higher is its number. If a larger size jet is needed, on no account attempt to ream the existing jet, but obtain a new one of larger size.

The Needle and Needle Jet. The needle is attached to and moves with the throttle slide. Being tapered, it therefore permits more or less fuel to pass through the needle jet as the throttle is opened or closed respectively. This applies throughout the range of throttle openings, except at nearly full throttle and when "idling." The needle jet is of a specified size, and normally it should not be changed except when going over to alcohol fuels.

As may be seen in Fig. 6A, the position of the taper needle relative to the throttle opening can be adjusted according to the mixture required by securing the needle to the throttle with the needle spring clip in a particular groove, several of which are provided. Position No. 3, for example, means the third groove *from the top*. At throttle openings from one-quarter to three-quarters open, raising the needle enriches the mixture, while lowering the needle weakens it.

Throttle Valve Cut-away. The throttle on the atmospheric side is cut-away, and this affects the depression on the main fuel supply. The cut-away provides a means of tuning between the pilot and needle jet range of throttle opening. The actual amount of cut-away is denoted by a number marked on the throttle slide. Thus 6/4 means a throttle type 6 with a No. 4 cut-away. A throttle with a larger cut-away (say, 6/5) weakens the mixture. Conversely, a smaller cut-away enriches the mixture.

Tuning the Amal Carburettor. The standard setting is usually entirely satisfactory, but better results and more power may sometimes be obtained by the use of a slightly larger main jet or by making other adjustments. Various sized jets are obtainable from A.J.S. spare parts stockists, or from Amal, Ltd., of Holford Works, Perry Barr, Birmingham, 20.

Should the setting of this instrument not give entire satisfaction for particular requirements, there are four separate ways of rectifying matters as given herewith, and the adjustments should be made in this order: (a) Main jet (¾ to full throttle); (b) pilot air adjustment (closed to ⅛ throttle); (c) throttle valve cut-away on

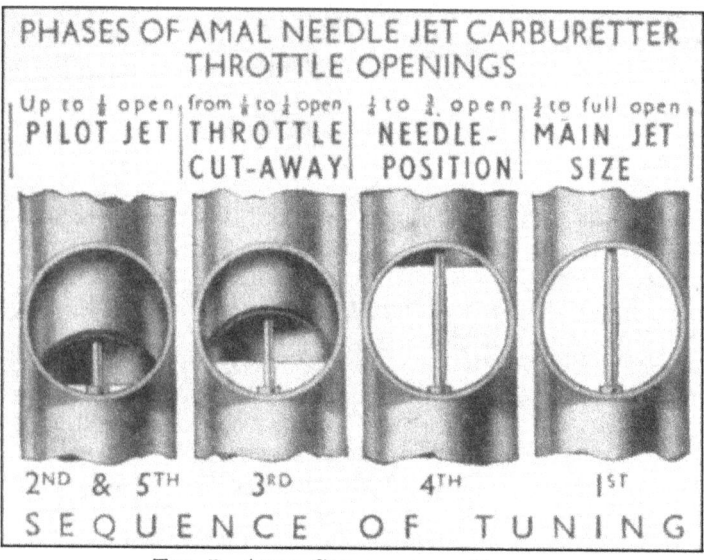

Fig. 7. Amal Carburettor Tuning.

the air intake side (⅛ to ¼ throttle); and (d) needle position (¼ to ¾ throttle). The diagram (Fig. 7) clearly indicates the part of the throttle range over which each adjustment is effective.

The Amal carburettor is throughout the throttle range entirely automatic, and the air lever should be kept wide open, except for starting and until the engine has warmed up properly. It is assumed that normal petrol is used for tuning, which should be done in the sequence described below. Throttle openings to be used in the five tuning operations are those indicated in Fig. 7. By following these tuning instructions (recommended by Amal. Ltd.) you will be assured of obtaining the most satisfactory performance with maximum economy of fuel. For tuning purposes it is advisable to get your A.J.S. started up on a quiet road having a slight up gradient, so as to impose a small load on the engine.

First Operation. Checking Size of Main Jet. Accelerate up to full throttle and carefully note the response of the engine to twist-grip action. Should power output appear better with the air lever very slightly closed or with the throttle not completely open, this indicates that the main jet is too small, and the next larger size should be tried. Similarly, if there is a tendency for the engine to run "heavily" on full throttle, this denotes that the main jet is too large and the next smaller size should be experimented with.

If tuning for speed, be careful to choose a main jet of size sufficient to maintain the engine in a cool condition. Make a run at high speed, pull up and stop the engine immediately. Remove the sparking plug and closely inspect it. If the business end of the plug is sooty, the mixture is too rich. Should the body be dry grey in colour, the mixture is on the weak side, and a larger size jet is required. With a properly proportioned mixture, the plug body should have a bright black appearance. Also, when running, observe the sound of the exhaust; it should be crisp and have no trace of "woolliness." Black smoke at the exhaust shows that the mixture is much too rich.

Second Operation. Pilot Jet Adjustment. Allow the engine to idle at an excessive speed, with the twist-grip closed and the throttle slide abutting the throttle stop screw. The ignition lever should be set to obtain the best slow running.

Loosen the nut on the throttle stop adjusting screw, and unscrew the latter until the engine slows up and begins to stall. Then screw the pilot air screw in or out as required to enable the engine to run regularly and faster.

Next, gently lower the throttle stop screw until the engine again begins to falter. Now lock the throttle stop adjusting screw with the lock-nut and commence to readjust the pilot air screw to obtain the optimum slow running. Should this second adjustment cause the engine to tick-over at an excessive speed, repeat the adjustment a third time. When perfect slow running has been obtained, tighten the lock-nut on the throttle stop screw without disturbing the position of the screw.

Third Operation. The Throttle Cut-away. Should appreciable spitting-back at the carburettor occur on accelerating from rest with the engine idling, stop the machine and slightly enrich the mixture by screwing the pilot air screw in approximately *half a turn*. If this does not effect the desired result, screw it back to its former position and fit a throttle slide having a smaller cut-away.

If there is no spitting-back, but the engine jerks under load, this shows an over rich mixture, and the remedy is to fit a throttle slide with larger cut-away, or else to lower the throttle needle.

Fourth Operation. Position of Needle. The tapered needle influences a wide range of throttle openings and affects acceleration.

Check performance with the needle in as low a position as possible, i.e. with the clip in the groove nearest the end of the needle. If acceleration of your A.J.S. declines, and improves by partially closing the air lever, raise the position of the needle by two grooves. If a marked improvement is thereby obtained, try the effect of lowering the needle by one groove, and leave it in the position where the best performance is obtained.

It should be noted that if the mixture is still excessively rich with the needle clip in groove No. 1 (nearest the end), wear of the needle jet has probably occurred and renewal of the jet is called for. The needle itself is of hard steel and wear does not take place, even after a big mileage.

Fifth Operation. Check over the idling adjustment and make any final small adjustment which is required to obtain perfectly smooth tick-over, neither too fast nor too slow.

Obstruction in Pilot Jet. If the pilot jet adjustment does not obtain the desired results and the engine will not idle nicely with the throttle almost closed, the air lever three-quarters open, and the ignition lever about two-thirds advanced, it is possible that the pilot jet is obstructed. The jet passage, actually a duct drilled in the jet block, is very small and can easily become choked.

To gain access to the pilot jet, remove the jet plug and the float chamber (see Fig. 6), and then detach the jet block by pushing it out of the mixing chamber. The pilot jet can then be cleared by means of a fine strand of wire.

Adjustment of A.J.S. Twist-grip. Adjustment should be such that the grip is free and easy to twist, but "stays put." The spring tension on the twist-grip rotating sleeve is regulated by a screw incorporated in one-half of the twist-grip body. To increase the tension, loosen the lock-nut and screw the screw into the body as required.

It is possible to move the complete twist-grip on the handlebars by slackening the two screws which clamp it in position. The best position of the twist-grip is that which gives the cleanest and straightest path to the throttle cable between the handlebars and the under side of the petrol tank. Should a new cable have to be fitted, do not forget to grease it with a graphite lubricant.

High Fuel Consumption. If in spite of careful checking up on the tuning of the carburettor, high fuel consumption continues, it is likely that one or more of the under-mentioned causes is responsible for wastage of precious fuel. Late ignition timing will eat into your petrol supplies quickly. The same applies to poor engine compression due to badly fitting piston rings or valves. Also take into consideration the question of flooding due to a faulty float, air leakage at the joint between the carburettor and engine, weak valve springs, insufficient taper needle extension, etc.

STANDARD AMAL CARBURETTOR SETTINGS FOR 1935 A.J.S. MODELS
(APPLICABLE ALSO TO CORRESPONDING 1936-7 MODELS)

Model	Carburettor	Main Jet	Needle Jet In.	Needle Position	Throttle Valve
35/5	5/148	100	·1065	4	5/4
35/4, 35/14	6/165	130	·1065	2	6/4
35/9	76/004	150	·1065	3	6/4
35/2	76/012	140	·1065	2	6/3
35/12, 35/22	75/154	120	·1065	2	5/3
35/16, 35/26	75/154	150	·1065	3	6/4
35/18	89/148	180	·1065	2	29/4
35/6 (350 O.H.V.)	76/014	150	·1065	2	6/4
35/8 (500 O.H.V.)	89/148	180	·1065	3	29/4
35/7 (Competition)	6/139	160	·1065	2	6/4
35/7 (Racing)	T15TT32	270	·109	4	4
35/10 (Competition)	6/164	160	·1065	2	6/5
35/10 (Racing)	10/TT32	310 c.c.	·109	3	4

Possible Causes of Bad Slow-running. If it is found impossible to obtain good slow-running by making the pilot air adjustment as described in the second operation on page 15, it is probable that some defect other than carburation is responsible for preventing the engine running slowly at low revolutions. Air leaks are a possible cause which should be looked for. They may be due to a poor joint at the carburettor attachment to the cylinder and/or a worn inlet valve guide. Badly-seating valves will also weaken the mixture. Defects in the ignition system may also be responsible for poor tick-over. The sparking plug may be oily, or the points set too close (see page 49). Possibly the spark is excessively advanced or the contact-breaker needs attention (see page 51). Examine the slip ring for oil and see that the pick-up brush is bedding down and in good condition. Also examine the H.T. cable for signs of shorting.

For Racing. A 50 per cent petrol and 50 per cent pure benzole mixture is suitable with a medium compression piston, but for speed work with an alcohol fuel fit a high compression piston. Tune for speed and disregard fuel consumption. The main jet may be increased by about 10 per cent for speed work (much more for alcohol fuels). In the case of early overhead camshaft models, a special road-racing carburettor is substituted for the standard carburettor. This racing carburettor has been used by the A.J.S. racing men with great success in all the big international road races. It goes without saying that to obtain very high speeds, in addition to tuning the carburettor with great care, it is essential to tune the engine thoroughly, cut down weight where possible, and select the most suitable gear ratios for the particular purpose in mind.

Down-draught Carburettors—Important Warning. On certain models with down-draught carburettors, including Models 35/12, 35/16, 35/22, 35/26, it is very important to turn off the petrol immediately after a run. The reason is that with a downswept inlet port there is a decided risk of neat petrol entering the cylinder in the event of the carburettor flooding. If this should occur it would not only thin down the oil but also subject the machine to a grave risk of fire and engine seizure.

Maintenance of the Amal Carburettor. Periodical cleaning is necessary to maintain efficient functioning of the carburettor, and should be carried out quarterly in the following sequence—

Disconnect petrol pipe. Unscrew holding bolt Q (Fig. 6) and remove float chamber complete. With box or set spanner, slacken the mixing chamber union nut E. Mixing chamber complete may now be removed from engine, either by unscrewing the clip pin or the two nuts holding the carburettor flange. Unscrew mixing chamber lock ring Z (held by clip $Z1$), and pull out throttle valve, needle, and air valve. Remove main jet P and needle jet O. Mixing chamber union nut E may then be removed and jet block completely pushed out. If this is obstinate, tap gently, using a wooden stump inside the mixing chamber. Unscrew float chamber cover W, after slackening lock screw X. Withdraw the float by pinching the clip V inwards, and pull gently upwards.

Generally it is sufficient to wash all the parts in clean petrol, but if the carburettor has had extended service, check the following—

(a) FLOAT CHAMBER NEEDLE U. If a distinct shoulder is visible on the point of seating, renew this as soon as convenient.

(b) THROTTLE VALVE. Test in mixing chamber, and if excessive play is present it is advisable to renew this without delay.

(c) THROTTLE NEEDLE CLIP. This part must securely grip needle. *Free rotation must not take place*, otherwise the needle groove will become worn and necessitate a new part being fitted. *Be sure to refit the clip in the same groove.*

(d) JET BLOCK. If trouble has been experienced with erratic "idling," ascertain by means of a fine bristle that the pilot jet J is clear, and that the pilot outlet M in the mixing chamber is unobstructed.

To Reassemble. Refit jet block F with washer on underside, and screw on lightly mixing chamber union nut E. Screw in needle jet O and main jet P. Open air lever $\tfrac{7}{8}$ in., throttle lever half-way; grasp the air slide between the thumb and the finger; *make sure that the needle enters the central hole in the barrel H.* Slightly twist the throttle valve until it enters the barrel guide, when on pushing down the valves the air valve should enter its guide. If not, slightly move the mixing chamber cap Y,

THE AMAL CARBURETTOR

when the air valve will slide into place. Screw on mixing chamber lock ring Z. *No brute force is necessary.*

Attach carburettor to the cylinder, pushing right home, and examine washer if flange fitting. Insert holding bolt Q, and thoroughly tighten union nut E by means of a fixed spanner. Refit float and needle, holding the needle head against its seating by means of a pencil until the float and the clip V are slipped into position. Make sure that the clip enters the groove provided. Screw on the cover tightly and lock in position by means of the lock screw X. The float chamber holding bolt has one washer above and one below the lug. Screw holding bolt into mixing chamber and lock securely. Clean petrol pipe and filter if fitted and replace. It will be necessary to re-check the pilot setting if this has been disturbed.

Persistent Flooding. Possible causes of flooding are (a) a bent float chamber needle, (b) a distorted needle clip, (c) dirt or grit

AMAL CARBURETTOR SETTINGS FOR 1938-9 A.J.S. MODELS

Model	Carburettor	Main Jet	Needle Jet (in.)	Needle Position	Throttle Valve
250 c.c. O.H.V.	75/014	120	·1065	2	5/3
350 c.c. O.H.V.	76/014	150	·1065	3	6/4
500 c.c. O.H.V.	89/004	180	·1065	3	29/4
500 c.c. S.V.	76/001	150	·1065	3	6/4
1000 c.c. S.V. (Home)	76/012	130	·1065	2	6/4
1000 c.c. S.V. (Export)	6/168	140	·1065	2	6/3

AMAL CARBURETTOR SETTINGS FOR 1945-8 A.J.S. MODELS

Model	Carburettor	Main Jet	Needle Jet (in.)	Needle Position	Throttle Valve
350 c.c. O.H.V. (16M)	76D/IJ	150	·1065	3	6/4
500 c.c. O.H.V. (18)	89B/IAK	180	·1065	2	29/4

lodged between the needle valve and its seat, (d) a punctured float. When dismantling the carburettor, clean the float chamber very thoroughly and renew any damaged parts. Polish the valve by pulling the needle against its seat and rotating it, but be sure to hold it vertical.

Wear of Needle Jet. The needle itself does *not* become worn. Should the mixture be still too rich with the clip in No. 1 groove (nearest the end), it is probable that the needle jet requires replacement due to wear. This is assuming that the carburettor has been correctly tuned and that no flooding is taking place.

CHAPTER III

ALL ABOUT LUBRICATION (1932-9)

THE lubrication system on A.J.S. models has been steadily improved during recent years and all 1935-9 engines incorporate the most modern type of automatic dry sump or constant circulation system, ensuring correct lubrication of all the working

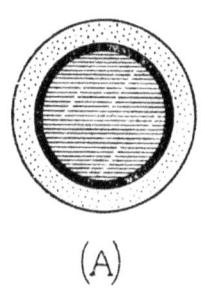 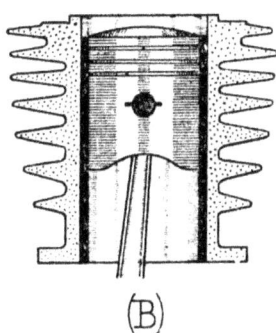

FIG. 8 SHOWING GENERAL PRINCIPLE OF LUBRICATION
The diagrams at A and B show how an oil film keeps a shaft apart from its bearing and a piston apart from its cylinder respectively.

parts with the minimum amount of attention. Some attention on the part of the rider is, however, necessary and can never safely be neglected if a host of evil troubles is to be avoided. Motorcycling can be cheap, but it can also with neglect be quite the reverse.

What Lubrication Is For. The fundamental principle of lubrication is that to avoid friction and heat, or in other words wear and tear, between close-fitting moving surfaces it is imperative to maintain an oil or grease film between them which does in effect actually keep them apart. The idea is made clear in Fig. 8. On a motor-cycle the oil film has a thickness varying from about ·0002 in. to ·0008 in. and the duty of the rider in regard to engine lubrication is to see that: (a) good quality oil is used, (b) a sufficient quantity of oil is kept in circulation, (c) the oil is kept clean and free from dilution (petrol gradually creeps past the piston rings).

1932–36 Improved Mechanical Lubrication. All 1932 to 1936 engines, except the dry sump lubricated engines, incorporate an improved mechanical lubrication system quite different from the dry sump system in principle as well as design. The oil in the tank is not kept in constant circulation, and the duplex pump (Fig. 30) is gear-driven from the crankshaft.

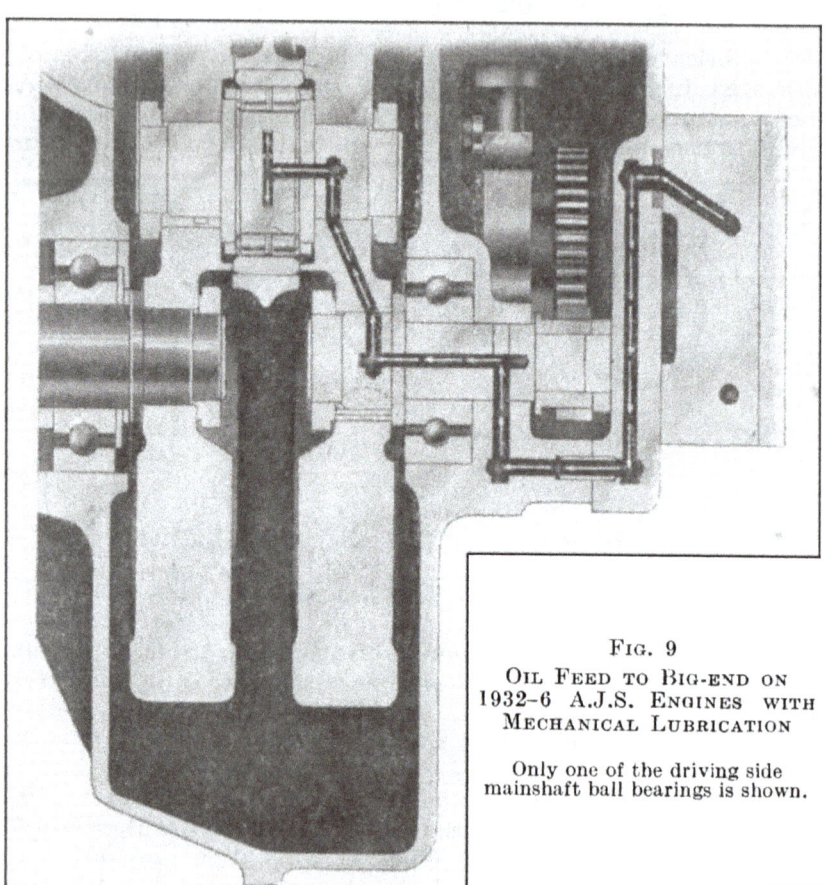

FIG. 9
OIL FEED TO BIG-END ON 1932-6 A.J.S. ENGINES WITH MECHANICAL LUBRICATION

Only one of the driving side mainshaft ball bearings is shown.

The upper plunger of the pump takes oil from the tank via the delivery pipe, and delivers it direct to a false bearing on the timing side, not the driving side, of the crankshaft. The oil-way is totally enclosed, no pipe being used as on earlier systems. The oil is then pressure-fed to the big-end bearing, as shown in Fig. 9. Some of it is also forced to the timing gear. Surplus oil drops down from the big-end on to the flywheels and is distributed by splash throughout the engine. The lower pump plunger collects some oil from a by-pass from the main feed and returns it to the tank via the return pipe, from whose orifice oil may be seen emerging on removing the filler cap. There is no separate oil feed to the cylinder walls as on the D.S. system, but the main oil supply can be controlled by means of the regulator on top of the pump. The oil return to the tank only shows that the pump is working and is not infallible proof of proper lubrication. Once the correct pump setting has been obtained no attention is necessary other than tank replenishment and occasional draining of the crankcase.

The Dry Sump Lubrication System (Big Twins). The lubrication system described below applies to all 1932-9 twin-cylinder engines.

It is a force-feed, constant circulation type with dry sump. Briefly its working is as follows: Oil, fed from the tank, is distributed throughout the engine, and finally returned to the tank by a duplex internal pump. This comprises a single double-acting, steel plunger (Fig. 10), housed in the crankcase casting below the timing case between two rectangular end caps horizontally and at right angles to the crankshaft axis, and able simultaneously to rotate and reciprocate. This dual action of the plunger is obtained, as is more fully explained on page 24, by the fact that while a positive rotation at one-fifteenth engine speed is effected by direct engagement of the spiral gear portion with a worm cut on the mainshaft, an endwise movement is secured by having an annular cam groove cut in the plunger body in permanent contact with the hardened end of a fixed guide screw. The actual oil circulation is brought about by alternate displacements and suctions at the delivery and scavenge ends of the reciprocating plunger, the latter being of greater diameter than the former to ensure complete scavenging of the sump and the return of all surplus oil to the tank. Two segments cut in the plunger body constitute the main ports which regulate the circulation. There is no adjustment however. A point worthy of notice here is that the crankcase cannot safely be split until the pump plunger has first been removed.

With regard to the actual oil distribution, the system adopted is made clear by reference to Fig. 10. The small end of the plunger (i.e. the front one) injects oil into the timing case to a predetermined level, such that the camshaft bearings and drive are adequately lubricated. All surplus oil overflows into the flywheel chamber, and is eventually returned to the sump, although a little is caught up by the flywheels and splashed upon the big-ends and the cylinders. Splash lubrication, however, is not relied upon to any extent owing to the small volume of oil remaining at any time in the sump. Oil is forced under pressure direct to the big-end bearings and to the crankshaft bearing on the timing side by means of carefully drilled passages in the flywheel, the crankpin and the off-side mainshaft. Oil is also fed to three points on each of the cylinder walls in such a position that the bulk of the oil is discharged on to that part of the thrust side of the cylinder walls where the maximum cooling effect upon the pistons is required. A ball valve regulates the supply.

The constant circulation system with fabric filter (see page 25) guarantees a continual supply of clean, cool oil to the engine whenever the latter is running. The oil circulation may be verified occasionally by removing the oil tank filler cap and noting whether oil is being ejected from the return pipe orifice. This check upon the oil circulation should be made preferably upon starting up the engine from cold. Remember the fact that when the engine has been left stationary for some time, oil from various parts of the engine has drained to the sump, and, until this surplus has been cleared, the return to the tank is very positive, whereas normally it is somewhat spasmodic and, perhaps, mixed with air bubbles, due partly to the fact that the capacity of the return part of the pump is greater than that of the delivery portion, and partly to the fact that there are considerable variations in the amount of oil held in suspense in the crankcase. For example, upon suddenly accelerating, the return flow may decrease entirely for a time, only, of course, to resume at a greater rate than before when decelerating. It may be mentioned that on most 1933-8 Big Twins the provision of a tell-tale on the instrument panel, illuminated at night, enables oil circulation to be noted while riding (only after oil warms up), the oil supply to the timing-chest being first by-passed up to the panel. It is important that no air leaks occur in this system.

The Double-acting Oil Pump. A general description of the twin dry sump lubrication system has already been given, and Fig. 10 shows how the oil is circulated. It remains to deal with the action of the pump, which also applies to most of the 1935-9 single-cylinder models.

The pump has only one moving part—a steel plunger driven at $\frac{1}{15}$ engine speed by a worm cut on the engine mainshaft. This plunger slowly oscillates to and fro, its precise travel being determined by the relieved end of a guide screw (Fig. 10) screwed into the rear of the pump housing and engaging with a profiled cam groove at the large return end of the plunger. This groove plays an all-important part. In addition to causing the plunger to oscillate and thereby obtain a pumping action at each end (for the plunger is completely enclosed by its housing and end caps), its carefully planned contour enables the pumping impulses to be synchronized with the opening and closing of two main ports and a small auxiliary port, thus definitely regulating the oil circulation and controlling the supply of oil to the engine and the return of oil to the tank.

The plunger itself has two diameters, and, because the capacity of the return portion of the pump is greater than that

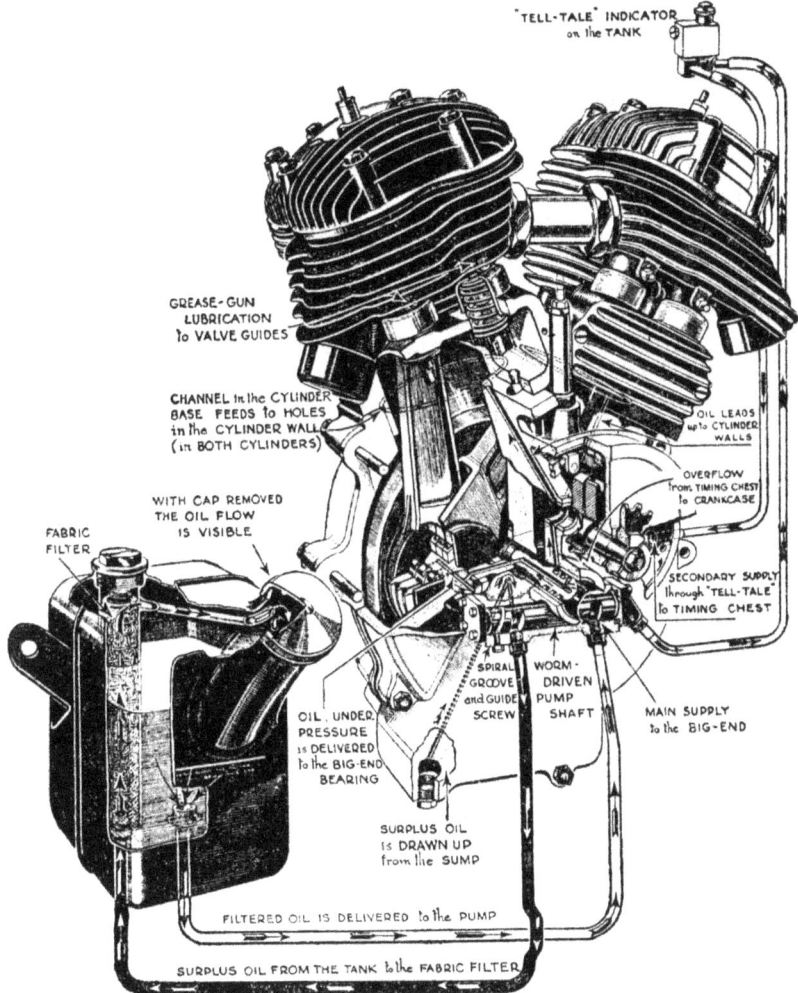

Fig. 10. Details of the Dry Sump System on the 1937-8 A.J.S Big Twins

of the delivery portion, therefore the sump is always kept clear of oil. Fig. 10 enables the action of the pump to be understood. Oil flows by gravity, assisted by suction, from the tank to a point in the pump housing, such that no further passage can take place until the plunger has moved to a point, approximately, as shown when oil flows into the hollowed end via the cut-away segment constituting the delivery port. Then as the plunger continues to advance with simultaneous rotary motion, the oil which has completely filled the hollowed end is momentarily retained and the bulk of it finally ejected by displacement from this port into an oil passage opposite the point of entry, and forced to the cylinder walls and main engine bearings. During the advance of the plunger culminating in the automatic injection of fresh oil into the engine, the receding of the large end of the plunger causes a strong vacuum directly opposite an oil passage leading from the sump base, and communicating with the plunger interior only when the return port is in a suitable position. All surplus oil in the sump is, therefore, sucked up as the plunger advances, and retained when the port closes until the plunger begins to reverse its motion, when, the return port coming into line with the return pipe passage, the oil is forcibly ejected by displacement into this pipe, and so to the oil tank, where its intermittent emergence can, though a tell-tale (Fig. 15) is provided (1933–8), be observed.

Thus it will be seen that so long as the engine is running, fresh oil is being constantly fed to it and then, after circulation, sucked from the sump and forced up back into the tank to be recirculated *ad infinitum*. Coincident with the ejection of oil from the main delivery port a supply of oil is forced out of an auxiliary port to the timing chest. Where a tell-tale is fitted it is first forced up into the panel, whence it flows by gravity to the respective parts requiring lubrication. Only a small portion of the total oil feed to the engine is diverted in this manner, but this portion is important and a definite index as to the correct functioning of the whole D.S. lubrication system, for only when the pump is forcing oil into the engine at a certain pressure can the rise of the tell-tale plunger be observed. The action of the pump plunger is almost fool-proof, but care must be taken to remove the plunger before separating the crankcase, and the guide screw must always be kept fully tightened. A point worthy of note is that with the plunger stationary no oil can possibly enter the engine. For this reason no oil taps are provided.

The Dry Sump Lubrication System (S.V. and O.H.V. Singles). The dry sump lubrication system provided on 1935–9 S.V. and O.H.V. singles is substantially similar in principle and design to the system employed on the Big Twins as may be realized by comparing Figs. 10 and 12. As may be seen in Fig. 12, a double-acting oil pump of the same type as that already described draws oil from the tank and forces it through the drilled timing side mainshaft and flywheel to the big-end bearing and crankshaft bearings. From the big-end some oil is splashed on to the cylinder

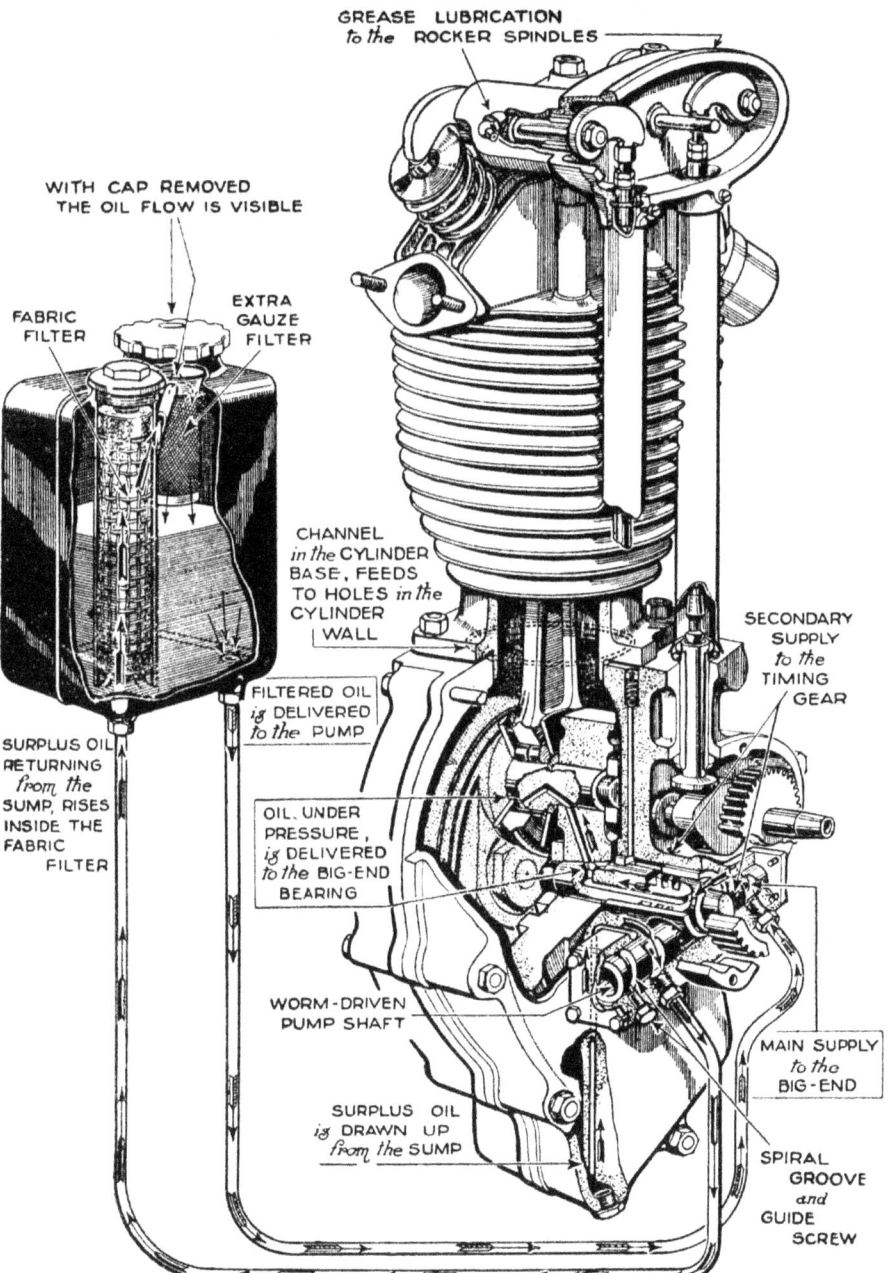

FIG. 11. SHOWING THE DRY SUMP LUBRICATION SYSTEM ON MOST 1935–6 S.V. AND O.H.V. SINGLES

The general arrangement is similar to that provided on the Big Twins (see Fig. 10). Above is illustrated a partly sectioned and cut-away 2·46 h.p. O.H.V. engine. Note the ball valve which controls the oil supply to the holes in the cylinder wall. The 1937-8 O.H.V. engine is shown on page 31.

walls, but cylinder lubrication relies mainly on oil fed from a channel to holes in the cylinder wall. A secondary supply is taken to the timing gear and rocker-box (1937-9 O.H.V.), surplus oil draining into the sump from which it is drawn by the large end of the worm-driven pump plunger and returned to the tank which has an ample system of filtering the oil. In addition to the gauze screen in the filler cap orifice which filters the oil during replenishment, a large fabric filter is included. This comprises a felt cartridge through which the oil from the return pipe is forced to pass before emerging from the orifice just below the filler cap. With this D.S. lubrication system no attention is necessary other than regular replenishment, checking oil circulation by removing the filler cap, and cleaning the filter when decarbonizing.

Dismantling Oil Pump (Dry Sump). See notes on page 66.

Use Recommended Engine Oils Only. The importance of using nothing but recommended brands of lubricating oil cannot be over emphasized. The use of inferior quality engine oil even for a short period may have very serious consequences and any attempt to economize on lubricating oil is likely in the long run to prove very expensive indeed. All A.J.S. engines are of the high-efficiency type and will only give the performance they are designed to give for long periods provided they are correctly lubricated. Five suitable engine oils are: Castrol "Grand Prix" ("XXL" during winter), Triple Shell (Double Shell during winter), Mobiloil "D" ("BB" during winter), Price's Motorine "B" de Luxe ("C" during winter), and Essolube Racer. All these oils have good heat-resisting qualities and their viscosity gives easy starting in cold weather. If a sports model is used for competition or racing purposes, Patent Castrol "R" is suitable, but it should be particularly noted that this oil must *on no account* be mixed with other mineral-base oils, such as Patent Castrol "XXL." When replenishing with Patent Castrol "R," the oil tank should first be completely drained and cleaned out with petrol.

No Oil Pump Adjustment Provided on Dry Sump Models. The dry sump lubrication system fitted on most 1932-9 S.V. and O.H.V. models is designed to deliver the correct amount of oil to the engine under all running conditions and therefore no adjustment whatever is provided. On the 1937-9 O.H.V. models, however, there is an adjustment for the feed to the inlet valve guide.

To Adjust Oil Pump on Mechanical Lubrication Models. An oil regulator is provided on 1932-6 mechanical lubrication models and on new engines this is set to deliver a rather liberal supply of oil. After running-in has been completed it is usually found desirable to cut down the supply a little. See also page 65.

Frequent Replenishment Is Advised. On dry sump models it is advisable to replenish the oil tank frequently. The oil level should be maintained as far as possible within *one inch* of the return pipe orifice below the filler cap (Fig. 12) and must never be allowed to fall below the half-full mark with the engine cold. The more oil there is in the tank, the cooler will it be, for with D.S. lubrication the whole of the oil is in constant circulation. Further, the oil is less likely to become contaminated or diluted, both of which are very detrimental to the engine.

In the case of models with mechanical or "wet sump" lubrication the actual amount of oil in the tank is immaterial so long as there is sufficient to ensure the oil pump being fed properly. No heating up of the oil occurs, as this is not in constant circulation throughout the engine and tank as with the D.S. lubrication system.

To Verify Oil Circulation (Dry Sump). On the 1932-9 dry sump models it is possible to check oil circulation by removing the oil tank filler cap and observing whether oil is being ejected steadily from the return pipe orifice. This check should be made prior to every run. On 1933-7 Twins with D.S. lubrication and a flush-fitting instrument panel on the tank an eye should be kept on the oil tell-tale (Fig. 15). Although, as has been mentioned on page 26, only a small portion of the main oil supply is diverted to the tell-tale, this portion provides definite evidence as to the correct functioning of the whole lubrication system. In the event of the tell-tale plunger failing to rise with the engine running, stop the engine and investigate the cause immediately.

To Check Pump Working (Mechanical Lubrication). Remove the tank filler cap and see if oil is issuing from the return pipe orifice. If it is, all is well with the oil pump, but as has been mentioned on page 23, this is no proof of oil circulation through the engine, which can be verified only by noting the exhaust and the behaviour of the engine.

Clean Oil Tank and Replenish with New Oil About Every 5000 Miles (Dry Sump). At least once every 5000 miles (or once every season) the entire oil tank on the 1932-9 dry sump models should be removed from the machine, washed out with petrol and after refitting replenished with new oil up to the correct level. In order to avoid undue waste, it is quite in order to arrange for this to be done when the oil is at the lowest recommended level, although ordinarily the oil should be kept well above the half-way mark. Clean the filter(s) with petrol when decarbonizing.

Drain Crankcase Every 2000-3000 Miles (Mechanical Lubrication). Every 2000-3000 miles all oil should be drained from the crankcase of mechanical lubrication models and replaced by ½ pint of clean oil. A plug at the base of the crankcase and another near the base of the cylinder on the driving side are provided for this purpose. Do not swill out the crankcase with paraffin or petrol as this may subsequently be difficult to remove completely.

Grease Overhead Rockers Every 500 Miles. Some oil mist reaches the 1932–6 rockers via the push-rod covers, but this is insufficient for adequate lubrication of the O.H. rockers and the grease gun should be applied to the nipples provided at least once every 500 miles, earlier if much hard riding is undertaken. Grease should be injected until it begins to exude at the bearings. A good heat-resisting grease such as Price's H.M.P. should be utilized for lubrication of the O.H. rockers. (See also pages 35, 36.)

Lucas " Magdyno " and Magneto Lubrication. The bearings and gears are packed with grease during assembly and for this reason no lubricators are provided. However, after approximately 10,000 miles running, the instrument should be returned to the makers for dismantling, cleaning, and repacking of the bearings with grease. A wrinkle worth remembering is to put just a spot (no more) of oil on the heel of the contact-breaker rocker arm which, if allowed to operate quite dry, is apt to wear somewhat more quickly. But beware of getting oil on the contacts. This applies to ring cam type contact-breakers of earlier design. If the rocker arm is stiff, put a spot of oil on its pivot.

In the case of later instruments with ring type cam, withdraw the ring cam and put a few drops of oil (thin) on the felt wick. Lubrication of the wick should be attended to about every 5000 miles. All 1938–9 magnetos have a face cam type contact-breaker, and to gain access to the wick it is necessary to remove the spring arm which carries the contact and withdraw the screw to which the wick is attached. When refitting the arm be sure that the small backing spring is correctly replaced. Every 5000 miles a few drops of thin oil should be inserted through the lubricator provided on the brush gear cover of the dynamo portion of later type "Magdynos." (See also page 87.)

Dynamo Lubrication (Coil Ignition Models). The Miller type dynamo on 1935–9 coil ignition models requires some periodical lubrication in order to maintain its efficiency, but oil should be used very sparingly. Every 500 miles insert a drop of oil through the lubricator on the driving end of the dynamo. The armature bearings are packed with grease on assembly, and under normal conditions this grease should suffice for 10,000–15,000 miles. At the end of this period the dynamo should be returned to a Miller agent for dismantling, cleaning, and re-greasing.

Dynamo Lubrication (Magneto Ignition). The bearings on the Lucas type dynamo (magneto models) are packed with grease before leaving the manufacturers and consequently no lubricators are provided. After a big mileage has been covered

ALL ABOUT LUBRICATION (1932-9)

it is advisable to return the instrument to a Lucas Service depot for dismantling, cleaning, adjustment, and repacking of the bearings with grease.

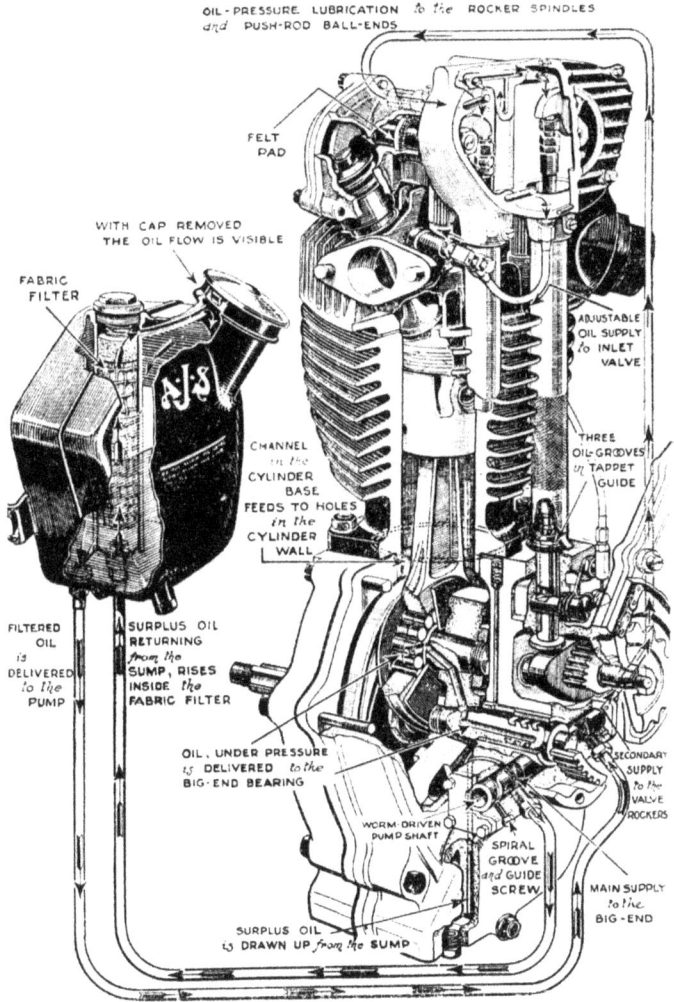

Fig. 12. Showing Constructional Features and Lubrication System of the 1937-8 O.H.V. Engine

Burman Gearbox Lubrication. New Burman gearboxes are charged with sufficient grease for at least 1000 miles' running without any attention. At the end of this period and subsequently every 1500 miles the gearbox should be replenished with 2-3 oz. of grease. In order to obtain the most satisfactory results the gearbox should always be maintained about *one-third* full. On no account replenish with thick grease, as this may cause damage to the gears and bearings. Suitable greases for Burman gearbox lubrication are: Castrolease Medium, Mobilgrease No. 2, Shell Retinax Grease C.D., Price's Belmoline D, and Esso Grease. In case of emergency it is permissible to use a thicker grease mixed with engine oil. For long distance racing or very fast road work it is advisable to add about 25 per cent of engine oil to the grease, and for sprint work engine oil alone may be used temporarily.

In the case of 1937 and earlier gearboxes having an external clutch operating lever (also on some 1939 models) it is best to inject the grease through the aperture on top of the gearbox after removing the oval metal cap, which is secured by two nuts. These nuts need not be actually removed as the cap is slotted at one end to enable it to be twisted round until the gearbox aperture is exposed. With this type of gearbox a small quantity of grease should be injected into the grease nipples about once a week. Two nipples which should not be overlooked are those for the kick-starter axle and the foot change mechanism (where fitted). Both are screwed into the gearbox end cover. This does not apply to 1938–9 models.

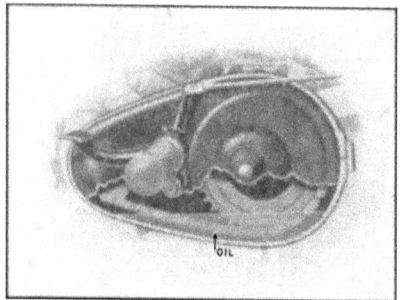

Fig. 13. The 1932-5 Oil Bath

1935–9 A.J.S. models with coil or magneto ignition have the primary and dynamo chains completely enclosed in an oil-bath chain case (Fig. 14).

On most gearboxes fitted during 1938 onwards the clutch-operating mechanism is completely enclosed and "one-shot" lubrication is provided, a single grease nipple sufficing to lubricate the entire gearbox, including the gear change and kick-starter mechanism. Replenish with grease as indicated in a previous paragraph. Gentle operation of the kick-starter will assist filling.

Occasionally it is desirable to remove the clutch operating rod and also the clutch cable and grease them thoroughly. About every 5000–7000 miles the clutch roller race should be repacked with grease.

Sturmey-Archer Gearbox Lubrication. This gearbox fitted on many 1932–5 models requires lubrication at the same period as the Burman gearbox. Every 1500 miles a small quantity of Castrol D gear oil should be injected into the gearbox. Occasionally verify the level of lubricant in the gearbox, which should be from *one-third to half full*. If the period recommended above for gearbox lubrication does not maintain this level, reduce the period accordingly.

Replenish Oil-bath Chain Case When Necessary. On all 1932–9 models the primary chain (and on most models the dynamo chain also) runs completely enclosed in an oil-bath chain case, and in order to ensure thorough lubrication of the chain all that is necessary is to remove the inspection cap on the chain case occasionally and replenish the oil-bath with engine oil (see page 28). The inspection cap orifice determines the correct oil level and oil should be poured in until it begins to trickle out through

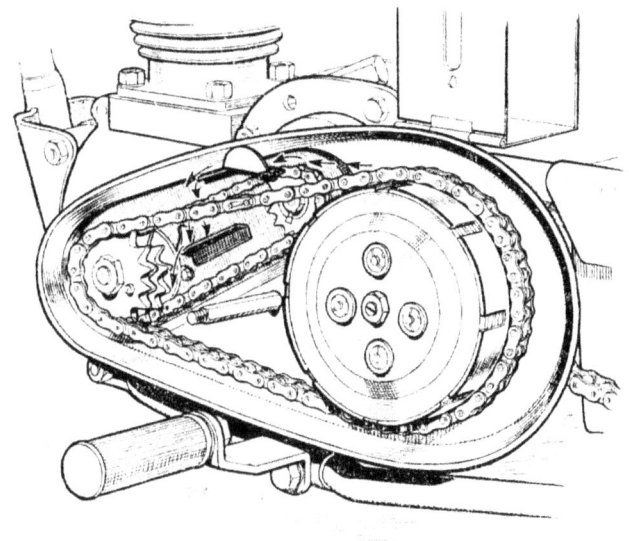

(From "The Motor Cycle")
Fig. 14. The Oil-bath Chain Case on Magneto, Coil Ignition Models (1935–9).

the filler orifice. Obviously it is a practical impossibility to overfill the chain case.

To obtain the most satisfactory service from the primary chain the oil-bath chain case should be kept filled to the correct level by frequent (say, weekly) examination of the oil level and replenishment when necessary. It is exceedingly important that the oil level should not fall more than about $\frac{3}{16}$ in. below the bottom edge of the filler orifice, otherwise there is a risk of the chain running in a semi-dry state which will cause rapid wear of the rollers and quick breaking up of the chain.

Secondary Chain Lubrication. On all 1932–9 models the secondary chain should be smeared with grease whenever it appears to be dry. About once every 1500–2000 miles in summer and every 1000 miles in winter it is advisable to take the secondary chain off the sprockets and immerse it in a paraffin bath, allowing it to soak thoroughly so as to remove all traces of dirt. After being carefully wiped the chain should then, before being refitted, be dipped in a bath of molten tallow, or as a poorer substitute, engine oil. If engine oil is used the chain should be allowed to soak overnight so that the oil can penetrate to all the link joints.

Dynamo Chain Lubrication. On the 1935-9 models with separate dynamos the primary chain is enclosed together with the dynamo chain in an oil-bath chain case (Fig. 14) and therefore, provided the primary chain is properly lubricated, it necessarily follows that the dynamo chain is also.

Magneto Chain Lubrication. On pre-1938 models with forward magneto the chain case is packed with grease during assembly and this grease will be found ample for at least 5000 miles, after which the case should be taken off and packed with fresh grease. When doing this, check, and if necessary adjust, the chain tension. (See also page 36.)

Grease Fork Spindles and Steering Head. About every 1000, 500 miles, respectively, the grease gun should be applied to the nipples provided for lubricating both the steering head and the fork spindles. If the former is neglected some steering stiffness may arise and the bearings become damaged. If the latter are overlooked nice front fork action will be unattainable. Suitable greases to use for these and all other grease gun points are: Castrolease Medium, Mobilgrease No. 2, Shell Retinax Grease C.D., Esso Grease, or Price's Belmoline " D." Castrolease Medium can incidentally be obtained in special push-down lid canisters for easily filling the grease gun.

Also Both Hubs. The roller bearing hubs are tightly packed with grease on assembly, but to prevent the ingress of mud and water while riding it is advisable to inject a small quantity of grease through the hub greasers about every 500 miles, or more frequently in very dirty weather. Where a sidecar is attached do not forget the sidecar hub. Avoid injecting excessive grease, owing to the danger of its getting on the brake linings and spoiling the efficiency of the brakes.

Points Which Should Not Be Overlooked. When lubricating the machine many riders are apt to overlook some small points which although not in themselves enormously important do materially contribute to general efficiency. Among such points may be mentioned moving parts such as the brake pedal bearing, and the brake cam nipple. These should be greased occasionally, especially in bad weather. Thin oil is quite suitable for brake rod joints, control levers, etc.

Worth Buying. For a few shillings it is possible to buy a special oil gun for lubricating the Bowden control cables on later A.J.S.

models, and the author strongly advocates the purchase of one of these guns by all readers of this book. It will enable all control cables to be kept lubricated such that they slide without friction in their casings, and frequent fraying and breakages become a thing of the past. With the specially designed oil gun it is possible to flood a Bowden cable with oil in a few seconds and the effect is surprising to those who have never before tried it. Oil is injected through a small bared patch on the outer casing and is forced through the spiral casing along the inner wire. A metal clip protects each bared patch which is near the centre of the casing. To apply the oil gun it is only necessary to slide the clip along the casing to permit of the oil gun being clamped with

(From "The Motor Cycle")

FIG. 15. SHOWING THE OIL TELL-TALE ON THE 1933–8 BIG TWINS

An instrument panel is fitted as standard on all 1939 models except the competition models.

the bared patch occupying a central position on the rubber pad on the nozzle of the oil gun. Then to flood the cable with oil it is only required to give a few turns to the screwed plunger.

Lubrication of Overhead Valve Gear (1937–8 Models). As may be seen from the illustration on page 31, the 1937–8 O.H.V. engine has a force feed to the rocker-box, the rocker spindles and ball ends of the push-rods thus being lubricated automatically. No grease nipples are provided. Automatic lubrication of the inlet valve guide is also included and the oil supply is capable of being adjusted if necessary by means of a needle-pointed screw-down control which once properly regulated needs practically no further attention unless valve squeak develops or the valve stem becomes gummy due to excess oil. To obtain approximately the correct setting the control should be screwed until it is *one-sixth to one-half (maximum) of a complete turn from the fully-closed position.* Excessive oil consumption, an oiled plug, a smoky exhaust, and oil leakage from the rocker-box are symptoms of the needle valve passing excessive oil.

Lubrication of Valve Stems (1937-9 S.V. Models). On the 500 c.c., 990 c.c. side-valve models grease nipples are provided for lubrication of the valve stems and a small quantity of grease should be injected every 500 miles.

Lubrication of Overhead Valve Gear (1939 Models). On the 1939 O.H.V. engines a separate feed from the oil pump front housing cap is led by an external pipe to the rocker-box and force feeds the rocker spindles as on 1937-8 engines. There is also an adjustable feed to the inlet valve guide, the supply of oil being regulated by a needle valve (see previous paragraph). The 1939 engines, however, have no external pipe as used the previous year and the exhaust valve guide receives a supply of oil from the rocker-box through a diagonal drill-way in the cylinder head. Surplus oil passes from the guide through another drill-way to the push-rod tube holes and then drains to the timing case and crankcase. This method of lubrication prevents the oil becoming burnt and thereby choking the passage. Surplus oil from the rocker spindles drains on to the push-rod cups and into the push-rod chamber; it is from this point that the oil is conducted to both the inlet and exhaust valve guides.

Magneto Chain Lubrication (1938-9). The magneto chain case is packed with grease on assembly and subsequently at intervals of 1000 miles a small quantity of grease should be injected through the grease nipple provided on the outer cover.

Possible Cause of High Oil Consumption. If an A.J.S. engine begins to run up big oil bills, suspect a choked or dirty oil filter cartridge (Part No. STD786). Replace the cartridge immediately if thorough soaking and washing in petrol does not remedy matters.

To Lubricate Speedometer. Inject about every 500 miles some grease into the speedometer gearbox nipple. The gearbox is located on the front brake cover plate and the nipple is sunk in its end.

Lubrication of 1945-8 Models. Detailed instructions for the correct lubrication of the post-war Models 16M and 18 will be found in Chapter VI of this handbook.

CHAPTER IV

OVERHAULING (1932-9)

IF a machine is to be kept in efficient condition and its depreciation and repair bill reduced to the absolute minimum, it is essential that the rider should devote some considerable time to its periodic overhaul. Overhauls are of two types—(1) the complete overhaul, (2) the ordinary overhaul. A *complete overhaul* is necessary only at long periods, recommended as seldom as possible. This overhaul should be treated seriously, and the whole machine should be dismantled completely. Every component should be cleaned, scrutinized and, if necessary, replaced. The engine and gearbox must, of course, be removed from the frame for this operation. Special points to be noted in the complete overhaul are set out herewith.

FRAME. Alinement, existence of damaged tubes, play in spring forks, looseness of steering head, wear caused by friction of all attached parts, condition of enamel.

WHEELS. Condition of taper roller bearings, truth of wheels, alinement, loose spokes, condition of rims, wear of tyres, valves.

CHAINS. Excessive wear, cracked or broken rollers, joints.

ENGINE. Oil leaks, compression leaks, main bearings, valves, valve guides and tappets, overhead valve rockers, valve springs, valve seats and faces, cotters, condition of cylinder bore, piston, piston rings, play in big-end and small-end bearings, timing wheels, shafts and bearings, cams, cleanliness of oilways.

GEARS. Condition of teeth on sprockets and pinions, damaged ball races, and loose parts generally. Do not forget the kick-starter and foot gear change mechanism.

The examination should also include all control rods and cables, tank filter(s), clutch and brake linings, etc. To sum up, everything should be dismantled, cleaned, and readjusted.

An *ordinary overhaul* should be undertaken every 1500–2000 miles. This should comprise decarbonizing of the engine, valve clearance adjustment, adjustments of contact-breaker and plug points, valve grinding, general lubrication (see previous chapter), and sundry adjustments.

Apart from these overhauls the rider should make a point of regularly going over the various nuts with a spanner. Vibration frequently loosens them. All working parts must also be kept well lubricated with oil or grease as required, and odd adjustments made as they are needed. The rider who callously runs a machine until " something happens " is asking for trouble and, moreover, will assuredly get it! If a machine is properly overhauled and cleaned the owner will be amply rewarded for his pains.

Cleaning. Cleaning the machine is highly important; it is a necessary preliminary to overhaul. If neglected it renders overhaul difficult and results also in great deterioration of the plating and enamel, and the machine soon becomes shabby, and its market value rapidly falls. After a dirty ride in wet weather cleaning may occupy at least an hour. It entails the use of stiff bristle brushes and paraffin for removing the filth from the lower part of the machine, together with cloths, leather, and polishes for the bright upper surfaces. On no account should the machine be left soaking wet overnight. A serious amount of rusting may occur. If the rider has not the time available for systematic cleaning, the machine should be thoroughly greased all over before use.

Do not rub or brush the mud off enamelled parts dry. Use a hose, or wipe over, using a sponge and pail of water. Dry with a chamois leather, and polish with dusters and wax polish.

In the case of the chromium-plated parts, on no account use metal polish or paste; all that is necessary is to clean them frequently with a damp and soft chamois leather. If the lustre deteriorates after some time, apply some special chromium cleaning compound. (See also notes on page 118.)

Valve Clearances. In order that the valves shall seat properly at *all* engine temperatures it is necessary that clearances should exist between the valve stems and the rocker arms or tappet heads, as the case may be, when the engine is warm. The clearance should be checked now and again with the feeler gauge on the magneto spanner, although it is unlikely that adjustment will be required unless the valves have been ground-in or the engine partly dismantled. In the case of a new engine, however, the clearances will increase until the engine has been thoroughly run-in. Fig. 16 illustrates the point where the clearance should exist (C) and the means of adjustment (A) on 1932-5 S.V., O.H.V. type engines. This clearance should, on the 1932-9 S.V. models be ·004 in. and ·006 in. in the case of the inlet and exhaust valves respectively with a *warm* engine. In the case of 1932-4 O.H.V. models and Models 35/6, 35/8, 35/18, 36/8, 36/18 (mechanical lubrication) the correct inlet and exhaust valve clearances with a *warm* engine are ·006 in. and ·008 in. respectively. On all other 1935-9 O.H.V. models (D.S.) the clearance recommended with the engine *cold* is the nearest approach to nil possible.

Turn the engine over until compression is felt; then raise the exhaust lifter and turn over a trifle more until the piston is at the top of its stroke. Before checking the clearance make quite sure that the exhaust valve lifter is not determining in any way the position of the exhaust valve tappet head or the rocker. There should be a small interval between the time when the lifter is raised and the tappet head or the O.H.V. rocker commences to move. If this is not so the tappet foot or the toggle will not be resting on its cam. If the valve clearances are not correct they must be rectified. In the case of the S.V. engine, hold the tappet body with a spanner and loosen the lock-nut (*B*) above with another spanner; now screw up or unscrew the tappet head (*A*) until the correct clearance is obtained, and retighten the lock-nut.

Check again after tightening the nut. In the case of the 1932–3 O.H.V. engines, first loosen the lock-nut (*B*) which is provided for securing the adjustable grub screw (*A*), adjust the latter, check the clearance at (*C*), and retighten. Check again afterwards. It is worth while adjusting the valve clearances carefully, for excessive clearance will produce noise accompanied by considerable loss of power, while insufficient clearance may cause actual damage to the valves, especially the exhaust valve, as well as loss of power. In the case of the the 1934–5 O.H.V. engines with mechanical lubrication the valve clearance adjusters are situated at the bottom of the push-rods, and to adjust the clearances it is necessary to telescope each push-rod cover, loosen lock-nut *B* (Fig. 16, inset), and adjust each hexagon *A*.

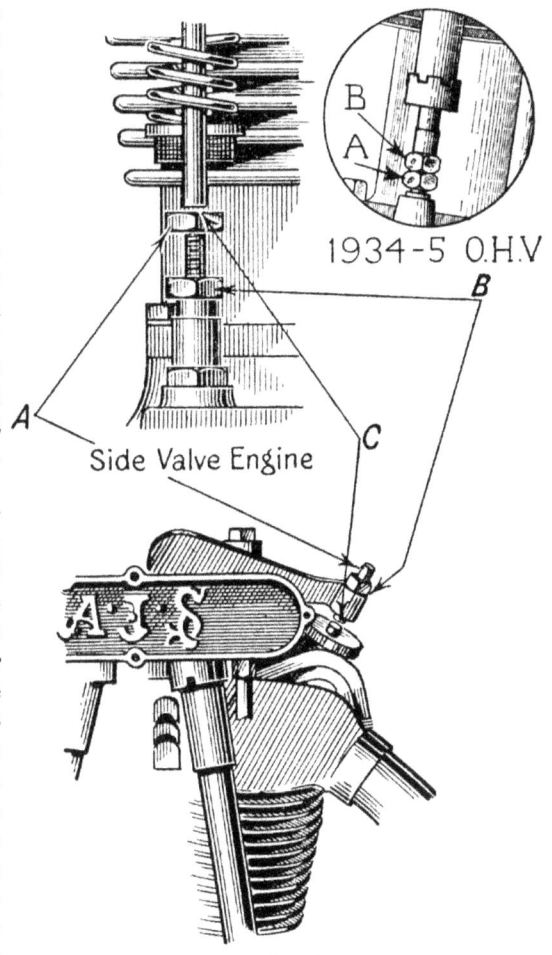

Fig. 16. VALVE CLEARANCE ADJUSTMENT (1932–3)

All 1935 and later models with D.S. lubrication have an adjustment as shown on page 119.

To adjust the valve clearances on the 1935-9 O.H.V. models with D.S. lubrication it is first necessary to remove the rocker-box cover by taking off the securing nut(s). Then revolve the engine until both valves are closed and loosen the lock-nut securing the adjustable push-rod end. Next screw up or unscrew the adjustable push-rod end until the correct clearance is obtained (see Fig. 11), afterwards tightening the lock-nut and checking the clearance. The push-rods should be just free to rotate without causing any rocker movement.

Hardened steel valve end caps are provided on some O.H.V.

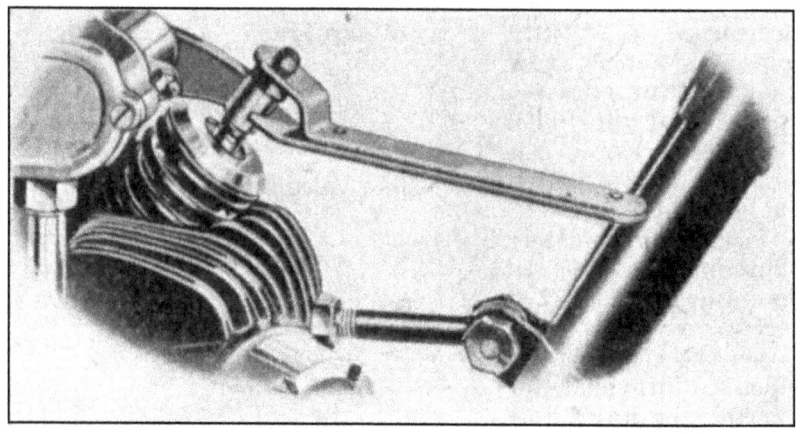

Fig. 17. The A.J.S. Push-rod Extractor (1932-3)

engines, and when the valve clearances are correctly adjusted it should be possible to revolve these freely without there being any perceptible up-and-down movement of the rockers.

On the 1939 O.H.V. engines with the entirely new type of rocker-box there are two screwed caps immediately over the valves and rocker arm ends. When checking the valve clearances (see above) these caps should be removed by applying a spanner to the hexagons provided. The caps are provided solely for inspection purposes. On 1937-8 engines the detachable valve spring caps are each secured by cheese-head screws. In the case of all engines of later manufacture, it is extremely important when checking the valve clearances first to see that the piston is at *the extreme top* of the compression stroke, for only in this position are the tappets absolutely clear of the cam quietening curves. This applies also when retiming the valves (on the exhaust stroke). When replacing the rocker-box cover, avoid excessive tightening of the nut(s) because on most engines the joint is made with a rubber fillet, and only a reasonable pressure is needed to provide an oil-tight joint.

Decarbonizing the Engine. After about 1500-2000 miles the exhaust note becomes " woolly," instead of being a crisp " bark," and the engine sluggish and very prone to " knock." These symptoms clearly indicate that the time has arrived when the engine must be decarbonized, that is to say, all carbon deposits on the piston head and in the combustion chamber must be removed after taking off the detachable cylinder head(s). Carbon deposits, incidentally, are due to three things—(1) incomplete combustion of fuel, (2) carbonization of road dust entering the cylinder, (3) burnt lubricating oil. When decarbonizing (every alternate decarbonizing on the S.V. models) it always pays to inspect the valve faces and seats, and grind in the valves if necessary and also every alternate decarbonizing to remove the piston and inspect the piston rings. In any case, removal of the valves enables the combustion chamber and also the ports to be very thoroughly cleaned. Dismantling is quite simple and whether the engine is a single S.V., a twin S.V., or an O.H.V. model, the procedure is much the same. Overhead valve mechanism is apt to frighten some people, but actually there is nothing in it at all. All A.J.S. engines, except some 1932-6 3·49 h.p. lightweights, have detachable cylinder heads. This greatly facilitates cylinder removal; there is no expert juggling required to get it off. Furthermore, the carbon may be removed if desired without disturbing the cylinder at all.

Initial Preparations. In the case of *Model* 35-6/5 the cylinder barrel and head are in one piece and the latter cannot therefore be detached as on other models. Preparatory to removing the cylinder barrel on this machine it is necessary to detach the H.T. lead to the sparking plug, and disconnect the exhaust pipe and the steady between the cylinder and front down tube. Remove the steady bolt. The Amal carburettor may either be left in place on the cylinder by removing the slides, and the petrol pipe from the base of the float chamber, or, alternatively, the carburettor may be taken off by undoing the screw-in fastening.

If dealing with *Model* 35-9/9 with detachable aluminium alloy head the only preliminary operation necessary before removing the head is to remove the sparking plug. In the case of the twin cylinder engine disconnect the H.T. leads and remove the plugs. If your own mount is of the O.H.V. type, first disconnect all fitments, such as exhaust pipe(s), carburettor slides, cylinder steady when fitted, plug, petrol pipes, rocker-box pipe, etc., and then proceed to remove the push-rods and rocker-box.

On Models of O.H.V. Type. Complete removal of the petrol tank is a necessary preliminary to decarbonizing the 1939 O.H.V.

models, except in the case of the 250 c.c. machines, where it is possible to decarbonize after first raising the tank. Raising of the tank is also sufficient in the case of most pre-1939 models. Obviously on the S.V. machines with detachable cylinder heads it is quite unnecessary to disturb the tank at all.

To raise the petrol tank, first remove the petrol pipe and drain the tank of petrol. Then remove the tank connection pipe and unscrew the four base fixing bolts. Now raise the tank and slide back on to the nose of the saddle, at the same time supporting the front end by placing a suitable block of wood across the support bars.

Removal of the petrol tank on 1939 models is simple, as the tank has been redesigned to permit of removal without interfering with the wiring of the panel which houses the ammeter and lighting switch. To remove the tank, first disconnect the main lead from the battery so as to avoid the risk of a short circuit. Next remove the petrol pipe, drain the tank and remove the connection pipe. Having done this, proceed to remove the four base bolts and the inspection lamp from the panel. The three screws holding the panel to the tank can then be taken out and the tank itself lifted away. While doing this, pass the panel through the slot between the two halves of the tank.

Push-rod Removal. To remove the push-rods on 1932-3 O.H.V. engines the special extractor tool illustrated in Fig. 17 must be used after shortening the two covers by undoing the lock-nuts and telescoping them. The end of the tool is arranged to fit over the rocker adjusting screw (Fig. 17) in such a way that by pressing the tool handle down it compresses the valve spring. Press down on this tool and seize the base of the push-rod tube with the other hand. The push-rods may then be withdrawn by lifting their hollow cups off the tappets complete with covers. The rocker-box should now be removed.

On 1934-9 O.H.V. engines the extractor tool mentioned cannot be used and removal of the push-rods is not a necessary preliminary to rocker-box removal. All that is necessary is to unscrew the lower push-rod cover tube nuts (where fitted) and telescope the tubes by forcing the bottom portion upwards. On 1937 O models, remove the detachable valve spring caps.

Rocker-box Removal (1932-3). To remove the rocker-box for the purpose of giving access to cylinder removal, the lock-nuts at the top and bottom of the push-rod covers will, of course, have to be dealt with as just described. Next unscrew the four pins holding down the rocker-box. The two pins at the right or push-rod side of the rocker-box need only be unscrewed until they are free, but those nearest to the valves must be withdrawn entirely. The rocker-box can now be drawn off the cylinder head from the right side.

OVERHAULING (1932–9) 43

Rocker-box Removal (1934–8). After telescoping the push-rod covers (used on some 1934–5 models), rotate the engine until both valves are closed and then unscrew the four bolts which secure the rocker-box assembly.

The rocker-box can then be lifted off together with the push-rods and covers.

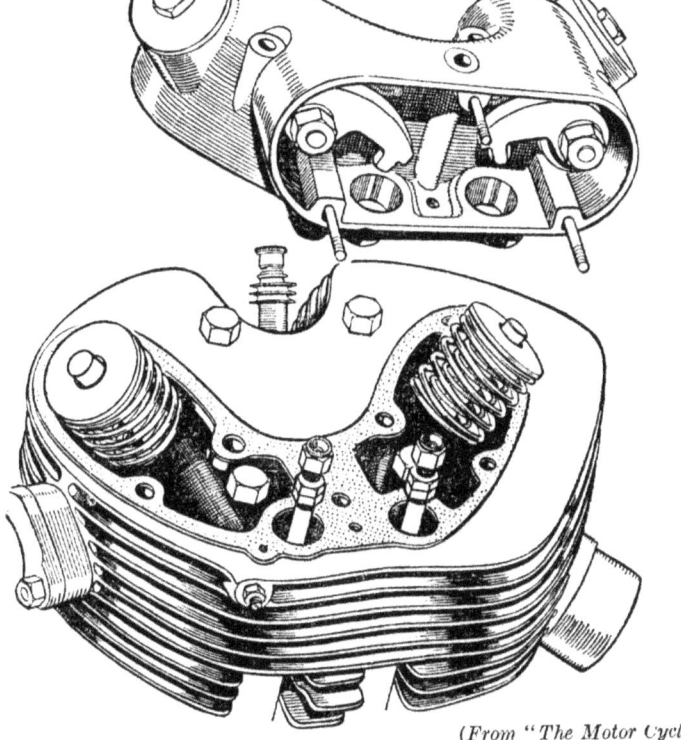

(*From "The Motor Cycle"*)

FIG. 18. THE 1939 O.H.V. CYLINDER HEAD AND ROCKER-BOX
Note the method of valve enclosure, the upper push-rod adjustment, and the neat rocker-box with Hallite washer.

Rocker-box Removal (1939). Unscrew the four bolts which pass vertically downwards through the rocker-box and lift the latter off. A Hallite washer is fitted between the rocker-box and cylinder head and care must be taken not to damage this, otherwise oil leakage will result. On the 1939 engines the push-rod covers do not extend to the rocker-box and are removed with the cylinder head (see page 44). After removing the rocker-box, withdraw both push-rods.

Removing Cylinder Head. Next remove the bolts or nuts holding down the head, and remove the latter. Care should be taken to relieve the pressure evenly on both sides while untensioning the bolts. The head can then be removed by lifting it off the cylinder barrel. No difficulty should be experienced in breaking the joint by hand pressure only. Afterwards cover up the cylinder bore with a rag. Avoid scratching the cylinder head or the gasket, and be most careful not to lose the small hardened steel valve stem end caps where fitted.

If during cylinder head removal the fixing nuts or bolts are found to have a dry, rusty appearance, they should be soaked with paraffin before applying the spanner. The copper or copper and asbestos washer should be thoroughly cleaned on *both* sides and deposited in a safe place, and the same applies to the rocker-box. To facilitate subsequent reassembly, the rocker-box end cover should be removed, if this has not already been done. It is also a good plan to smear some graphite paste on the threads of the cylinder head bolts or studs.

On 1939 Engines. The cylinder head (see Fig. 18) should be removed with the push-rod cover tubes attached at their upper ends to the head. The two one-piece covers are sandwiched between the head and the top face of the crankcase, oil leakage being prevented by a composition joint at the top and a rubber gland (like an umbrella rubber ring) joint at the bottom. If these joints should be damaged, immediate renewal should be made.

Drawing off Cylinder Barrel. Undo the base nuts. It is then a simple matter to draw off the cylinder barrel. When doing this the engine should be turned over until the piston is at the lowest position of its stroke, and the barrel gently slid off, care being required to prevent the loose piston falling sharply against the connecting-rod which might damage or distort the piston skirt. Be careful with the cylinder base washer.

It should be noted that on the Big Twin one of the cylinder barrel retaining nuts is *inside* the valve chest and on this model it is necessary to remove the inlet manifold before the cylinders can be withdrawn.

Having removed the cylinder, wrap a clean rag round underneath the piston, so as not to allow dirt or foreign matter to enter the crankcase. Remember, that should you by some mischance allow even the smallest article to fall into the crankcase (which the author confesses to having done once) it may be necessary to take the engine right out of the frame in order to extract the offending article. Anyway, fishing for a small nut with a piece of wire is at the best of times depressing, especially on a fine afternoon! Before actually starting to remove any carbon the piston should be be taken off. It is desirable to mark the interior of the piston to ensure its correct replacement.

Piston Removal. Decarbonizing can be carried out without removing the piston, but each alternate occasion it is advisable to remove the piston so that the ring grooves can be cleaned. On all A.J.S. engines the gudgeon-pin is of the "floating" type, and is secured in position by two small retaining springs, one on each side. These springs fit into recessed rings in the piston bosses, and to be withdrawn the ends must be squeezed together with a pair of small round-nose pliers. Afterwards the gudgeon-pin may be pushed out from the driving or timing side. The piston can then be removed from the connecting-rod. On replacing, see that the split on the skirt faces to the front and on a Big Twin see that there is no possibility of the two pistons being interchanged.

Removing the Valves. Valves of the side-by-side type can be removed, if desired, without disturbing the cylinder. Take off the valve chest cover and the valve caps in the case of a 35-6/5 engine, or remove the cylinder head in the case of other engines and place the hooked end of a proprietary valve spring compressor such as the Terry illustrated in Fig. 19 on the top of the valve and the forked end over the lower valve spring cap. Then exert sufficient leverage to lift the valve spring to allow the split collet to be withdrawn. The valve can then be pushed up and drawn out of the head. Remove the other valve similarly. Remember that side valves are readily removed with the cylinder in situ and a stout screwdriver can be used.

FIG. 19. TERRY VALVE SPRING COMPRESSOR FOR S.V. ENGINES

In the case of the engine with overhead valves it is necessary to remove the cylinder head entirely from the engine to enable the special valve extractor (see Fig. 20) to be used. This is a clamp-like tool for extracting the valves readily. For portability the tool is made to fold up. Unfold it and place the end opposite the screw over the upper valve spring cap in the manner illustrated on the next page. Screw up until the point of the screw presses inside the hollow of the valve head. Hold the cylinder head firmly, keep screwing, and it will be found that the spring is compressed. Then the two small split cones can be taken away from the recess in the valve stem, and the valve may be withdrawn. Repeat this operation for each valve. When removing valves, note where they come from and replace them in the same order. The valves are interchangeable on some engines, but it is best never to change them about.

Removing the Carbon. Procure an old screwdriver, or similar tool, and scrape off all carbon from the piston head. If this is done with the piston not removed be careful not to impose side strain on the connecting-rod. The piston may then be polished with very fine emery cloth, but do not touch the sides of the piston at all. With aluminium pistons the use of emery cloth is not advised, and if used great care must be taken to remove abrasive particles. If the deposit is very hard it may be necessary to allow the piston to soak in paraffin in order to soften the carbon. Now

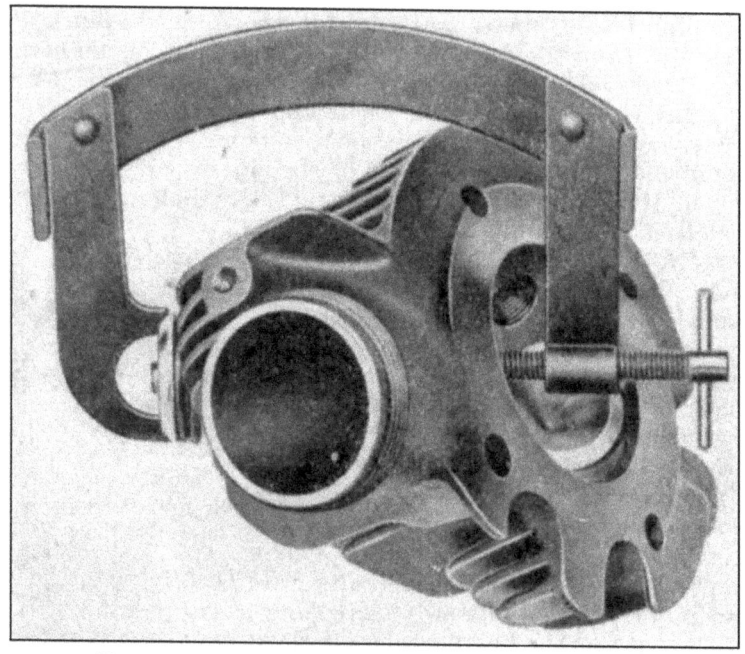

Fig. 20. The A.J.S. Overhead Valve Extractor

The extractor illustrated above is unsuitable for 1939 engines. If no extractor is available, shape a piece of wood to fit the combustion chamber, and then press down on the valve spring caps with a spanner or other tool.

scrape off all deposits in the cylinder head, being careful not to scratch deeply the walls of the combustion chamber during this operation. Incidentally, it should be mentioned that carbon deposits form less rapidly on smooth surfaces, and therefore it is worth doing the job thoroughly. On no account use emery cloth or, indeed, any abrasive on either the combustion chamber or cylinder walls. Any abrasive particles left would cause very serious damage in the event of their finding their way between the piston and cylinder. Chip off all deposits around the valve pockets and the ports, afterwards wiping all surfaces over with a clean rag slightly damped with paraffin.

Grinding-in the Valves. Should the valves or valve seats show signs of " pitting," the valves will have to be ground-in. This requires considerable patience and care. We will deal first with the S.V. type of engine. Stuff a rag into the combustion chamber or cylinder to prevent dirt getting in, and then, if removed, place the cylinder firmly on a bench with valve seats uppermost. The best preparation for valve-grinding is a compound such as Richford's (supplied in two grades, coarse and fine).

Smear the valve face lightly with some of the coarse carborundum paste, and insert the valve on its seat. Only use a little of the compound at a time. Now oscillate the valve repeatedly

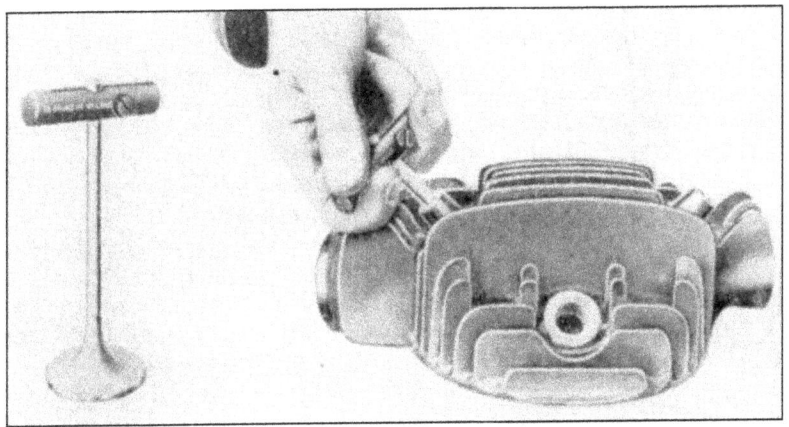

FIG. 21. USING A.J.S. VALVE GRINDING TOOL

On S.V. engines with detachable heads not housing the valves grinding-in does not necessitate cylinder removal, but care should be taken to screw down the tappet heads a few turns to ensure the valves seating with piston at T.D.C.

under moderate pressure with the aid of a screwdriver or a screwdriver blade gripped in a brace. Lift the valve at intervals, and turn it round a few degrees before dropping it again. Remove it at intervals, wipe and inspect the face. If there are still signs of " pitting," apply more paste and carry on. When there is a matt ring contact all the way round, and the little brown or black pock-marks have disappeared, the valve is a good fit again, and may be refitted. It is a refinement to finish off with a fine grade of abrasive, or even with rouge or metal polish. After grinding-in both valves, carefully remove every particle of abrasive from the cylinder head. Never attempt to grind-in a very badly pitted valve ; it should be returned to the makers to be refaced. To grind-in such a valve effectively would cause very bad wearing down of the valve seat, and would ultimately result in the valve becoming "pocketed," with consequent loss of power. A light spring under the valve head will assist grinding-in.

Grinding-in overhead type valves is very similar to the procedure described above; but, of course, the valves, instead of being pressed down upon their seats, have to be pulled up against them. For this purpose a special tool is obtainable (see page 124).

Having ground-in the valves and thoroughly cleaned out all dirt and abrasive, as well as any fluff on the valve seats, proceed to replace the valves and valve springs, together with the valve caps in the case of 3·49 h.p. lightweight Models 32–6/5. When replacing valve caps, smear a jointing medium, such as "Metalestine," on the threads, also see that all copper-asbestos washers are in sound condition. Valves should be replaced in their correct places. The colour of the steel usually indicates which is the exhaust valve. As a rule this valve is rather blue. If it is greatly discoloured it is a sign of overheating having occurred.

Examining and Removing Piston Rings. The piston rings are the main-guard of the compression. They must, therefore, be full of spring, free in their grooves, and set with their slots equally spaced round the piston to maintain compression. If all the rings are bright all the way round they are obviously being polished against the cylinder walls, and are perfect, and should be left alone. If, on the other hand, they are dull or stained at some points, they are not in proper contact with the walls of the cylinder. Perhaps they are stuck in their grooves with burnt oil, and will function properly if the grooves are cleaned. If vertically loose in their grooves or very badly marked, the rings must be renewed. Piston rings are of cast-iron, and being of very small section must be handled very, very carefully. If not, they will certainly be broken. They cannot safely be opened out wider than will allow them to slip over the crown of the piston. Therefore, to put them on or remove them requires the insertion of small strips of metal, about ¼ in. wide, which are placed in the manner illustrated by Fig. 22. When fitting new piston rings, thoroughly clean the grooves into which they fit, as any deposit left at the back of new rings forces them out, and makes them too tight a fit. Paraffin usually loosens stuck piston rings. Piston

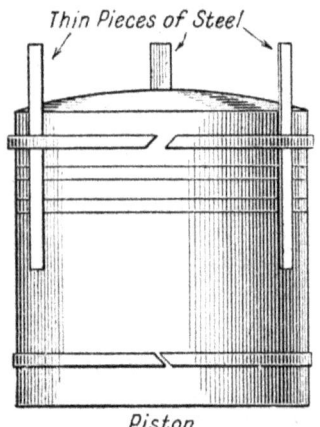

FIG. 22. HOW TO REMOVE PISTON RINGS

The above is the accepted method, unless one has a special tool available.

rings are made to very accurate dimensions, and it is very bad practice to attempt to "fit "oversize or undersize rings unless you know exactly what you are doing. Lapping-in oversize piston rings is a skilful job, and unless the slot sizes are exactly right the rings will not function well, and may even produce an engine " seizure." Therefore, always use piston rings guaranteed to be of A.J.S. manufacture. On O.H.V. engines of 350 c.c. the correct slot sizes are ·006 in. for the top ring, ·006 in. for the middle ring, and ·004 in. for the bottom ring. For 250 c.c. and 500 c.c. engines deduct ·001 in. or add ·001 in. respectively. All pistons are fitted with three rings, the bottom ring being extra wide on later engines to allow of a scraper ring being fitted if desired after a considerable mileage.

Lubricating O.H.V. Rockers. 1932–6 rockers have grease nipples provided (see page 30). A nipple is also provided to lubricate the upper ball joints of the push-rods. In the centre of the cover will be found a " Tecalemit " grease gun nipple.

Grease should, *with both valves closed*, be forced through this nipple, when it will automatically find its way to the two ball joints. It is important when this is being done that both valves are in a closed position. If the inspection cover is removed, care should be taken to see that the two coil springs, which fit inside the rocker spindles, are not lost. These coil springs press against the inside of the cover, and have their other bearing against the end of the hollow rocker spindle.

Cleaning the Outside of Cylinder. Rain and heat soon make the outside of an air-cooled cylinder look red and rusty. This does not affect the running, but does not improve the appearance of the machine, and to a very small extent reduces heat radiation. To remedy this the cylinder head and the cylinder radiating fins should be cleaned with a stiff brush soaked in paraffin, and afterwards painted with cylinder black. There are plenty of such compounds on the market.

The Sparking Plug. Occasionally clean the sparking plug with petrol and scrape the electrode points lightly with a sharp pocket-knife, afterwards checking the gap between them, which should be ·020 in.–·025 in. with "Magdyno" and magneto ignition, and the same gap with coil ignition. The reach of the plug should be $\frac{1}{2}$ in. The sparking plug should be frequently inspected. It is susceptible to oiling-up, especially during the running-in period and after decarbonizing or reboring.

An excellent gadget for quick plug cleaning consists of a metal reservoir containing petrol and steel wires. The plug is screwed into this and then vigorously shaken until clean. However, at considerable intervals dismantle a Lodge or K.L.G. and clean it thoroughly, which is not really possible without removing the insulated electrode of the plug from the body. When dismantling, first unscrew the gland nut with a K.L.G. tool or else with a box spanner. On no account squeeze the body in a vice. All metal parts should be scraped with a knife and then rinsed in petrol. Do not scrape the Sintox or Corundite insulation; but if coated with oil or soot, wash in petrol or paraffin. Next remove carbon deposits with fairly coarse emery cloth and again wash in petrol or paraffin. After cleaning the components, polish the electrode points with some *fine* emery cloth and reassemble, taking care not to over-tighten the gland nut, and to see that there is no grit between the insulator and body. Also make sure that the internal washer is correctly seated so as to give a gas-tight joint. Smear some thin oil on this washer. Finally check the gap, examine the copper washer, and clean the threads.

Suitable Plugs. All later type engines require 14 mm. plugs, but 18 mm. plugs are needed on some earlier models. Suitable 18 mm. plugs for S.V. engines are the Lodge C3, K.L.G. M30, or Champion 7. Suitable 14 mm. plugs for S.V. engines are the Lodge C14, K.L.G. F50, or Champion L-10. On O.H.V. engines taking 18 mm. plugs, fit a Lodge H1, K.L.G. M60, or Champion 16. For O.H.V. engines requiring 14 mm. plugs, use a Lodge H14S (or H14), K.L.G. F70, or Champion L-10 or L-10S. An excellent 14 mm. racing plug is the Lodge R51.

Reassembly of Engine. After thorough decarbonizing, the engine may be reassembled. Care should be taken to replace all paper washers and C. and A. or soft copper washers if fitted; any damaged washers should be at once renewed when reassembling.

On O.H.V. engines having a soft copper cylinder head gasket if signs of leakage are observed it is advisable to anneal the gasket before replacing it. To do this, heat it to a dull red and then suddenly plunge it into cold water. It is not necessary and not advisable to use any form of jointing compound where a cylinder head gasket is provided.

The piston should be oiled after being attached to the connecting rod with the gudgeon pin. It must be replaced the same way round as taken off, with the rings properly spaced. Do not forget the retaining circlips. They must be a snug fit. Hold the cylinder in the front angle of the frame, and place the piston a little before bottom dead centre on the downward stroke. By pressing the rings in with the fingers without disturbing the slot positions, the barrel may be slid over the piston. When replacing the cylinder on early models remember that it must be tightened down before the steady is again attached to the down tube. When the cylinder has been finally tightened down, then the stay of the steady can be adjusted so that the pin passes through the clip on the down tube and eye of the stay without force. The rest of the assembly is quite straightforward. There are three points to be noted, however: (1) Be careful to tighten all cylinder and cylinder head nuts and bolts evenly. They should be tightened finger-tight first and then done up in a diagonal order ¼ of a turn each until all are quite tight; (2) see that the overhead valve rocker bearings are lubricated; (3) make certain that the hardened steel caps on the ends of the valve stems are properly replaced and that the valve clearances are correct (page 38). Before replacing the rocker-box on the O.H.V. engines it is advisable to remove the cover plate so as to verify that the O.H. rocker ends properly enter the cupped push-rod ends. Be sure push-rods engage the tappets.

After assembly, test the engine compression by trying to pull the rear wheel over with top gear engaged and throttle open. Do not stand on the kickstarter, as this may strain the gear-box layshaft bearings. It should offer powerful resistance for several seconds on full compression. But bear in mind that the compression will improve still further when the oil has circulated again throughout the engine, and the valves and piston rings have rebedded themselves again. The machine is now ready for the road again, but before putting it on "active service" warm up the engine and then check over the various nuts and bolts (especially the cylinder head bolts), tightening those which are found to "give" to a spanner.

Carburettor Fitting. All 1932–9 machines, except a few, have flanged fitted carburettors, and if the carburettor is removed great care must be taken to ensure on refitting an absolutely airtight joint. If the washer is damaged, fit a new one at once or the bad joint will result in air leaks and erratic running of the engine due to a weak mixture.

Engine Lubrication. Full particulars concerning engine lubrication will be found on pages 21–30.

Care of Lucas Magneto. The Lucas magneto is provided with ball bearings throughout, which are packed with grease before leaving the manufacturers. Fresh lubricant should not be required under normal circumstances before some 10,000 miles (see page 30).

The contacts of the contact-breaker should be examined on a new magneto after the first 100 miles, again after 500 miles, and subsequently about every 2000 miles, and, if the "break," with the contacts full open, should be considerably more or less than will just hold a 12 thou' blade of a feeler gauge, they should be adjusted. Too great a gap will advance the timing. A special magneto spanner is provided, which includes a gauge for checking the "break." It is unnecessary to remove the contact-breaker to make this adjustment. All that is necessary is to revolve the engine until the contacts are wide open, slacken the nut securing the fixed contact screw and then adjust the screw until the correct gap is obtained.

If it becomes necessary to take a ring cam type contact-breaker off, unscrew the long taper fixing screw, and withdraw the contact-breaker bodily. The contacts only need attention at long intervals, and the reader should not interfere unnecessarily with them. The contact points must only be dressed with a fine carborundum stone or emery cloth if the surfaces have become at all pitted, and then the least possible amount taken off. The greatest care must be exercised. Always keep the contact-breaker scrupulously

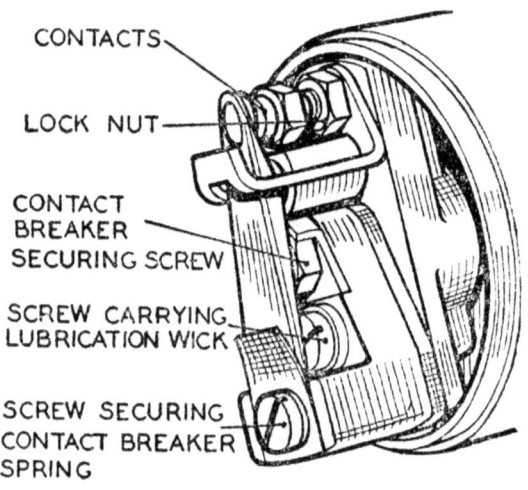

Fig. 23. The Lucas Face Cam Type Contact-breaker

This contact-breaker is fitted on all 1938–9 magnetos, but is not used on the 1935–9 "Magdynos." (See also Fig. 61.)

clean and free from oil. To remove the rocker arm, proceed as described on page 55. When replacing the contact-breaker, be sure that the projecting key on the tapered portion of the contact breaker base engages the key-way cut in the armature spindle, otherwise the timing of the magneto will be upset. Also, when tightening the fixing screw, be most careful not to use excessive force. Lubrication has been already dealt with on page 30.

All 1938–9 Lucas magnetos have a face cam type contact-breaker (Fig. 23), and in order to clean and dress the contacts the spring arm carrying the moving contact should be removed by withdrawing the fixing screw. When replacing the arm, make certain that the small backing spring is fitted in its original position, i.e. immediately beneath the securing screw and spring washer, with the bent portion facing outwards.

OVERHAULING (1932-9)

The moulding of the H.T. pick-up should occasionally be cleaned with a dry cloth and the pick-up brush should be examined. The brush should move freely in its holder and bed down on to the track of the slip-ring. Avoid undue stretching of the brush spring.

It will prevent misfiring and render starting easier if the slip-ring is cleaned occasionally. This is done by taking off the H.T.

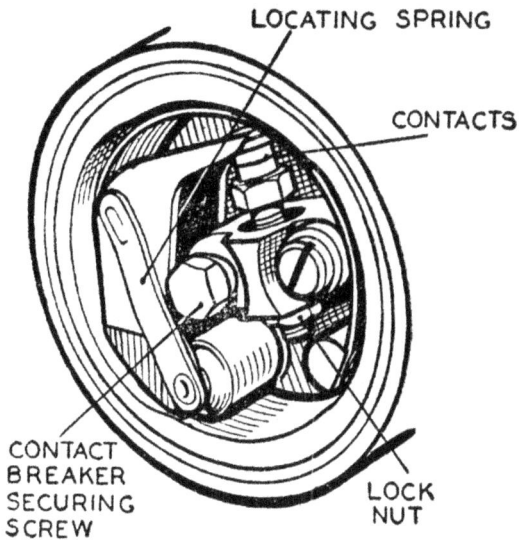

FIG. 24. THE LUCAS RING CAM TYPE CONTACT-BREAKER

This design is provided on 1938-9 "Magdynos" and has been used on 1932-7 pattern magnetos.

terminal and, while the magneto is being revolved by slowly turning the engine over, inserting a lead pencil, the end of which is covered with a clean rag moistened with petrol. The pencil should be pressed against the rotating slip-ring.

Beyond the above-mentioned points, the magneto should not be interfered with. If internal trouble develops, return the instrument to the makers for repair.

When Ignition Trouble is Suspected. Before interfering with the magneto verify that the sparking plug, the cable, and connections are correct. If these are in order turn the engine over slowly and watch if the contact-breaker arm works properly. This is bedded in a fibre insulating bush, and in moist weather there is an occasional danger of the material swelling. If this happens prise the rocker arm off its bearings and clean the pin on which it works with fine emery cloth, and smear a very small quantity of oil on it before replacing. Do not take the magneto to pieces needlessly. It is easily possible to damage it.

Care of "Magdyno" (Ignition Unit). Little attention is required (for maintenance of dynamo unit, see page 86), and if any serious trouble arises it is best to return the instrument to the makers for attention. Never attempt to remove the armature.

The contact points of the contact-breaker should be kept adjusted so that they open to an extent equal to the thickness

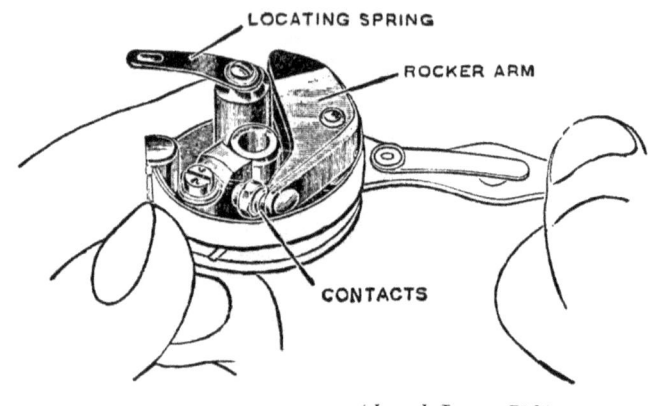

(*Joseph Lucas, Ltd.*)

FIG. 25. SHOWING "MAGDYNO" CONTACT-BREAKER AND METHOD OF REMOVING THE ROCKER ARM FOR POLISHING THE CONTACTS

of the gauge on the magneto spanner (·012 in.). One of the contacts (Fig. 24) will be found to be adjustable, and care must be taken to slacken the lock-nut before attempting to adjust the contact. The contact-breaker is designed to run without lubrication, and, except for very occasionally putting a spot of oil on the wick, if dry, to prevent wear of the fibre heel of the rocker arm, no lubrication is necessary (see page 30).

Occasionally, if the machine has been kept in a damp place, the fibre bush on which the rocker arm works will swell and cause the arm to stick causing irregular firing of the engine. If the contacts remain permanently open the engine cannot be started, for no spark at the plug can occur. The best cure is to remove the contact-breaker and rocker (see below) and rub the whole of the inside of the rocker bush with the head of a live safety match, which is usually sufficient to effect a cure. In exceptional cases something rougher may be needed.

The contact points themselves must be kept scrupulously clean. On examination after a big mileage the contacts may be found to have irregular and dull surfaces due to burning (especially if the contacts have not been kept clean and properly adjusted), and if such is found to be the case it is necessary to polish them up, otherwise misfiring and rapid deterioration of the contacts will inevitably follow. To polish up the contacts, use a fine carborundum stone or emery cloth (do not use a file) and with the contact-breaker and rocker arm removed polish the contacts until all pitting is removed and the contact surfaces are bright all over. Be careful to keep the surfaces "square" as well as uniform. To remove the contact-breaker and rocker arm, proceed as follows—

Withdraw the contact-breaker from its housing by unscrewing the hexagon-headed screw (Fig. 24) in the centre by means of the magneto spanner. The complete contact-breaker can then be pulled off the tapered end of the armature to which it is keyed. Next push aside the locating spring and with the magneto spanner prise off the rocker arm from its bearings as shown in Fig. 25. After polishing the contacts wipe away all traces of dirt and metal dust with a rag moistened in petrol. When refitting the contact-breaker be very careful to see that it engages the key-way on the end of the armature properly, otherwise the ignition timing may be upset.

Occasionally remove the H.T. pick-up (there are two on the Big Twin) and examine the carbon brush. It should work freely in its guide and not be unduly worn. When examining the brush avoid stretching the pick-up brush spring unduly, or a new one will be required. Renew both the brush and spring if they are in questionable condition. Also occasionally clean the slip ring track and flanges by inserting a small rag wrapped around a pencil through the pick-up hole and slowly revolving the engine. Little attention is required in regard to lubrication of the armature bearings and this is referred to on page 30.

The Miller Contact-breaker (Coil Ignition). Occasionally remove the moulded cover and inspect the contact-breaker which is fitted on the timing case of coil ignition models. The Miller contact-breaker is somewhat different to the Lucas contact-breaker. There is an adjustable contact point attached to an insulated terminal post; and a second contact, fixed to an uninsulated lever on which is a pad, which presses firmly on a cam fixed to the exhaust camshaft. Every two engine revolutions, the lever pad coming upon the raised portion of the cam, causes the contacts to open momentarily. During the remaining period of the cam's rotation, the cam leaves the pad, and this allows the contacts to meet and close the primary coil circuit. The contacts should be pressed firmly together by means of the spring. Binding at the pivot-pin bearing will weaken this pressure and prevent the smart make-and-break so essential for satisfactory results. To obviate this, occasional lubrication is necessary. The cam should be smeared lightly with vaseline and the rocker-arm bearing pin, if tight, should be oiled slightly.

About every 1000 miles the contact-breaker cover should be removed, and the contacts should be examined and the "break" checked with a feeler gauge. This should be ·018 in. to ·02 in. If the clearance is excessive, the timing will be advanced, and the primary circuit will not remain closed sufficiently long. Misfiring of some kind will probably occur. Provided the contacts are kept clean and free from oil, adjustment is required only at long intervals. If adjustment is required, rotate the engine slowly until the points are fully open; and then, using the magneto spanner, slacken the lock-nut and rotate the fixed contact screw by its hexagonal head until the correct "break" is obtained, as indicated by a suitable feeler gauge. Afterwards retighten the lock-nut. Check the "break" after the first 100-300 miles.

If examination reveals that the contacts, instead of having a grey-frosted appearance, are burned or blackened (due to the presence of dirt or oil), it is advisable to clean them with *very fine* emery cloth and afterwards wipe over with a cloth damped in petrol. Every trace of dirt and oil must be removed. Should the contact surfaces be pitted and uneven, it is necessary to true them up with a fine carborundum stone. Only the barest amount of metal must be removed, and it will greatly facilitate matters if the contact-breaker mechanism be first taken off the timing-case cover.

Retiming the Ignition (1932-6 Single-cylinder Models with Mechanical Lubrication). If the magneto or "Magdyno" has been removed from the machine, or the drive disturbed, it will be necessary to see that it is retimed correctly after it is fitted again. The engine magneto driving sprocket is secured to its shaft by means of castellations, which render wrong replacement impossible. The sprocket on the armature shaft of the magneto is supplied with a Vernier timing adjustment (see Fig. 26), which allows a very accurate and certain method of fixing the drive after the correct setting has been arrived at. The setting of this Vernier adjustment may at first sound a trifle complicated, but in reality it is perfectly simple.

Keyed to the armature shaft of the magneto or "Magdyno" is a sleeve (1) which has thirteen holes ranged in a circle. Fitting over a collar on this sleeve is the chain sprocket (2), which has twelve holes similarly arranged. Now on the sprocket on the engine camshaft and the magneto shaft an arrow will be found. These must point to each other before anything else is done. The first thing then in retiming is to set these arrows so that they exactly face towards each other. To do this turn the engine over until the arrow on the driving sprocket is pointing directly towards the arrow on the magneto sprocket. The latter should be held free in the fingers and moved a tooth backwards or forwards in the chain until the correct setting is arrived at. When this is so, place the magneto sprocket on to the sleeve, and rotate armature shaft of magneto until a mark found punched over one of the twelve holes on the sprocket exactly registers with a similar mark on the outside of the sleeve collar. It will now be found that the marked holes in sleeve and sprocket, respectively, coincide exactly, so that all that has to be done is to push the peg washer (3) into these holes. This effectively prevents the sprocket from moving from its correct setting, and tightly screw up the sleeve lock-nut (4), which can be done without fear of the timing shifting in the process, as is often the case with other methods. Set the piston at its correct distance (given in a later paragraph (page 59) from the top of the compression stroke—make sure that it is not on the exhaust stroke. With the engine in this position, take off the sleeve lock-nut on magneto sprocket, and remove peg washer. This will now leave the armature free from the engine drive, but still connected via the chain to the engine. See that the sprockets have their arrows facing

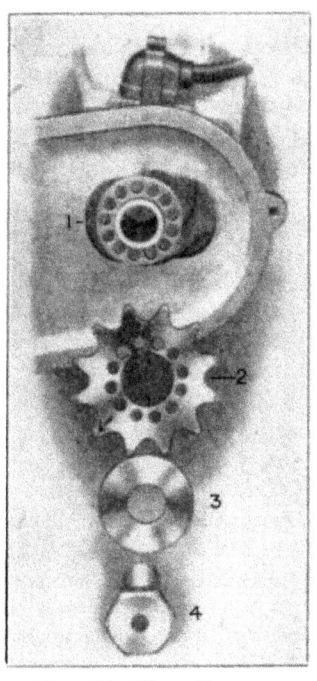

FIG. 26. THE VERNIER TIMING ADJUSTMENT

as previously mentioned. Move the spark lever to the limit of its motion of advance. Remove the cover of contact-breaker and slowly turn the armature till the fibre block of the make-and-break lever rises on the inclined plane of the steel segment sufficiently to just separate the contact points. This is the firing point, and in this position the markings previously referred to on the sleeve and sprocket should register if correctly fitted up. If so, the drive should be fixed up as before detailed. It is, however, always advisable to check the timing after tightening up.

It can be understood that so long as the sleeve (No. 1) has not been removed (i.e. its position relative to the armature shaft altered), all components can be replaced exactly as taken off, and therefore the timing is unaltered, but it should be checked.

The taper on the sleeve is very gradual, and hence the sleeve will remain firm even with the lock-nut removed. Should the sleeve have to be taken off, the magneto will have to be timed in the usual way, and the correct sleeve position on the armature shaft found afterwards. In the case where the sleeve is keyed the Vernier adjustment always holds good.

Retiming Ignition (Big Twins). In the case of the 1932-9 Big Twins, the "Magdyno" must be timed on No. 1 cylinder, that is, the one that fires first. This is the back cylinder and No. 1 cam is the one farthest from the rear cylinder when looking at the contact-breaker end (the lowest, 1937-9). The "Magdyno" chain sprockets have a plain taper bore, and to retime after dismantling, reassemble in the usual manner and tighten the sprocket on "Magdyno" armature securely, but leave the sprocket on the camshaft loosely fixed. Then revolve the engine by hand until the back piston is approximately one-quarter of an inch from the top of the compression stroke (i.e. the stroke upwards immediately after inlet has closed). Then with ignition lever in fully advanced position, and camshaft sprocket loose on shaft (the other sprocket having been previously tightened) turn the "Magdyno" armature backwards until the points are just about to break on the No. 1 cam. Holding carefully in this position, tighten up the camshaft sprocket nut.

There are two important points to which the author would draw attention. Firstly, do not forget to check the contact-breaker gap before commencing to retime; secondly, should it be necessary to remove the sprocket from the "Magdyno" armature for any reason, remember that it is absolutely essential before removing the sprocket locking nut first to detach the spring locking ring which encircles the nut and the locking washer next to it.

The "Magdyno" terminals are numbered on the body of the instrument, and care must be taken to see that the H.T. leads are connected to the corresponding cylinders.

The Lucas "Maglita." Vernier timing is not used in conjunction with the Lucas "Maglita," fitted to 1932-3 Models T5 and TB6 and driven by a special duplex chain off the inlet camshaft.

To Retime Ignition (All Coil Ignition Models). First remove the bakelite contact-breaker cap and slacken the screw securing the contact-breaker cam. Then with a small punch inserted in one of the slots in this cam, give a sharp but light tap. This will loosen the cam on the taper end of the shaft to which it is fitted. Now set the piston the correct distance before T.D.C. and the ignition lever fully advanced, after which gently turn the cam with the fingers in an anti-clockwise direction until the contact points are just about to part, in which position carefully retighten the cam fixing screw and replace the bakelite cap. It is essential, in this ignition setting operation, to obtain exactly the prescribed piston setting on the compression stroke, i.e. the stroke at the top of which both valves are closed, and to check the contact-breaker gap before setting the timing.

To Retime Ignition (Models with Separate Magnetos). First remove the outer portion of the aluminium magneto chain cover and slack off the nut securing the lower sprocket. Then, with a stout screwdriver, or the hooked end of a stout tyre lever, gently lever the sprocket loose from the taper on the camshaft to which it is attached. Then carefully turn the engine until the piston is at the correct distance before T.D.C., observing that it is on the stroke at which both valves are closed. Now fully advance the ignition and remove the contact-breaker cap, after which gently turn the magneto with the fingers in its ordinary direction (i.e. counter-clockwise when looking at the sprocket end) until the contact points are just about to break, in which position the sprocket fixing nut must be carefully retightened. Needless to add, it is of vital importance to obtain exactly the correct piston position and to secure the chain sprocket at the exact position at which the contact points commence to part. To find the exact point of break, place a piece of tissue paper between the points and turn the magneto armature until the paper is just released, and no more, upon a gentle pull.

1932–9 Ignition Settings. The correct procedure for retiming the ignition on the various 1932–9 models has already been described, and it remains to give the actual settings of the piston before the top dead centre (B.T.D.C.) on the compression stroke when the "break" should occur with the spark lever fully advanced. These settings are as follows: On Models 32–5/5, 32–4/B6, 33–4/12, 33–5/2 the spark should occur $\frac{3}{8}$ in. B.T.D.C. On Model 32–5/6 the setting is $\frac{7}{16}$ in. B.T.D.C. On Models 32–5/8, 32–4/B8 and 32–5/9 the correct setting is $\frac{1}{2}$ in. B.T.D.C. In the case of Models 35–9/12 and 35–9/16 give an advance of $\frac{5}{16}$ in. B.T.D.C. Give $\frac{1}{4}$ in. in B.T.D.C. for Model 35/4; $\frac{1}{8}$ in. B.T.D.C. for Model 35/14; and $\frac{7}{16}$ in. B.T.D.C. for Models 35–9/22, 35–9/18, 36–9/8 and 35–9/26; $\frac{1}{4}$ in. for Model 37–9/9 and Models 37–9/2, 37–9/2A.

To measure the distance which varies on different engines as given above, the cylinder head need not be removed.

On side-valve, overhead-valve engines it is only necessary to remove the sparking plug and gauge the distance by means of a piece of wire inserted through the plug hole. Two marks must, of course, be scratched on the wire, one indicating top dead centre, and the other above it the spark advance.

Some riders prefer to time the ignition by measuring degrees of crankshaft rotation, and in this case a degree disc must be attached to the crankshaft. The author is of the opinion, however, that this method is really "splitting hairs" and quite unnecessary and apt to entail a considerable amount of bother. Measurements taken on the piston stroke are sufficiently accurate.

"**Magdyno**" **Chain Adjustment.** Examine the driving chain occasionally and, if slack, tighten it until there is a whip in the centre of the upper chain run of about $\frac{1}{4}$ in. to $\frac{3}{8}$ in. when the chain is pressed lightly up and down. If chain adjustment is needed, the outer half of the aluminium chain case should first be removed. Then with a spanner slacken off slightly the two "Magdyno" platform fixing bolts and insert a lever or suitable tool under the front end of the platform and gently lever it up

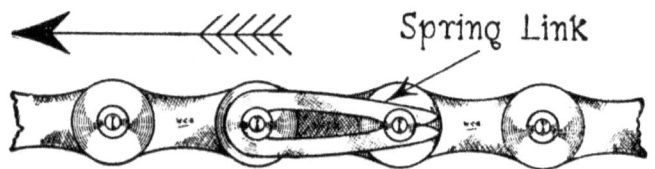

FIG. 27. THE CORRECT METHOD OF REPLACING THE SPRING LINK ON A CHAIN
It is unsafe to fit a spring link with the open end facing the direction of motion.

until the above-mentioned chain tension is obtained. Afterwards firmly retighten the platform fixing bolts, grease the chain if it appears to be dry, and finally refit the chain case cover. It should be noted that the platform fixing bolt nearest the cylinder operates in slotted holes to permit of the necessary tilting being obtained.

To Adjust Dynamo Chain (**All D.S. Singles**). On the 1935-9 single-cylinder models with dry sump lubrication to adjust the dynamo chain it is necessary to rotate the dynamo in its cradle mounting until there is a movement of $\frac{1}{4}$ in. to $\frac{3}{8}$ in. as the top run of the chain is lightly pressed up and down in the centre. Always check the chain whip with the chain in its tightest position. To adjust the chain tension, first slacken the dynamo clamp bolt and then twist the unit in its mounting *anti-clockwise* to tighten. It should be noted that it is possible to check the tension of both the dynamo and primary chains by passing the fingers through the inspection cap orifice. To release the cap unscrew the knurled edge screw.

When turning the dynamo in its mounting a spanner should be applied to the flats cast on the dynamo end plate. A suitable spanner is provided in the tool-kit to enable this operation to be done positively, readily, and safely.

An Essential Precaution. Owners of single-cylinder models should note that if for some reason removal of the dynamo sprocket becomes necessary it is essential to hold the sprocket with a spanner applied to the flats on the sprocket boss when loosening or tightening the nut. Unless this precaution is taken, there is risk of subjecting the dynamo armature to a bending strain with serious consequences. Before removing the sprocket nut, first remove the spring locking ring which encircles the nut and the locking washer adjacent to it.

To Adjust Magneto Chain (Magneto Ignition). If the magneto chain has a whip of more than about $\frac{1}{4}$ in. when the chain is gently pressed up and down mid-way between the chain sprockets it should be retensioned by tilting the magneto bodily upon the lower crankcase bolt on which the magneto platform is mounted, the upper fixing bolt holes being slotted for this purpose. To retension the chain, first remove the chain case cover, slacken off slightly the two crankcase bolts securing the magneto platform and then insert a lever or screwdriver under the top edge to force the back end up until correct chain tension is obtained. Afterwards securely retighten the two fixing bolts and before refitting the chain case cover smear the chain with grease if necessary (see page 34).

Engine Timing. No useful results can be obtained by tampering with the valve timing. On the contrary, all results following such action are likely to have a negative value, if they do not completely spoil the engine performance. The makers have arrived at the setting after very careful consideration, and have marked the pinions with a dot system of identification (line marks used 1937 onwards) to enable the setting to be always kept. The correct valve timings in degrees of crankshaft rotation for the single-cylinder and twin-cylinder engines are shown in Fig. 29.

To reset the valve timing after dismantling a single-cylinder engine, proceed as follows. Rotate the engine until the mark on the small timing pinion is in line with the centre of the inlet (rear) camwheel bush. Then insert the inlet camwheel so that the mark on it meshes with the marked tooth on the small engine pinion. Now rotate the engine slowly *forwards* until the mark on the engine pinion is in line with the centre of the exhaust (front) camwheel bush. Finally, insert the exhaust camwheel so that its mark is in mesh with that on the engine pinion.

The Big Twins have a single camwheel timing gear (Fig. 28A), and in order to obtain the correct valve timing it is only necessary to replace the camwheel such that its mark exactly faces the mark on the small engine pinion. To facilitate replacement of the camwheel the valve pressure should be taken off the cam followers by placing bolts or pieces of metal rod (four), about $1\frac{3}{8}$ in. long,

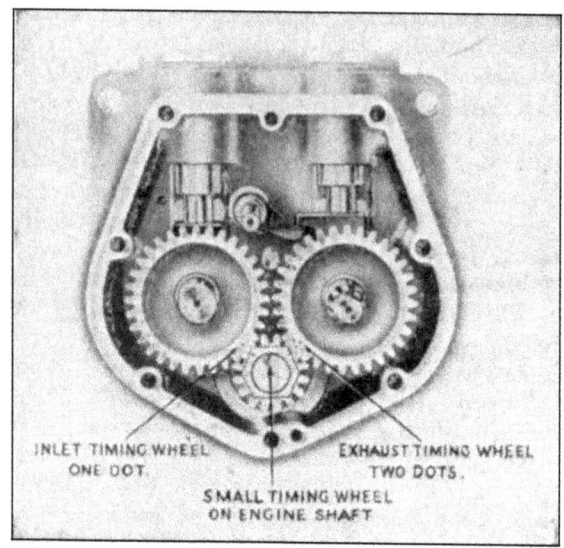

FIG. 28. SINGLE-CYLINDER TIMING GEAR (1932-5)

The timing gear on the 1935-9 D.S. models is slightly different and includes flat base tappets (Fig. 11).

FIG. 28A. TWIN-CYLINDER TIMING GEAR (1932-5)

between the valve spring bottom collars and the base of the valve chest.

An unusual feature about the Big Twin engine is that the timing gears run submerged in oil, and if the timing cover is removed for any purpose, a dish or some other receptacle should be used to catch the oil. It is unnecessary to fill the timing chest before replacing the cover, as a special feed is carried from the oil pump to the timing gear chamber for this purpose, and after the engine has been started up the correct level is quickly obtained.

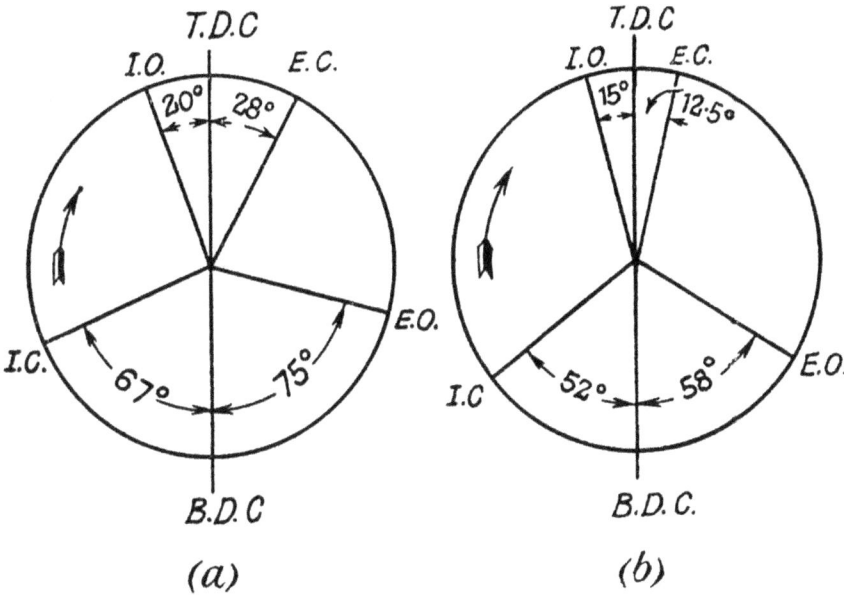

Fig. 29. Valve Timing Diagrams for A.J.S. Engines

The timing shown at (a) is correct for single-cylinder engines made since 1935 with the exception of the 1935 models 5, 6, 8, 18 and the 1936 models 5, 8, 9, 18. On these models the same valve timing is employed as for the corresponding 1934 models. At (b) is shown the correct valve timing for all twin-cylinder engines made in 1932 onwards. Note that timing must be checked with ·016 in. valve clearance (both valves) for single- and twin-cylinder engines

To Dismantle Single-cylinder Timing Gear. The gear-change foot pedal (where fitted) should be removed. On machines with magneto ignition, remove the magneto chain case cover by taking out the six screws. Then unscrew the nut retaining the sprocket to the magneto armature and remove the nut and the washer behind it. By levering with a suitable tool, or using a sprocket drawer, the sprocket may be taken off. Next unscrew the nut (R.H. thread) securing the sprocket to the camshaft and remove the nut and its washer. Having done this, remove the camshaft sprocket similarly to the magneto armature sprocket. With both magneto driving chain sprockets removed, take out the five screws from the timing case and remove the cover. In the case of the coil ignition models there is, of course, no driving chain to remove and the timing case cover can immediately be removed after first removing the contact-breaker and cam.

To dismantle the timing gears, unscrew the nut which retains the small engine pinion (L.H. thread) and remove the nut. Afterwards rotate the engine until both valves are closed and pull away both camwheels in turn. Then remove the small engine pinion with a withdrawal tool or by leverage. It should be observed that the pinion is a taper fit on the mainshaft, and is located by a key. To reassemble, reverse the above procedure, taking care not to over-tighten the nut which secures the small engine pinion.

Maintaining Compression. If piston rings and valves are in good condition, the only other possible sources of leakage are the valve caps, the cylinder head joint, and the sparking plug. The washers belonging to all these parts should be renewed as soon as they become at all distorted or uneven, and a jointing medium should be used when screwing up the valve caps. Test for compression leakage by putting thick oil on the sides of the joints and observing whether bubbles occur when the engine is running.

Testing for Spark at the Plug. The accepted method of doing this is to place a wooden-handled screwdriver with steel blade across the terminal and just touching a cylinder fin. Now depress the kick-starter and see if there is any sparking at the blade tip. It is just possible that the plug insulation is defective if the foregoing experiment produces a "juicy" spark, and yet the engine refuses to fire, assuming there are no carburation troubles. In this case take the plug out and lay it on the cylinder head, taking care that the terminal is insulated from the cylinder, and reconnect the H.T. lead. Now again depress the kick-starter and see if anything happens. If no spark occurs now, we may take it that the plug is faulty, and it should be scrapped.

Air Leaks in Induction System. The chief source of air leaks, apart from leaks at induction pipe connections and carburettor, is at the inlet valve guide. Should this guide become badly worn it must be renewed or the engine will run irregularly at low speeds. The occasional addition of a little upper cylinder lubricant such as "Mixtrol" undoubtedly lengthens the life of the valve guides.

Absence of Compression after Valve Grinding. This temporary phenomenon is common to all engines. Usually it is due to some foreign particles existing between the valve seats and faces. After a short mileage the engine regains its full compression.

Cleaning Dirty Exhaust Valves. Sometimes, when an exhaust valve is removed, the portion of the bevel face which does not bear on the seat is found to be thickly carbonized (due usually to running on an over-rich mixture). This deposit should be cleaned off before the part of the face which beds on the seat is attended to; otherwise the upper portion of the valve face may be damaged and in any case it will prevent the valve head from taking a central bearing on its seat during the operation of valve-grinding. Such carbon is fairly easy to remove when it has been soaked in paraffin for an hour, after which a stiff brush will scour it off.

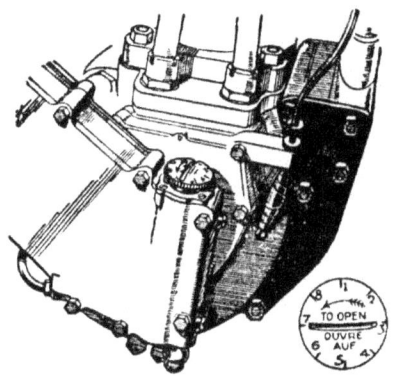

FIG. 30. OIL PUMP ADJUSTMEMT (1932-6 MODELS)

The regulator shown is used on 1932-6 models with mechanical lubrication (page 28) and a normal adjustment is to turn the knob half a turn from the fully closed position.

If an exhaust or inlet valve stem is discoloured, clean with some fine emery cloth held between the thumb and forefinger.

Paper Washers. These are useful in preventing leakage, and may be made by placing a sheet of paper over the part for which the washer is intended and rubbing round the edge.

Fitting New Small-end Bush. Amateurs sometimes drive out these bushes with disastrous results. The correct procedure is as follows: Get an old bush slightly smaller than the one which is to be extracted and a larger one for it to fit into. An iron bolt is then run through the connecting-rod, and the two bushes placed one on each side of the latter. By slowly tightening a nut on the bolt with a long spanner, the bush in the connecting-rod can be slowly pressed out. A new bush may be fitted in like manner, and if a trifle large externally can be eased off with emery cloth. See that oil grooves are provided on the new bush.

Assembling Flywheels. Strictly speaking, a lathe and dial indicator are required for this job, but it can be done with a vast amount of patience. The final test of truth is the absolute free running of the wheels when the crankcase is bolted up. The slightest suspicion of binding indicates that the wheels are not true. When the time comes for separating the flywheels in order to fit a new big-end bearing the best plan is to forward the complete crankcase to Plumstead.

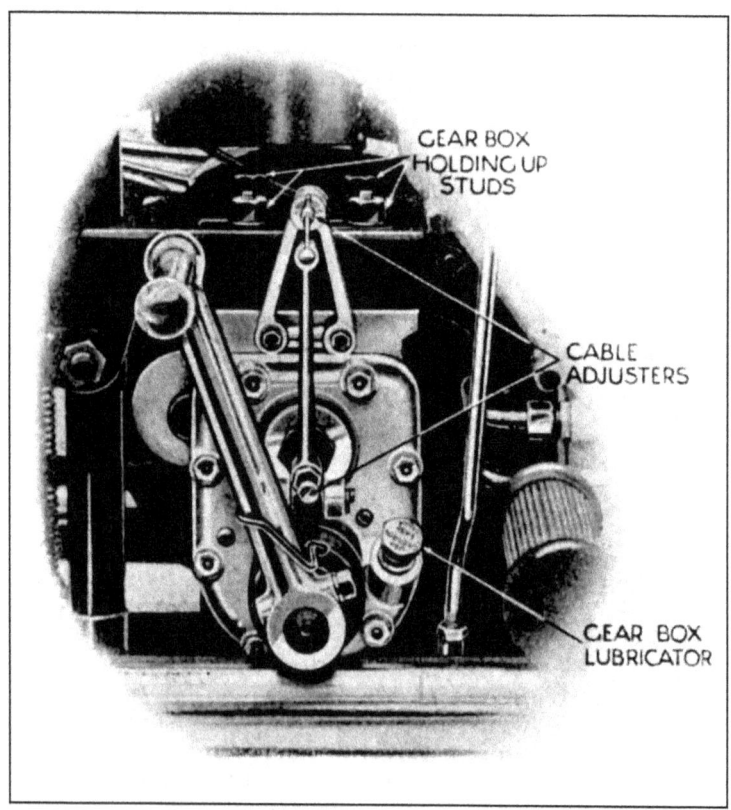

FIG. 31. THE HEAVYWEIGHT STURMEY-ARCHER GEARBOX (1932-36)

If You Do Split the Crankcase. Be very careful first to withdraw the oil pump plunger on the dry sump models, otherwise serious damage will be caused. In order to withdraw the plunger first remove both end caps and also the guide screw and then push the plunger out large end first. When reassembling, the plunger must be replaced after the crankcase halves have been bolted together, and *before* you replace the end caps you must refit the guide screw with its relieved tip engaging the profiled cam groove in the plunger. By moving the plunger to and fro while introducing the guide screw it is possible to find the correct location of the groove. The guide screw must finally be firmly screwed home.

How to Use the Foot Gear Control Without Causing Damage. There is one very important point which should be mentioned and this is the need for care in avoiding the application of excessive leverage on the foot pedal. With foot control it is very easy, especially in the case of muscular individuals, to put excessive force on the lever and possibly damage the control mechanism or gear selectors. On no account give a violent kick to the pedal, a steady pressure being quite sufficient. When changing gear the clutch should be released and the pedal moved simultaneously with

FIG. 32. THE TRANSMISSION SHOCK-ABSORBER

No attention in regard to lubrication or adjustment of the engine shaft shock-absorber is needed.

a steady movement of the toe. On reaching the end of the pedal travel the pedal should be firmly held with the foot until the clutch has been re-engaged. It is not sufficient to merely kick the pedal and remove the foot when the end of the travel has been reached.

Primary Chain Adjustment (Burman Gearbox Models). To adjust the primary chain, it is possible to swing the gearbox bodily on its lower pivot bolt, and to carry out this adjustment the following instructions should be observed. Loosen pivot bolt nut. Then offside nut on the top gearbox fixing bolt must be slackened off. In tightening the front chain first slack off the nut on the adjuster bolt nearest the engine and turn the nut farthest from the engine clockwise, until a correct chain tension is obtained. To ascertain this, remove the small inspection disc on the chain cover; the tension of the chain can then be felt with the fingers. It is most important to leave about $\tfrac{3}{8}$ in. up-and-down chain movement. When the correct chain tension has been arrived at, retighten the nut nearest the engine on the adjuster and also the gearbox fixing bolts. Always adjust the primary chain before the secondary, and after making an adjustment check, and if necessary adjust the gear control.

Adjusting the Primary Chain (Sturmey-Archer Gearbox Models). To adjust the chain slack off the nuts on top of bracket and slide the box bodily backwards by means of the adjusting bolt the necessary amount. It is important that the nuts are screwed tightly again after adjustment. The chain should be adjusted, and kept adjusted, so that the bottom run of the chain (visible on detaching the oil-bath inspection cover) can be pressed up and down in the centre with the finger about $\frac{3}{8}$ in. After primary chain adjustment it is usually necessary slightly to alter the adjustment of the gear control, as described below.

Adjustment of Rear Chain. On all 1932-9 models, adjustment of the rear chain is obtained by sliding the rear wheel bodily backwards in the slotted fork ends. To adjust, first slack off the nuts on each side of wheel axle and screw the adjuster bolt in each fork end to exactly the same extent, taking care to leave the wheel in correct alinement (see page 79). It may be found that moving the wheel back will cause the rear brake to bind. This possibility should not be overlooked, and the necessary adjustment is easily made by means of the brake rod adjustment. The correct adjustment for the rear chain should allow a movement of $\frac{3}{8}$ in. to $\frac{1}{2}$ in. as the chain is lightly pressed up and down midway between the sprockets. It should be noted that it is advisable to check and if necessary adjust the tension of the primary chain before dealing with the secondary. For shortening a chain, a rivet extractor can be obtained from most accessory dealers for a few shillings.

In the case of machines with quickly detachable wheels (above 350 c.c.) it is necessary when slackening the wheel spindle nuts preparatory to chain adjustment also to slacken the large nut securing the brake drum dummy spindle. Both nuts are on the near side and concentric to each other.

Gear Control Adjustment (Hand). The Sturmey-Archer and Burman gearboxes have a system of internal indexing of the various gear positions which makes adjustment of the gear control very simple.

To check the gear control adjustment on hand control models proceed as follows: Place the machine on the stand and remove the split pin from the top gear rod yoke end pin (i.e. the pin which passes through the end of the gear lever). Also at the same time slack off the lock-nut securing this top gear rod yoke end. Now place the gear lever into third gear position, and after removing the top yoke end pin from which split pin has already been withdrawn, lightly alternately pull and push the gear rod by hand in order to feel the action of the gearbox internal spring indexing plunger. As the sliding gears move either side of the correct third gear position the resistance of the spring plunger will be plainly felt, and the exact position at which this plunger is in full engagement with the third gear notch must be accurately and definitely found. Having established this correct position, offer up the gear rod to gear lever, which latter must, of course, be in the third gear position, in the case of four-speed models (second gear position on three-speed models) and screw the top yoke end up or down as the need may be until the pin can be quite freely inserted. Before locking the yoke end into position, it is advisable to again obtain by hand the exact position of third gear as already described, and check the rod length for correct setting, after which the yoke end may be secured by means of its lock-nut and the pin refitted. It must be understood that if the correct adjustment is obtained for the third gear all the remaining gears will also be correct as regards rod adjustment.

Attention to Clutch (Sturmey-Archer). This has no adjustment for the spring tension and the pins must always be screwed up dead tight, but the rider should always see that there is a little backlash in the handlebar lever so that the clutch springs can always exert their full pressure. To give the correct (about $\frac{1}{2}$ in.) backlash in the Bowden lever on the handlebars, adjust on the S.A. gearbox models by means of the operating shaft adjustment screw shown in Fig. 31. A further adjustment is also provided at the arm through which the cable passes.

Attention to Clutch (Burman). Two separate adjustments are provided to compensate for stretch of the clutch cable and wear of the clutch thrust rod. With the clutch correctly adjusted it should be possible to move the handlebar lever about $\frac{1}{2}$ in. (measured at the lever end) before actual declutching commences. Minor adjustment may be made by means of the cable stop and lock-nut (see Figs. 33, 34). Major adjustment is effected as follows.

On the latest gearboxes with enclosed clutch mechanism (Fig. 34) the fulcrum of the gearbox clutch lever is adjustable. To adjust, remove the small raised plate secured to the gearbox end cover by two screws, and then turn the sleeve nut exposed *anti-clockwise* to take up wear between the clutch thrust rod and the operating lever, or *clockwise*, if the lever is bearing on the clutch thrust rod and causing slip. (See also Fig. 71.)

On some gearboxes (H.P. type) there is a centre screw and lock-nut in the clutch spring pressure plate (Fig. 33), and wear on the clutch thrust rod may readily be taken up by the screw.

On other gearboxes (CAP, BAP type) the adjustment consists of a screw on the clutch operating lever on the gearbox. Access

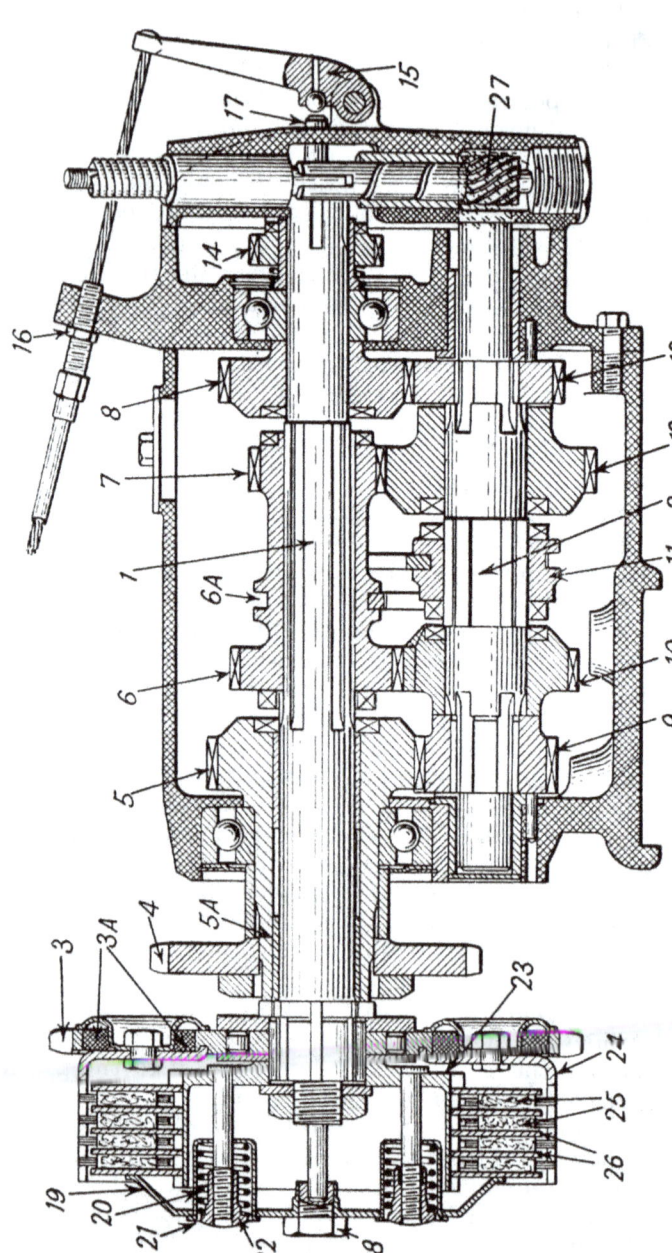

FIG. 33. SECTIONAL VIEW OF BURMAN FOUR-SPEED GEARBOX AND FOUR-PLATE SHOCK-ABSORBER CLUTCH
The key to the numbered parts is given opposite. This gearbox assembly is fitted to most 1932–7 models.

OVERHAULING (1932-9)

to the screw is by disconnecting the clutch cable from the operating lever. This enables the lever to be hinged downwards and the screw adjusted.

To Disconnect Clutch Cable. If it is necessary to disconnect the clutch cable for replacement or repair in the case of a gearbox with enclosed clutch mechanism, unscrew the large plated knurled nut on the top edge of the gearbox end cover, or on some 250 c.c. and 350 c.c. machines remove the steel plate (held by two nuts) from the front of the gearbox immediately below the point where the clutch cable enters.

If the Clutch Slips. First of all attend to the above adjustments, but if slip persists, screw in the spring adjuster nuts (22, Fig. 33)

KEY TO FIG. 33

  1 = Mainshaft (splined)
  2 = Layshaft (splined)
  3 = Clutch sprocket
  3A = Clutch shock-absorber
  4 = Gearbox sprocket
  5 = Mainshaft fourth gear
  5A = Mainshaft sleeve
  6 = Mainshaft second (sliding) gear
  6A = Groove for striking fork
  7 = Mainshaft first (sliding) gear
  8 = Mainshaft third gear
  9 = Layshaft driving pinion (keyed)
  10 = Layshaft second gear
  11 = Layshaft clutch
  12 = Layshaft first gear
  13 = Layshaft third gear (keyed)
  14 = Mainshaft K.S. pinion
  15 = Clutch actuating lever
  16 = Clutch cable adjustment
  17 = Clutch operating plunger
  18 = Clutch adjuster screw and lock-nut
  19 = Clutch spring plate
  20 = Clutch springs
  21 = Clutch spring cup
  22 = Clutch spring adjuster
  23 = Clutch centre
  24 = Clutch disked back-plate
  25 = Clutch friction insert plates
  26 = Clutch-driven steel plates
  27 = Worm speedometer drive

exactly *half a turn*, test for slip and repeat, if necessary. The correct adjustment of these nuts is normally *four* complete turns from fully home. Be very careful to tighten the nuts all the same amount and not excessively, otherwise difficulty in releasing the clutch will be experienced.

Dismantling Burman Clutch. To remove the clutch plates, unscrew the spring adjuster nuts and remove the springs, spring cups, and take off the outer pressure plate, when the other plates may be withdrawn. If desired, the complete clutch assembly may be removed after taking off the spring plate, by unscrewing the nut which holds the clutch body on the castellated mainshaft. All 1939 clutches have three friction plates, except those fitted to the Competition models, which have four.

Dismantling Sturmey-Archer Clutch. The Sturmey-Archer clutches used with the three-speed and four-speed gearboxes are of the single and multiple spring pattern. Dismantling of either type is a comparatively simple matter.

In the case of a single spring clutch, first unscrew the end cap, using either a special spanner or a hammer and punch. Note should be taken that it has a R.H. thread and must be unscrewed in an anti-clockwise direction. Now unscrew the clutch adjuster nut which is exposed and has also a R.H. thread. The clutch spring and collar can then be removed, allowing the clutch plates to be withdrawn. Be most careful when doing this to note the exact position of each plate so as to ensure their being replaced correctly. If the clutch inserts are thin but otherwise sound, extra spring tension may be obtained by removing one of the washers placed under the clutch adjuster nut. After reassembly be quite sure that the end cap is screwed up thoroughly tight.

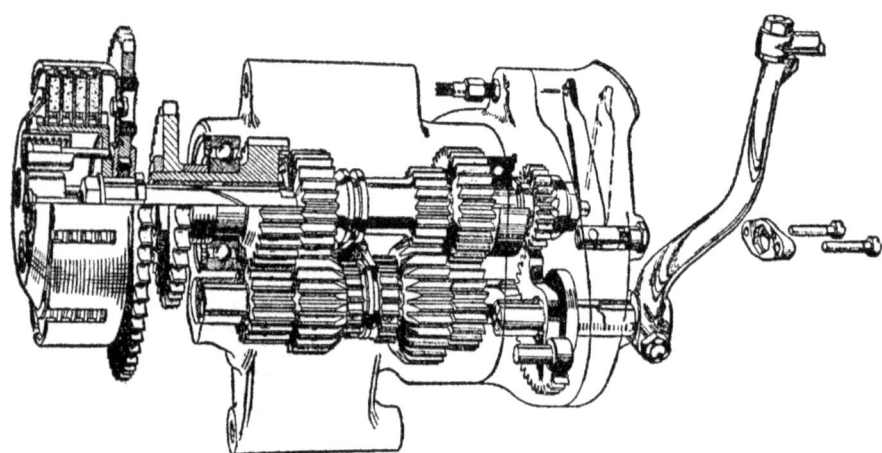

FIG. 34. THE BURMAN FOUR-SPEED GEARBOX WITH ENCLOSED KICK-STARTER AND CLUTCH MECHANISM (1938 ONWARDS)

With a multi-spring clutch unscrew the six screws which hold the clutch springs and then remove the springs and their boxes. It is then possible to lift off the spring box plate and withdraw the other plates as in the case of the single spring clutch. After reassembly it is important to tighten up fully each of the screws holding the springs so as to ensure the springs maintaining an even pressure all round. If this is not done some clutch "drag" may occur.

Removing Oil-bath Chain Case Cover. To do this on 1932–5 "Magdyno" singles, first remove the footrest arm and distance pieces, brake rod, yoke end pin and brake pedal. On 1938–9 Twins dismantle the clutch. Remove the securing pin in the aluminium band round the chain cover, after which it is possible to take away the outside half of the front chain cover. The replacement of these parts is quite a simple matter, and the remaking of an oil-tight joint round the edge of the cover is not difficult, as a rubber seal is used underneath the aluminium retaining strap. (See Figs. 13, 14.)

Coupling up a Chain. Always reconnect a chain with the spring link on a sprocket. This makes it perfectly easy, as all tension can be resisted by the teeth, and not by stretching the chain by hand. Also see that the open end of the spring faces the opposite direction of chain rotation. And fit the plate and spring clip so that they are on the outside of the chain.

Chain Repairs. Chain repairs are rarely necessary, but broken rollers may occasionally be found. When they are, they may be

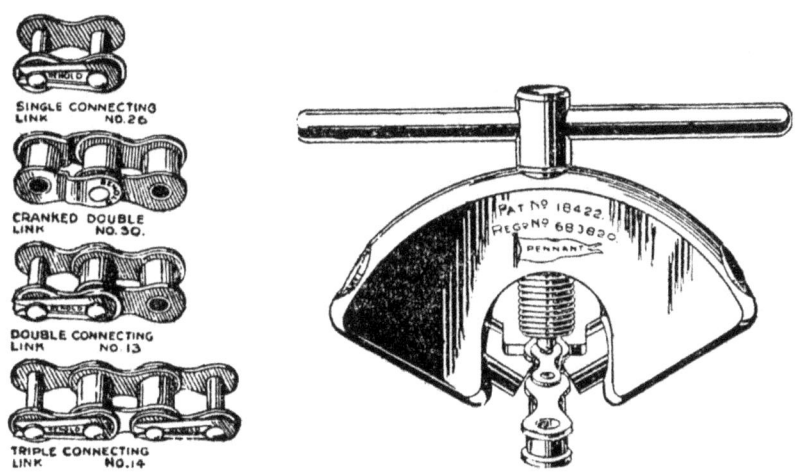

FIGS. 35, 36. CHAIN REPAIR PARTS AND RIVET EXTRACTOR

readily repaired with the aid of a box of chain repair parts and a suitable chain rivet extractor. Fig. 35 illustrates all the parts necessary to repair any fracture. To shorten a chain having an even number of pitches, replace by parts Nos. 30 and 26. To shorten a chain containing an odd number of pitches, replace by part No. 13. To repair a chain with a broken roller or faulty inside link, replace by part No. 14. For joining up lengths with inside ends, use part No. 26.

The "Pennant" rivet extractor is shown in Fig. 36, where the outer link of a chain is shown ready for rivet removal, the rivet which is case-hardened and incapable of being filed down, being forced through the bush by screw pressure. Before attempting to extract a rivet, compress the ends of the jaws to obtain a grip on the chain roller. To remove complete links, screw down the punch on to the head of each rivet in turn through the top plate (Fig. 36). Both rivets should be pushed out from the same side of the chain. To remove broken links, insert the chain roller between the jaws and then screw down the punch until the rivet head is pressed through the top plate. On removing the extractor the link will fall out.

Play in Steering Head. All play on earlier models should be taken up by means of the domed lock-nut and nut adjustment. The adjustment should not be too tight, or the balls in the steering head may be damaged. Keep this bearing well lubricated. To take up slack loosen the domed nut and screw down the nut below. It is advisable in all cases when adjusting the steering head to place a box or some other article beneath the engine so as to take the weight off the front wheel and allow the forks to move freely. Also slacken off the steering damper.

On all A.J.S.'s of later manufacture the steering head races are of the floating self-alining type with spherical seats. Occasionally test the head for slackness by exerting pressure upwards from the extreme tips of the handlebars with the steering damper completely slacked off. If any shake be noticed, slacken the pinch bolt of the handlebar clip lug which encircles the steering column, and screw down the large nut beneath the steering damper knob. As already stated, the front wheel should have the weight taken off it.

Handlebar Adjustment. All A.J.S. machines are fitted with adjustable handlebars. If the rider wishes to make any adjustments, slacken off the bolts which pass through the split lugs which connect handlebars to forks. It is important, however, that these bolts are carefully tightened up after this operation.

How to Adjust the Saddle Position. To adjust the position of the saddle, the pin and nut at the front (early models) should be unscrewed, and the nut that fastens the top of the coil springs to the undercarriage should be slacked off enough to allow the saddle to be moved into whichever of the three positions the rider desires. Afterwards the pin and nut must be tightened up and the rear spring again securely fastened down.

Spring Fork Adjustment. To take up any play that may have developed in the side links, unscrew the spindle lock-nuts on both sides of the forks and (looking at the machine from the front) turn the spindles by means of the hexagon heads seen on the left-hand side until all slack is taken up. Afterwards tighten up lock-nuts.

The need for adjusting the fork spindles is indicated usually by a click or creaking noise when the steering is sharply turned. To ascertain exactly which spindle or spindles require adjusting turn the steering head with the fingers partly over the spindle link end and partly upon the spindle lug. The spindles are tightened by *clockwise* rotation and, when adjusting, rotate half a revolution at a time before testing with the nuts tightened. Be careful not to overtighten the spindles, as this will cause unpleasant stiff fork action. The fork shock-absorbers have an entirely independent adjustment.

Fork Shock-absorber Adjustment. Ride the motor-cycle to a corrugated patch of road such as occurs on lively bus routes, and then tighten down the ebonite damper knob until the fork

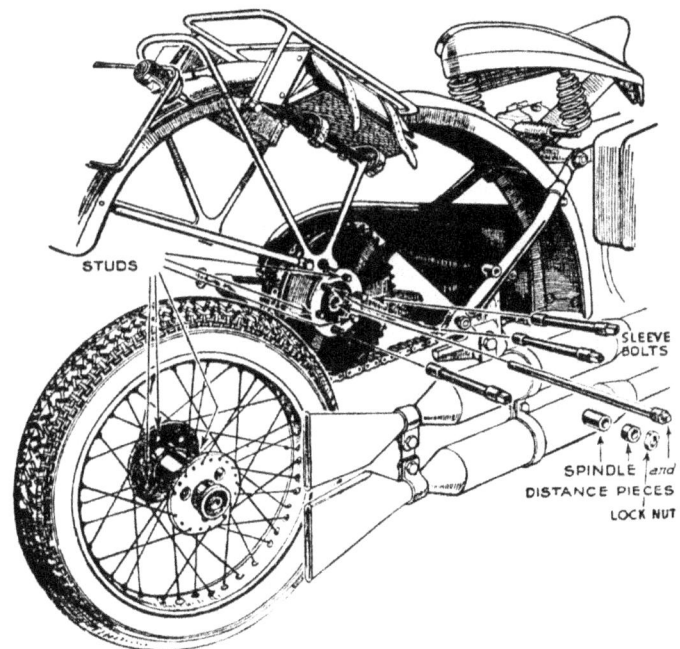

FIG. 37. SHOWING ARRANGEMENT OF QUICKLY DETACHABLE REAR WHEEL AND HINGED MUDGUARD

Above is shown the rear wheel removed from a Big Twin on which machine both wheels are quickly detachable and interchangeable. A quickly detachable rear wheel is also provided on 500 c.c. Models.

action becomes just sluggish. On normal roads maximum comfort will then be obtained.

Removing Rear Wheel. The rear wheel on many 1932-9 A.J.S. machines is of the quickly detachable type. It can be removed in 60 seconds! In the case of other models, the wheel and driving sprocket are permanently bolted together. To remove the wheel it is necessary to remove the rear chain guard and the adjustable nut on the brake rod, also the spring. Next proceed to remove completely the brake anchor plate pin and raise the tail portion of the rear mudguard by unscrewing the stay bolts. The wheel can then be removed after disconnecting the secondary chain and undoing the spindle nuts.

To remove the detachable wheel proceed as follows: On machines with the detachable wheel put the machine on the stand and unscrew the two pins, holding the stays of the hinged portion of the rear mudguard to the frame. This hinged portion can then be swung out of the way. Now remove the axle nut on the left-hand side, and with the box spanner provided then unscrew the three sleeve-nuts which pass through the hub flanges. These three sleeve-nuts extend right through the wheel and rear hub flange (as may be clearly understood by reference to the illustration on page 75), and screw on to the three threaded studs on the driving sprocket. There are also three plain studs on the sprocket which act as dummy drivers. These fit into the three remaining holes in the hub flange. After the sleeve-nuts have been unscrewed, then unscrew the centre pin and draw it out completely, together with distance piece(s). The space now left by the inner distance piece will enable the wheel to be drawn off the driving studs on the sprocket and removed from the fork ends.

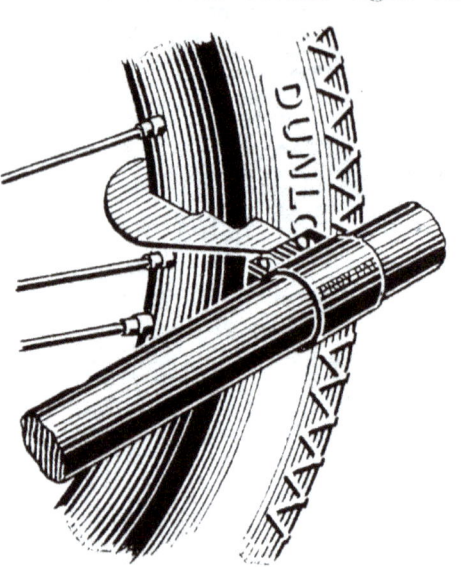

Fig. 38. Rear Wheel Alinement Gauge (1932–5 Heavyweights)

To replace the wheel, push it squarely on to the driving studs and next (with the distance piece(s) in position) screw up the centre pin moderately tight. The three sleeve-nuts can now be screwed up tightly, afterwards giving a final turn to the centre-pin. It is exceedingly important to realize that when the centre pin is removed, the wheel is hanging on one fork only, so any rough treatment must be carefully avoided, or there is great danger of straining or breaking the fork end. UNDER NO CIRCUMSTANCES MUST THE CENTRE PIN BE REMOVED UNTIL THE MACHINE IS JACKED UP, and the pin must always be in position before the machine is run off the stand. If the wheel is difficult to pull off the driving studs, screw in centre pin a few turns (without distance piece). This will steady the wheel while drawing off the driving studs. Periodically test the centre pin and sleeve-nuts with a spanner and keep them tight. If the sleeve-nuts are loose a dull hammering is perceptible at low speeds. If this is noticed, tighten instantly. If desired, of course, the wheel can be taken out complete with chain sprocket and brake drum, as in the case of models without quickly detachable wheels. All wheels are now disc-adjusting. Don't allow the hubs to run loosely, but see also that they are not over tight (page 78). Sidecar outfits have all three wheels interchangeable.

To Fit a Tube Without Removing the Wheel. On models having quickly detachable wheels a new tube can be fitted with the wheel in position. Lever off one side of the tyre cover and detach the tube in the usual way. Then remove the centre pin and distance piece only, leaving the sleeve nuts intact. This will leave ample room to enable the tube to be drawn out and other one passed through. Replace the distance piece and centre pin and proceed to refit the tube and cover in the usual way.

A Faulty Kick-starter Return Spring. If any difficulty is experienced with the return of the kick-starter crank after starting up the engine, this would be due to the spring not having enough tension. To overcome this difficulty, the kick-starter crank should be removed and also the cover for the spring. You will then notice that the end of the spring is fitted into the first of a series of holes to the right. To get additional tension, the end of the spring should be fitted into one or more holes farther to the right, which should produce the desired effect. Under no circumstances whatever should the spring be given an additional complete turn. The above applies to S.A. gearboxes.

Rear Wheel Alinement. On the right-hand side of the bottom chain stay is a piece of sheet metal, held in position by a clip, on some 1932-5 A.J.S. models. In the tool kit will be found a flat gauge that can be fitted round the rim (see Fig. 38). When replacing the rear wheel after removal, or after making a chain adjustment, place the gauge on the rim with the extension to the right and set the wheel so that the edge of the gauge just touches the plate that is held in position by the clip on the chain stay. This ensures the wheel being correctly alined, and must be done before finally tightening up the spindle nuts. Do not attempt to unscrew the clip from the chain stay, as the position of the plate is set correctly before the machine leaves the factory. It is important that the gauge should bed properly on to the rim on both sides; the best method of ensuring this is to see that the hooked end is properly encircling the bead of the rim. Then pull the gauge end into place firmly. Some pressure is necessary to apply the gauge when the tyre is highly inflated.

Care of Ball Bearings. Periodically shake and pull the road wheels sideways with machine on the stand to see if there is any shake. If any side play exists, slacken locking ring and turn adjuster ring until *all* play disappears. Then slacken ring one quarter of a turn and retighten locking ring. The wheel should be free enough for the weight of the valve to determine its position.

Dismantling and Reassembling Taper Roller Bearings. To dismantle, release the locking-ring and screw out the adjusting ring. The dished plate containing felt washer and plain plate will then drop out. Take out spring ring from the opposite side of hub and remove felt washer and holder consisting of two plates and retaining ring, the latter being between the two plates. The spindle can now be pressed or driven out from either end, bringng with it one of the outer races. The other race can then be driven out.

To reassemble, press in outer race on fixed or plain end of hub, *taking great care that it goes in square.* This race is pressed in about $\frac{1}{32}$ in. beyond its actual position, to enable the felt washer and its retaining ring together with the two plates to be put in, and the spring ring to snap into its groove. *Care must be taken to put the plate with the larger hole in last. This is most important.* This outer race can now be forced back until the plates are tight on the spring ring. The spindle can now be inserted, the short end being placed in first. *The long end of the spindle must be on the adjusting side.* The other race can now be pressed in until there is about $\frac{1}{16}$ in. *end play in the spindle.* Insert plain plate and dished plate with felt washer, screw in adjusting ring, *and gradually screw down until there is just a fraction of end play in the spindle.* This should be ·002 of an inch.

It is of the utmost importance that the bearings are not adjusted too tight, as this would ruin them in a few miles. Having got this adjustment correct, the locking ring can be put on and tightened up, *again taking care that the adjusting ring does not creep forward and make the bearings too tight.*

Removing Front Wheel. Disconnect cable or rod yoke end from brake operating lever, remove anchor plate bolt (where fitted) from fork end, and after slackening off spindle nuts the wheel will fall out of the slots in the fork ends.

Brake Adjustments. The brakes require no attention, with the exception of occasional adjustment of the control mechanism. In the case of the rear brake, this is effected by giving a few turns to the adjusting nut. The front brake adjustment is carried out in a similar manner by finger adjustment on top of the fork girder, or else on recent models by a milled nut at the side of the forks. If the ratchet rear brake on an "Export" model does not operate correctly, it is due to the brake adjustment being either too fine or the reverse. Move the adjuster at the end of the brake rod backwards or forwards until the position in which the ratchet device functions perfectly is found. (See also page 82.)

Frayed Control Wires. As soon as control wires show signs of bad fraying, renew. Once they start to wear badly their end is

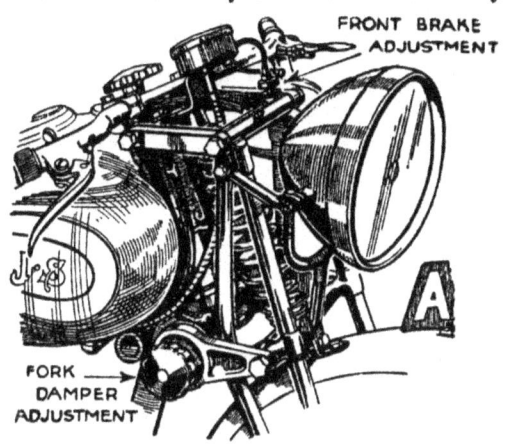

FIG. 39. 1935 FRONT BRAKE AND FORK DAMPER ADJUSTMENT

imminent, and should this take place while out on a long run great inconvenience may be caused. Always keep cables well lubricated at exposed places and where they bind. (See page 34.)

Loose Spokes. If spokes work loose in either wheel, retighten with a spoke key. Be careful while doing this to maintain the truth of the wheels. All spokes should be equally tensioned. On plucking with the finger they should all emit a note of the same pitch. The alinement gauge should assist truing the rear wheel, if this is required. Perhaps the best method of truing is to hold a piece of chalk against the rotating rim and observe by the chalk marks the evenness of contact, adjusting spokes accordingly.

Wheel Alinement. This is highly important, having regard to tyre wear. On a solo A.J.S., one straight edge or a plain board about 6 ft. long, 4 in. wide, and 1 in. thick is required. Place the machine upright on its stand with the wheels parallel to each other,

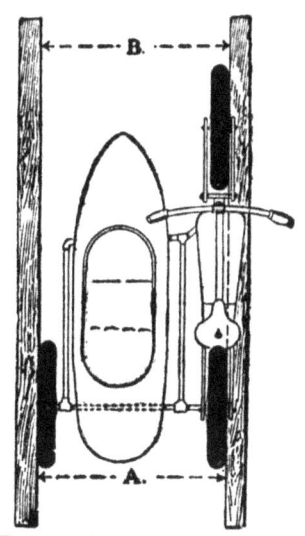

FIG. 40. SIDECAR ALINEMENT
The distances A and B must be compared.

and then check the alinement by holding the straight edge or board in contact with the front and rear tyres. If alinement is correct, it should contact each tyre at the front and rear.

Correct alinement is still more important on a sidecar outfit, in order to prevent excessive tyre wear and skidding. In this instance two plain boards, about 6 ft. long, about 4 in. wide, and about 1 in. thick, are needed. Both boards must have one true edge. A third similar type board, about 4 ft. long, is also required. A steel measuring tape and a pencil should be available when checking the alinement of the three wheels. When not using the above-mentioned boards, these should be kept quite flat to prevent warping, and care must be taken not to damage their planed faces.

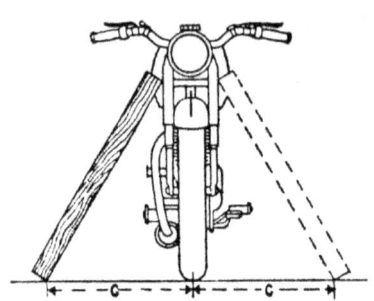

(*Dunlop Rubber Co., Ltd.*)
FIG. 41.   CHECKING WHETHER MOTOR-CYCLE OF SIDECAR OUTFIT IS VERTICAL

To verify whether all three wheels of a sidecar outfit are running in track, place the outfit on a smooth floor, preferably concrete. Then place one of the long boards alongside the front and rear tyres of the motor-cycle. Adjust the position of the front wheel to obtain the best contact, and note whether the board touches each tyre at two points, as already mentioned in the case of a solo machine. Now without disturbing anything, position the other long board with its true edge contacting the sidecar tyre, as shown in Fig. 40. Then measure dimension *A* and also dimension *B*, taking the measurements with the steel measuring tape as close to the tyres as possible. The sidecar wheel should not run absolutely parallel to the wheels of the motor-cycle, or there would be a tendency for the outfit to pull towards the left. To obtain the best results, distance *B* should be about $\frac{3}{8}$ in. smaller than distance *A*.

Besides checking the wheels for track, it is necessary to check that the motor-cycle itself is quite vertical. Usually it is possible to verify this point by visual inspection, but a dimensional check should be made while undertaking a wheel alinement check. Referring to Fig. 41, take the smaller board and rest it at a given point against the upper portion of the front forks. Where the board touches, mark the floor. Now transfer the board to the other side of the machine in a position so that it touches the front forks in an exactly corresponding manner. Again mark the floor where the board touches. The dimensions *C* should both be exactly the same if the machine is vertical.

Sidecar Alinement. If a sidecar outfit has a tendency to steer to the right or left due to reasons other than road camber, the motor-cycle is probably not upright or else the sidecar itself is

OVERHAULING (1932-9)

out of alinement (see page 80). After a new A.J.S. sidecar has done a considerable mileage it occasionally happens that the sidecar fittings take a permanent "set," causing the machine to lean slightly towards the sidecar. This trouble can be easily cured by means of the adjustable arms.

Keep Tyre Pressures Correct. Upon the maintenance of correct inflation pressures depends comfortable riding, freedom from skidding, and, most important of all, long life from the tyres.

TYRE PRESSURES FOR 1932-9 SINGLES

Tyre	Section	Pressure (Solo)	Pressure (With pillion)
Front	26 × 3·25	16–18 lb.	18–20 lb.
Front	26 × 3·00	20–22 lb.	22–24 lb.
Rear	26 × 3·25	20–22 lb.	22–24 lb.
Rear	26 × 3·50	16–18 lb.	18–20 lb.
Sidecar	26 × 3·25	—	14–15 lb.

Pressures should be checked weekly with a suitable pressure gauge, and if found above or below the recommended pressures, rectified accordingly. The correct pressures for A.J.S. machines

TYRE PRESSURES FOR 1932-9 BIG TWINS

Tyre	Section	Solo	Single S/c	Double S/c
Front	27 × 4·00	14–15 lb.	15–16 lb.	15–16 lb.
Rear	27 × 4·00	16–18 lb.	18–20 lb.	20–22 lb.

are tabulated above. If the driver is abnormally heavy or a heavy pillion passenger is carried, 2 lb. per sq. in. should be added to the rear tyre only.

A convenient type of pressure gauge is the Dunlop Pencil Type No. 6 gauge, illustrated in Fig. 42. To check the tyre pressure with this gauge, remove the valve cap and then press the gauge on to the open end of the valve. This has the effect of depressing the valve pin and enables air to enter the gauge. The calibrated piston is pushed out and the tyre pressure read off in lbs. per sq. in. Details of the valve fitted to all Dunlop tubes are shown in Fig. 42. The valve core embodies a non-return valve to facilitate pressure checking and inflation, and it forms an effective working seal. The valve cap, however, should always be fitted, as this excludes dirt and dust, and also provides a positive air seal. Keep the cap screwed down firmly by hand.

If a valve core requires to be removed for inspection or renewal, unscrew the valve cap and then insert the slotted end of the cap into the valve stem and use it as a screwdriver. Alternatively use the valve core key provided in the end of the piston of a Dunlop pencil type gauge.

Note Regarding 1939 Brake Shoes. The brake shoes on all 1939 models incorporate adjustable hardened steel pads to take the load of the brake expander cam and allow the full life of the friction lining to be utilized. To take up lining wear, remove the

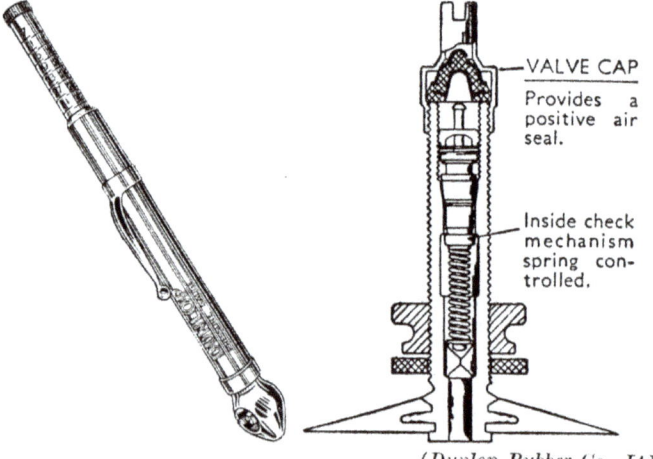

(*Dunlop Rubber Co., Ltd.*)
Fig. 42. Showing (Left) Dunlop Pencil Type Pressure Gauge and (Right) Details of Tyre Valve
The gauge shown has a valve core key incorporated in the end of the piston.

pads and place shim washers on the steel pad stems sufficient to centralize the brake expander. It is hardly necessary to mention that the steel pads prevent the wear that normally occurs when the expander bears directly on the aluminium shoes.

Removing a Wired-on Cover. First completely deflate the tyre by removing all valve parts, including the inside check mechanism (Fig. 42). Then push both beads off the rim seats. Now insert a tyre lever close to the valve, use some pressure on the lever, and push the beaded edge of the cover diametrically opposite to the valve into the well of the rim. Next insert a second tyre lever about 2½ in. distant from the first one, and progressively prise the bead over the flange of the rim. Continue cover removal with one tyre lever, while retaining the detached portion of the bead with the second one. Then withdraw the tube.

Stand the cover upright with the wheel in front. Then insert a tyre lever from the front between the flange and the bead, and carefully ease the cover back over the flange. If some difficulty is experienced in removing the cover, maintain the pressure on the bead with the tyre lever, and tap the cover off with a suitable mallet, preferably one lined with or made of rubber. It will, of course, be appreciated that complete removal of the cover is not essential in order to remove a tube and effect a repair, but it is always the best plan to remove the wheel from the machine.

Wired-on covers incorporate inextensible wires in the beads, and for this reason no attempt must be made to stretch the wire beads of the cover over the rim flange either during removal or fitting of the cover (see Fig. 43). Do not employ large tyre levers and always make sure that the wire beads are properly seated in the rim well.

Repairing Non-synthetic Tubes.

Auto-vulcanizing patches, such as the Dunlop "Vulcafix," are suitable for repairing tubes made of pure rubber or synthetic rubber. First thoroughly clean the tube in the vicinity of the injury, using fine sand-paper. Afterwards rub off all dust. Next select a suitable size patch and detach its linen backing by stretching the rubber. The patch may then be affixed with or without the application of solution. If solution is used, apply it to *the tube only* and wait until the solution becomes quite "tacky." Where solution is not employed, rub the prepared face of the patch with a cloth moistened with petrol and transfer the brown deposit on the cloth to the tube. Repeat this procedure, and give one minute for the patch and transferred deposit to dry. Then affix the patch to the tube, applying slight pressure, particularly around the edges. It should become automatically vulcanized. Finally rub some french chalk over and around the patch.

(*Dunlop Rubber Co., Ltd.*)

FIG. 43. REMEMBER COVER BEADS ARE INEXTENSIBLE

It is impossible to pull the cover bead at A over the flange of the wheel rim until the cover bead at B is eased off the rim shoulder C down into the well D. Brute force may damage the cover, but it will never stretch the beads

Repairing GR-S Synthetic Tubes.

A 1 in. diameter red disc

close to the valve or a stripe round the base of the tube identifies war-time synthetic tubes, many of which are still in service. For repairing such tubes, use the same materials as for non-synthetic tubes. Although it is satisfactory to effect an emergency repair of nail holes and other injuries up to $\frac{1}{4}$ in., it is better to remedy damage by vulcanizing. Where the injury extends for more than $\frac{1}{4}$ in., it is always advisable to have a proper vulcanized repair. The following points should be noted when effecting emergency repairs—

(I) Roughen the surface of the tube around the injury for an area slightly larger than the patch to be used. Remove all surface glaze with a wire brush or sand-paper. Then remove all dust.

(II) Select a suitable auto-vulcanizing patch (such as the Dunlop "Vulcafix") not smaller than $1\frac{1}{2}$ in. diameter.

(III) Apply one coat of solution to the tube and, before affixing the patch, permit the solution to dry.

(IV) Apply the patch and press it down firmly by hand. Finally dust the repaired area thoroughly with french chalk.

Care of Synthetic Tyres. Synthetic rubber tyres are more liable to injury and need greater care than is the case with pure rubber tyres. Avoid fierce acceleration and excessive speed. Also check the inflation pressures at least once a week, and remove all flints, etc., embedded in the tread. After repairing a tube, certain precautions are desirable during replacement. The following procedure is recommended by the Dunlop Rubber Co., Ltd.

Dust the inside of the cover evenly with french chalk. Then pump up the tube until it assumes a rounded form. Insert the tube in the cover. Then apply a frothy solution of soap and water liberally around the entire base of the tube, extending upwards between the tyre beads and the tube itself for at least 2 in. on both sides. Be careful not to allow any solution to run into the crown of the tyre. The condition of the solution should be such that it feels slippery when the fingers are wetted and rubbed together.

Mount the tyre on the rim immediately, while the soap solution is still wet and, before inflating the tube, check that the cover beads are clear of the rim right round. Inflate the tyre fully until all beads are fully seated. Then completely deflate the tube and re-inflate to the correct pressure. The purpose of double inflation is to allow any stretched portions of the tube to adjust themselves in the cover and thereby prevent the tube being strained. If soap solution is not available, french chalk can be used as a substitute, but this is not recommended.

Fitting a Wired-on Cover. Assuming the wheel is on the floor or bench, place the cover on top of the wheel and push as much as possible of the lower bead by hand into the well of the rim. Then insert a tyre lever and prise the rest of the lower bead over the rim flange. Round out the tube slightly by gentle inflation and insert it in the cover. Pass the valve through the hole in the rim. Now begin to fit the second bead of the cover by pushing it into the well of the rim in a position diametrically opposite to the valve. Lever the bead over the flange either side of this position and finish fitting the bead at the valve. Press the valve upwards in the rim hole to enable the beads to bed down properly and then pull the valve back firmly into position. Finally inflate the tyre to the correct pressure and verify that the beads are evenly seated round the rim. It should be noted that the moulded line on the cover serves as a guide.

CHAPTER V

CARE OF LIGHTING EQUIPMENT

THIS chapter deals solely with the lighting system, the ignition components having been dealt with in the previous chapter. On single-cylinder A.J.S. models of recent years a separate Lucas dynamo is fitted (magneto ignition machines) or else a Miller dynamo (coil ignition machines). Many earlier type singles, however, have Lucas "Magdyno" equipment, and this is provided on all the pre-war twin-cylinder models. Since 1937 compensated voltage control has been a feature common to all models. Conversion sets are available for earlier Lucas dynamos.

Equipment on 1945-8 Models. The post-war Models 16M and 18 both have a Lucas separate dynamo, type E3AR/AO5/1. This is mounted rigidly on the rear engine plates and is driven by a roller chain enclosed in the oil-bath chain case for the primary chain. The positive brush of the dynamo is insulated and the negative brush is earthed. Both terminals on the commutator end bracket are connected to a compensated voltage control unit.

The MCR1 type cut-out and regulator unit is neatly mounted beneath the spring-seat saddle, and ensures a dynamo output which varies according to the load on the battery and its state of charge. The battery itself is a lead-acid type PUW7E5 Lucas, mounted on a special platform below the saddle.

The "business end" of the lighting system comprises a Lucas type DU42 headlamp having a sturdy bracket fixing on the "Teledraulic" front forks. Incorporated on top of the headlamp is a panel housing the lighting switch and a type CZ27 Lucas ammeter. The tail lamp is also of Lucas manufacture and the dipping switch is located on the handlebars. A Lucas electric horn is mounted just behind the engine. An excellent A.J.S. pictorial wiring diagram of the complete lighting equipment is given on page 103.

DYNAMO MAINTENANCE

Before Removing the Dynamo Cover. Disconnect the positive lead of the battery* to prevent the possibility of the dynamo polarity being reversed or the battery being short-circuited and the ammeter burnt out.

On Lucas equipment a brass connector connects the lead from

---

* For safety's sake it is advisable to do this whenever any alterations to the wiring are made or whenever any of the leads are disconnected.

the positive terminal of the battery to the switch lead, and to disconnect, push back the rubber shield and then unscrew the cable connector, taking care that it does not touch any metal part of the frame. If it does touch, a spark will show that the battery has been well and truly shorted. Pull the rubber shield well over the connector when again reconnecting.

If at any time the motor-cycle must be ridden with the battery disconnected, or in any way out of service, it is essential to run

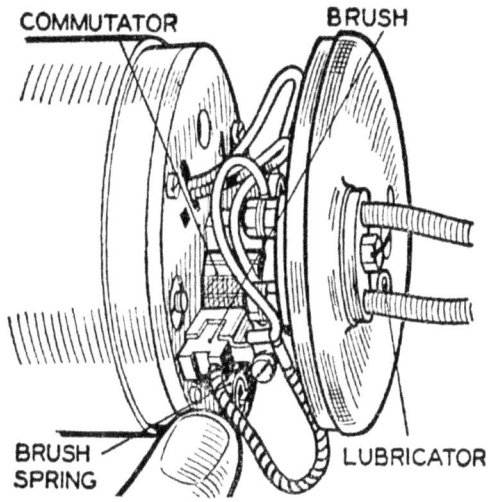

FIG. 44. COMMUTATOR END OF LUCAS DYNAMO WITH C.V.C.

As may be seen, the "third brush" and cut-out are omitted on all recent generators which have compensated voltage control. Some thin machine oil should be inserted in the lubricator every 4000-5000 miles.

with the switch in the "OFF" position. This does not apply where compensated voltage control is fitted.

The Commutator Brushes. With a brand new dynamo, no attention to the commutator is needed for many thousand miles, but afterwards it is advisable to remove the commutator cover about every six months and inspect the carbon brushes, which must be absolutely clean and able to move freely in their holders, on holding back the retaining springs and gently pulling the leads and then releasing them. There must also be perfect contact between the brushes and the copper segments; the brush faces in contact with the commutator should be uniformly polished. To clean the brushes with a petrol moistened cloth, pull back each brush-retaining spring and remove the brush by pulling on its lead, being careful to see that the brush pressure spring is clear of the brush holder. Examine the brushes for wear and unevenness, and true up if necessary. Generally it is best to replace the brushes before serious wear develops, as this prevents sparking, which causes blackening of the commutator and an unsteady charging current.

If Lucas brushes become so badly worn that it is necessary to remove them, this can easily be done as follows: Release the eyelet on the brush lead by unscrewing the hexagonal nut or screw at the terminal; then, holding back the spring lever out of the way, withdraw the brush from its holder. Replace with genuine Lucas brushes.

The brush springs should be inspected occasionally to see that they have sufficient tension to keep the brushes firmly pressed against the commutator when the dynamo is running. It is particularly necessary to keep this in mind when the brushes have been in use a long time and are very much worn down. Owners are cautioned that it is unwise to insert brushes of a grade other than that supplied with the dynamo, or to change the tension springs. The arrangement provided has been made only after many years' experience, and will be found to give the best results and the longest life. It is really best, when the brushes become so worn that they no longer bed down on the commutator, to go to a Lucas or Miller service depot, as this ensures the brushes being properly "bedded."

Commutator. The surface of the commutator should be kept clean and free from oil or brush dust, etc. Should any grease or oil work its way on to the commutator through over-lubrication, it will not only cause sparking, but, in addition, carbon and copper dust will be collected in the grooves between the commutator segments. The best way to clean the commutator is, without disconnecting any leads, to remove from its box one of the main brushes and, inserting a fine duster in the box, hold it, by means of a suitably-shaped piece of wood, against the commutator surface, causing the armature to be rotated at the same time. If the commutator has been neglected for long periods, it may need cleaning with fine glass-paper, but this is more difficult to do, and should not be necessary if it has received regular attention. The segments should be *dark bronze* and highly polished.

Cut-out (pre-1937). This is on the dynamo end bracket and constitutes an automatic switch whose duty it is to prevent the battery discharging into the dynamo when the engine is running slowly or is stationary. When the voltage at the dynamo exceeds the battery voltage as the engine is accelerated, the cut-out contacts close, and when the speed is reduced and the battery voltage exceeds the dynamo voltage the contacts open, so making it

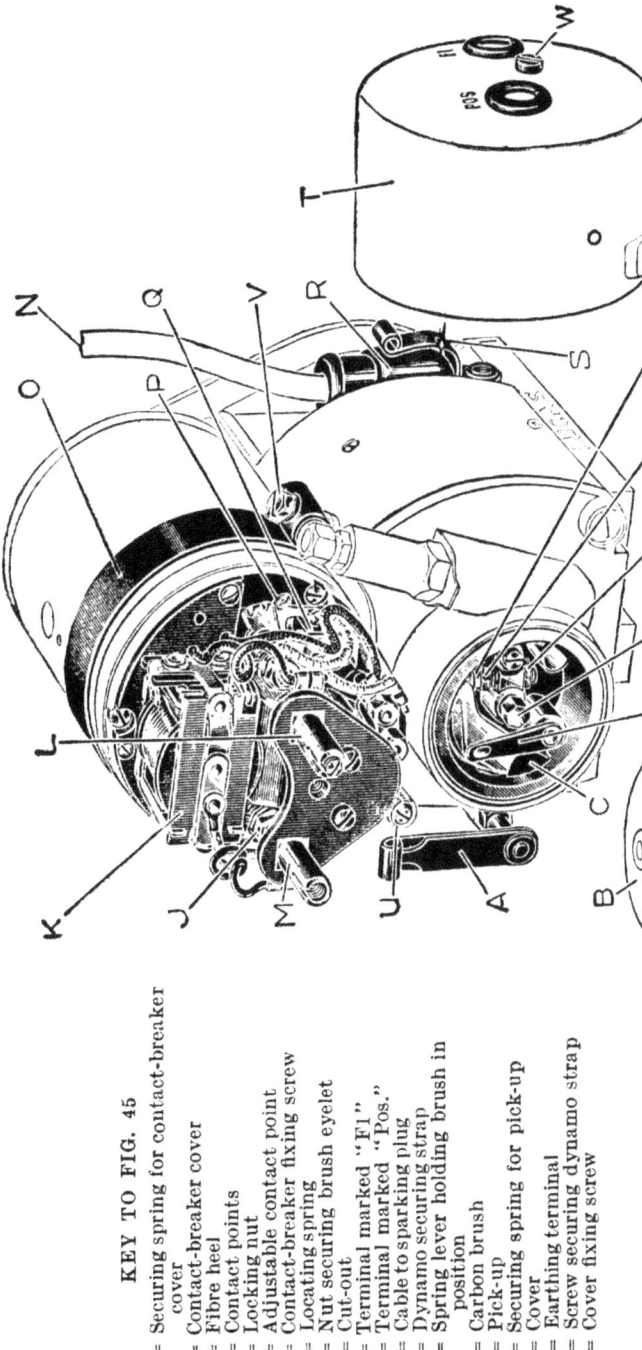

Fig. 45. The 1935–6 "Magdyno" without Compensated Voltage Control.

KEY TO FIG. 45

- A = Securing spring for contact-breaker cover
- B = Contact-breaker cover
- C = Fibre heel
- D = Contact points
- E = Locking nut
- F = Adjustable contact point
- G = Contact-breaker fixing screw
- H = Locating spring
- J = Nut securing brush eyelet
- K = Cut-out
- L = Terminal marked "F1"
- M = Terminal marked "Pos."
- N = Cable to sparking plug
- O = Dynamo securing strap
- P = Spring lever holding brush in position
- Q = Carbon brush
- R = Pick-up
- S = Securing spring for pick-up
- T = Cover
- U = Earthing terminal
- V = Screw securing dynamo strap
- W = Cover fixing screw

absolutely impossible for the battery to discharge back through the dynamo. It should be noted, however, that the cut-out is not intended to and cannot prevent over-charging of the battery. Compensated voltage control, however, does prevent it.

If by any unlucky chance the dynamo polarity becomes reversed, the remedy is to run the engine *slowly* with the switch in the "C" position and then press the cut-out contacts together momentarily. In the case of Miller dynamos, press the contacts together with the switch in the "H" position. (See below.)

Compensated Voltage Control (1937–47). It comprises the cut-out and voltage control (working on the trembler principle) neatly housed in a box on the machine. It is connected across

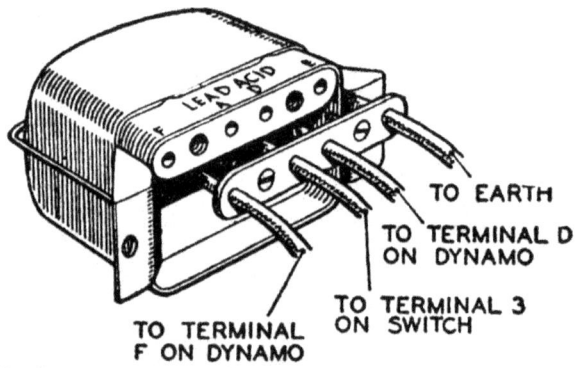

Fig. 46. Connections on Lucas Cut-out and Regulator Unit

the brushes and sees to it that the battery is kept properly charged automatically, the dynamo output varying according to the state of charge of the battery and the load. The regulator begins to operate when the dynamo voltage reaches about 7·3 volt. With this equipment the switch resistance is omitted and there are only three positions—"Off," "L," and "H," for the switch. In all three positions the dynamo gives a controlled output, thus relieving the rider of much responsibility. During daylight running when the battery is well charged the ammeter may indicate a charge of only 1 or 2 amperes, for the dynamo gives only a trickle charge. This may occur with the switch "Off."

If battery is low, the ammeter may show 6 amp. The voltage control unit is sealed by the makers and should not be tampered with, the only likely trouble being oxidizing or welding together of the contacts due to accidental crossing of the dynamo field and positive leads. If a "Lucas-Knife" battery is fitted, the regulator should be changed at a Lucas service depot. Excellent service is given at Lucas and Miller depots and the reader is advised to call at one whenever any spot of bother is encountered

CARE OF LIGHTING EQUIPMENT

in regard to the electrical equipment. On machines having C.V.C., if it is found that the battery is constantly in a low state of charge, or, if on the other hand, it is being overcharged by the dynamo, the setting of the regulator should be checked at a depot specializing in the type of equipment specified on the A.J.S. concerned. As previously mentioned, all post-war models have Lucas equipment.

Keep the battery connections clean and tight, otherwise the ammeter readings will suggest a fully charged battery when such is not the case. Also do not neglect a badly discharged battery. See that the dynamo to regulator cable insulations are correct and that the connections are good. The earth contact of the regulator must also be perfect. (For wiring diagram, see page 102.)

What the Ammeter is For. This centre-zero instrument which shows a charge on one side and a discharge on the other is provided to give a reading of the amount of current flowing to and from the battery. It indicates whether or not the electrical equipment is functioning satisfactorily.

Removal of Ammeter. Should it be necessary for some reason to remove the ammeter on a post-war A.J.S. having the ammeter incorporated on the headlamp, this can readily be effected. Referring to Fig. 47, detach the panel from the top of the DU42 Lucas headlamp by unscrewing the three retaining screws. Then unscrew the two ammeter terminal screws shown at *A* and disconnect the wires. Next bend back the four metal tags shown at *B*. When these have been dealt with, the ammeter can be removed bodily from the panel. To replace the ammeter, proceed in the reverse order of removal.

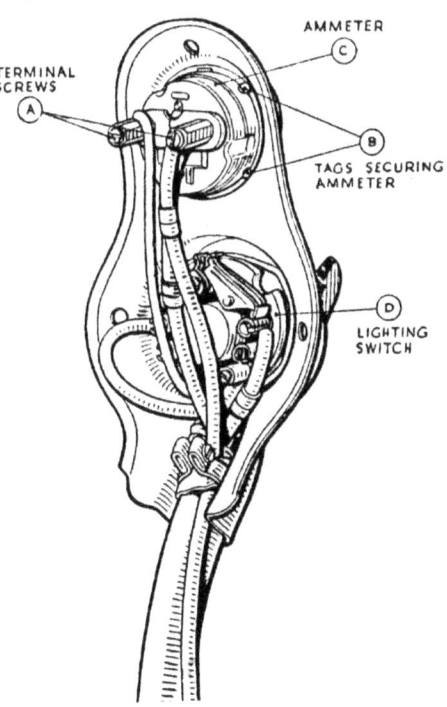

FIG. 47. PANEL REMOVED FROM TOP OF LUCAS DU42 HEADLAMP

Absence of Fuses. In order to simplify the system so far as possible, no fuse is provided. If all the connections are kept clean and tight, there is no possibility of any excess current causing damage to the equipment.

Lucas Terminals. The positive dynamo terminal, marked "POS," and the shunt-field terminal, marked "FI," are situated on either side of the cover (Fig. 45). To connect up, the cables merely have to be bared and clamped in their terminals by means of grub screws. This applies to 1935-6 dynamos.

On the later generator (Fig. 44) with separate voltage control unit the positive dynamo terminal is marked "D" and the shunt-field terminal "F" on the cover. To connect up, first slacken the fixing screw on the terminal block and remove the clamping plate. Then withdraw the metal sleeve from each terminal. The cables should then be passed through the clamping plate holes and bared at the ends for ¾ in. Now fit the sleeves over the cables, bend back the wires over them and push the sleeves home into the terminals, finally screwing down the clamping plate (see Fig. 46).

CARE OF THE BATTERY (LEAD-ACID TYPE)

It is of the utmost importance that the battery should receive regular attention to keep it in good condition.

The following are the most important maintenance hints—
1. Keep the acid level with the tops of the separators.
2. Add only distilled water, never tap water.
3. Test the condition of the battery by taking readings of the specific gravity of the acid with a hydrometer.
4. The battery must never be left in a discharged condition.

Topping Up. Examine the acid level about every two weeks, and even more frequently in hot weather and tropical climates. Unscrew the battery clamping screw and remove the battery. Then take off the battery lid and remove the three vent plugs. Inspect the hole in each vent plug and make certain that it is not obstructed. A choked vent plug hole will result in an increase of pressure in the cell due to "gassing," and this may cause trouble. Wipe the top of the battery clean with a rag and also verify that the rubber washer fitted beneath each vent plug, to prevent leakage, is in position. After wiping the top of the battery, either destroy the rag or else wash it thoroughly, using several changes of water. See that a supply of clean distilled water is to hand.

Be careful not to hold a naked light near the vents. If the level is below the tops of the separators, add distilled water as required. This should be added to each cell just before a charge run, as the agitation due to running and the gassing will thoroughly mix the solution. Acid must not be added to the electrolyte unless spilled. If the solution has been spilled by accident, add diluted sulphuric acid of specific gravity equal to that in the remaining cells.

CARE OF LIGHTING EQUIPMENT

When the inspection is carried out, hydrometer readings (specific gravity values) should be taken of the solution in each of the cells. The method of doing this is shown in Fig. 48. The hydrometer contains a graduated float which indicates the specific gravity of the battery cell from which a sample of electrolyte is taken.

After a sample has been taken and checked, it must, of course, be returned to the cell. The taking of S.G. readings with a hydrometer is the most efficient way of ascertaining the state of charge of the battery. The S.G. readings should be approximately the same for all three cells. Should the reading for one cell differ substantially from the readings for the others, probably some acid has been spilled or has leaked from the cell concerned. There is also a possibility of a short-circuit between the battery plates. In the latter case it will be necessary to return the battery to a service depot for attention. Under no circumstances must the battery be permitted to remain in a discharged condition for long, or serious deterioration will occur. After checking the S.G. readings and topping up, wipe from the top of the battery any spilled liquid; replace the vent plugs and battery lid. Then fit and tighten the battery clamping screw.

Always keep the battery connections clean and free from acid. To prevent corrosion they should be smeared with vaseline.

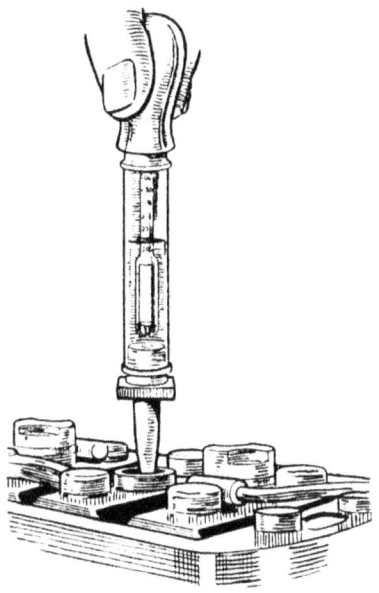

FIG. 48. CHECKING SPECIFIC GRAVITY OF ELECTROLYTE WITH LUCAS HYDROMETER

Specific Gravity Readings. For both Lucas and Miller batteries fitted to A.J.S. machines, the specific gravity readings at an acid temperature of approximately 60° F. should be: 1·280–1·300, battery fully charged; about 1·210 battery half discharged; below 1·150, battery fully discharged.

Charging Hints. The charging required on machines without compensated voltage control varies considerably owing to various running conditions. If the light is poor and falls off when the machine is standing, charging should be immediately carried out. It is difficult to lay down rigid instructions on the question of charging, since it largely depends upon the extent to which the lamps are used. With the coil ignition models more charging is necessary than with the magneto ignition models, since the current is used for ignition and lighting. The following suggestion may serve as a rough guide: leave the switch in the "charge" position during the day for about 50 per cent of the night riding (a slight charge should flow to the battery when running with lamps on). Charging a battery after discharge raises the specific gravity, and discharging lowers the specific gravity. Place on charge, either by running the engine or using an independent electrical supply, immediately any battery whose specific gravity

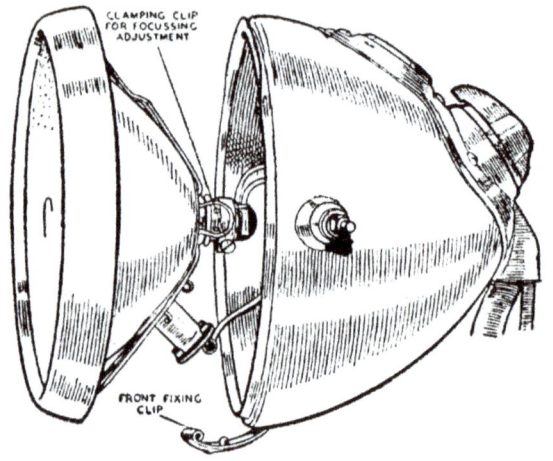

FIG. 49. LUCAS DU42 HEADLAMP WITH FRONT REMOVED

has fallen as low as 1·210. Take hydrometer readings whenever trouble is experienced with any part of the electrical system.

Storage. If the equipment is laid by for several months, the battery must be given a small charge from a separate source of electrical energy about once a fortnight, in order to obviate any permanent sulphation of the plates. In no circumstances must the electrolyte be removed from the battery and the plates allowed to dry, as certain chemical changes take place which result in permanent loss of capacity.

LAMPS

Lucas DU42 Headlamp. This headlamp fitted to all post-war A.J.S. machines is very similar to earlier Lucas types, except that the indirectly illuminated ammeter and the lighting switch are housed in a panel mounted on top of the lamp instead of being mounted on a fuel tank panel. On all Lucas headlamps a double-filament main bulb is used, one filament (that for normal driving) being placed at the focus of the reflector, and the other (that for the anti-dazzle dipped beam) slightly above it. The

CARE OF LIGHTING EQUIPMENT

change-over from the normal driving light to the dipped beam is effected by means of the dipping switch on the handlebars. A small pilot bulb is also incorporated for use when driving in well-lit streets and for parking purposes.

Switch Positions. The lighting switch incorporated on the tank panel, or on top of the headlamp in the case of recent models, has the following positions—

"Off"—Lamps off and dynamo charging (C.V.C. only).

"C"—Lamps off and dynamo delivering about half its normal output. On all machines fitted with compensated voltage control, the "C" position is omitted.

"H"—Headlamp (driving light), tail lamp, and sidecar lamp (where fitted) on; dynamo charging (maximum output (4-5 amp.) where C.V.C. is not fitted).

"L"—Conditions identical to position "H" except that the pilot bulb is illuminated instead of the main bulb.

How to Adjust Focus (Miller Headlamps). To detach the lamp front, release the spring clip at the bottom and pull the front off. To focus the bulb, insert it in the bulb-holder until the bayonet fixing pins are right home and give a further twist to the right. This will enable the bulb and holder to be slid backwards or forwards until the correct focus is obtained. On releasing the extra twist, the bulb is securely held.

A good method of alining the headlamp is to take the machine to a level plot of ground and place it so that the lamp is about 40 yards from a fence or wall and measure the distance from the centre of the headlamp to the ground and chalk on the fence or wall a mark at the same height. Then switch on the main bulb and note if the centre of the beam is slightly below the mark. If it is not, loosen the headlamp side securing screws and tilt the lamp as required. Then proceed to focus for intensity of light as described in the preceding paragraph.

How to Adjust Focus (Lucas Headlamps). On machines with or without an instrument panel the focusing of the headlamp is carried out in the same manner. To focus the main bulb it is necessary to remove the lamp front and reflector by pressing back the clip (Fig. 49). Then slacken the clamping clip which secures the bulb-holder and move the bulb-holder and bulb until correct focus is obtained. Afterwards tighten the clamping screw. To remove the bulb-holder it is only necessary to press back the two securing springs. When replacing the lamp front and reflector the top of the rim should be located first. When focusing a lamp, adjust until the smallest circle of light is obtained.

The Tail Lamp. The tail lamp (type WT203), fitted to all post-war

A.J.S. machines and many earlier models, is of Lucas manufacture and of the type shown in Fig. 50. The body of the lamp, complete with bulb holder, is secured to the rear number plate by means of three bolts, with appropriate washers and nuts. The portion of the lamp housing the red glass can be detached by giving it a half turn to the left and then pulling it outwards. When replacing the outer portion, engage the slots in the body with the two spring clips on the body of the lamp, and push right home to obtain full engagement.

Miller Bulb Replacements. The correct bulbs to fit are as follows. On coil ignition models fit a 6 V. 24–24 W. double-filament main bulb and 6 V. 3 W. S.C.C. sidecar, pilot and tail bulbs. For the ignition tell-tale a 2·5 V. flashlamp bulb is suitable except where compensated voltage control is fitted. In the latter case an 8 V. (·1 amp) bulb should be used.

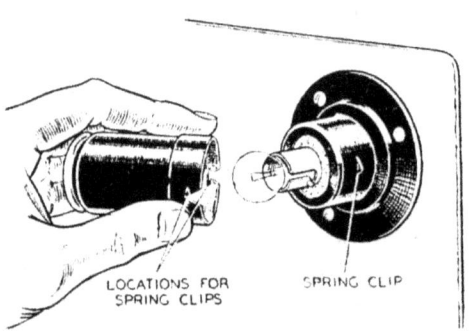

Fig. 50. Lucas Tail Lamp

Replacement of Lucas Bulbs. When the replacement of a bulb is necessary, a genuine Lucas bulb should be used. The filaments are arranged to be in focus, and give the best results with Lucas reflectors. When it is found necessary to replace the headlamp main bulb, screw it out two or three turns in an anti-clockwise direction. This will release the pressure on the bulb contacts and enable the bulb to be withdrawn easily. Care should be taken that the bulb is fitted the correct way round, i.e. with the dipped beam filament above the centre filament.· Always focus the headlamp after fitting a new bulb.

The number of the bulb for the headlamp driving and dipped beam light is 70; and that of the headlamp pilot, sidecar, panel, and tail lights, 200. The double-filament main bulb is 6 V,, 24 W , S.B.C. The other bulb is 6 V., 3 W., S.B.C.

Keep the Reflectors Clean. Wipe over chromium-plated surfaces with a damp cloth to remove dirt or dust and polish ebony black surfaces with a good furniture or car polish. Metal polish is taboo. Lightly polish with a soft cloth or chamois leather the transparent reflector covering.

Examine the Wiring Occasionally. See that none of the wires has become chafed or disconnected, particularly the battery leads and the positive lead from the dynamo to the switch panel. Should the dynamo go on strike, possibly it may be due to a

CARE OF LIGHTING EQUIPMENT

faulty lead. The ends of all the cables are identified by means of coloured sleevings, as shown on the following wiring diagrams.

HORN

Adjusting Lucas Electric Horn. Careful adjustment of the horn is made at the works, and subsequent adjustment is rarely called for. Normally the horn should give long service without any attention whatsoever. The vibrating parts do, however, gradually wear and, after very considerable usage, some roughness and loss of tone may develop. This can be rectified by means of the adjusting screw shown in Fig. 51.

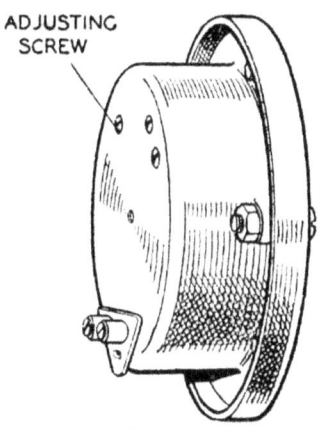

FIG. 51. TONE-ADJUSTING SCREW ON LUCAS HORN

To adjust the horn, turn the adjusting screw with a small screwdriver *two or three notches*. Clockwise turning is generally required and the under side of the screw is serrated to facilitate adjustment. Now check the tone of the horn and repeat the adjustment if necessary. An excessive clockwise adjustment of the tone adjusting screw must not be made, otherwise it may be found that separation of the contacts does not occur, although the armature pulls in. On no account unscrew the nut securing the tone disc or tamper with any screws other than that just referred to. After adjusting the horn, note its current consumption recorded at the ammeter. With the horn correctly adjusted, this should not exceed 4-5 amp.

While testing the horn, do not continue to depress the push switch if no sound is audible. Perhaps a faulty adjustment has resulted in the contacts failing to close, in which event no discharge is indicated at the ammeter.

If Horn Fails Completely or Partially. Do not immediately infer that the horn has broken down or needs adjustment. Possible causes of the trouble are: a loose fixing bolt; vibration of some adjacent part; a discharged battery; a loose connection; a short circuit in the wiring; or a defective push switch. The last-mentioned may be occasioned through poor electrical contact due to corrosion.

WIRE CONNECTIONS

Making Terminal Connection. The terminal connections in most cases comprise a metal sleeve which fits tightly into a metal socket. Where this type of connection is provided, the method of making the connection is as follows. First, withdraw the metal sleeve from the terminal socket. Then bare the end of the wire lead for about ⅜ in. Having done this, pass the wire into the metal sleeve and afterwards turn back the wire strands so that they lie outside the sleeve. Finally, push the sleeve into the socket.

Terminal Connections to Switch and C.V.C. Unit. In this case the wire is secured to a metal post by means of a binding screw. To connect, slacken the binding screw, bare the end of the wire for about $\frac{3}{16}$ in., push the wire through the slot in the side of the metal post, and tighten the binding screw.

Earth and High-tension Wires. Connections consist of solid sleeve-type terminals with an eye at the extreme end. To effect a connection, first bare the end of the wire for about ⅜ in. Then slip the terminal over the wire so that the bared end fully enters the reduced core of the terminal. Afterwards flatten this

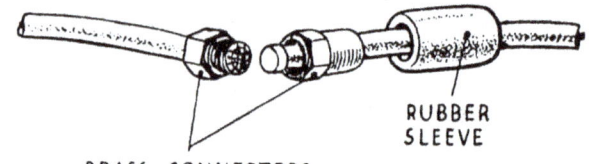

Fig. 52. Lucas Connector Incorporated in Rear Lamp Wire

portion of the terminal either by hammering it or squeezing it in a vice. The lighting system incorporates two important earth wires. One wire runs from the negative terminal of the battery and the other from the C.V.C. unit. The ends of both these wires have solid sleeve-type terminals of the kind just referred to and are secured to the saddle lug bolt situated beneath the saddle on the near side. See that the securing screw and also the connections are kept firmly tightened.

Rear Lamp Connection. To facilitate rear wheel removal, a Lucas detachable wire connector (Fig. 52) is incorporated in the lead to the rear lamp. It is situated just above the rear wheel spindle and consists of: a threaded sleeve; a collet; a gland nut; and a rubber sleeve. Referring to Fig. 52, make a connection in the following manner. First, bare the ends of the wire for about ¼ in. Then pass the rubber sleeve and the threaded sleeve over one wire, and slip the bared end of this wire through the collet and bend back the wire strands. Next push the bared end of the second wire through the gland nut and similarly bend back the wire strands. Now screw the gland nut into the threaded sleeve and complete the union by sliding the rubber sleeve over the metal parts. It should be noted that the rubber sleeve is important, as it insulates the exposed metal parts and also helps to prevent vibration working them loose.

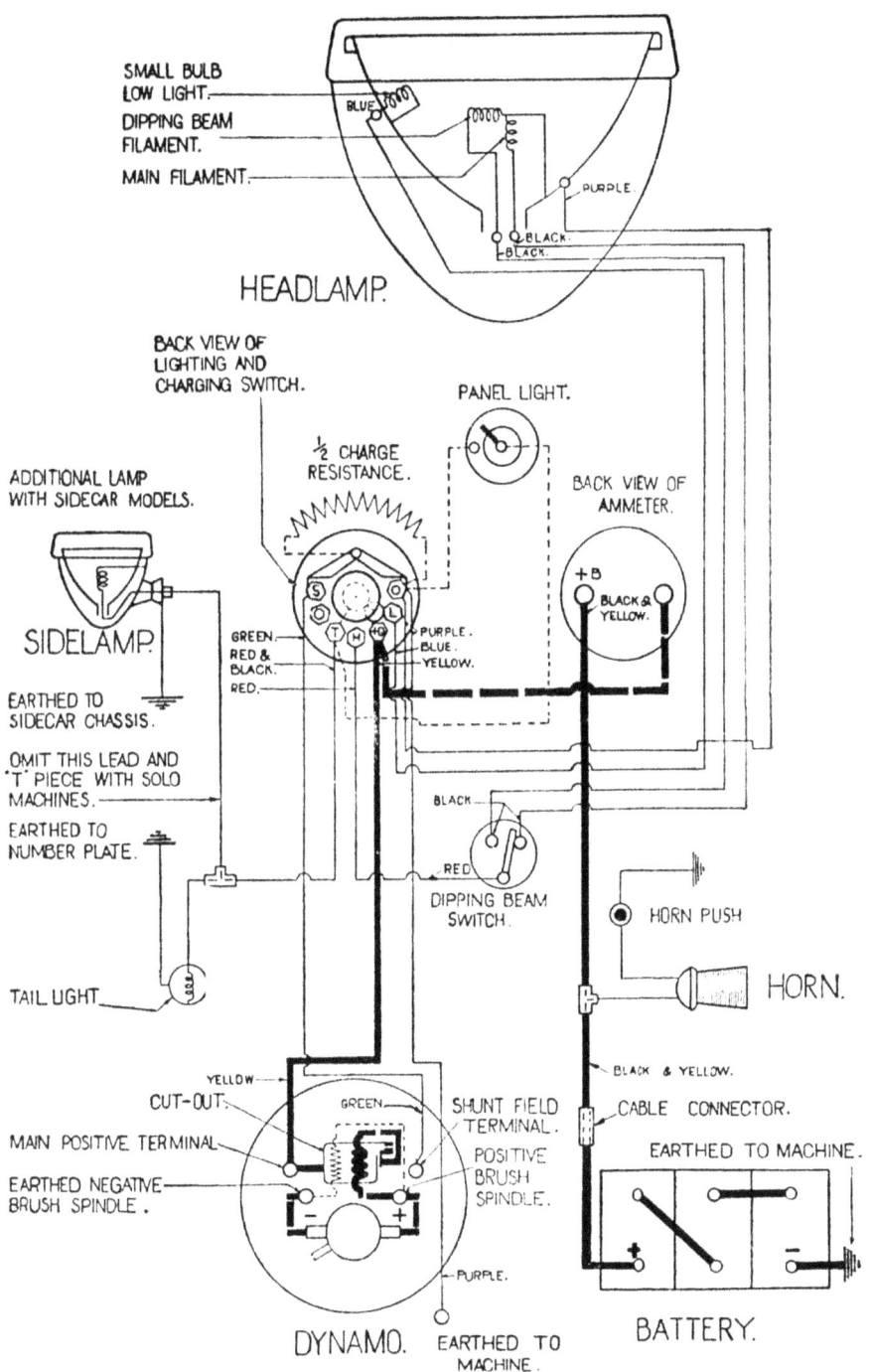

FIG. 53. WIRING DIAGRAM FOR THE LUCAS LIGHTING EQUIPMENT WITHOUT COMPENSATED VOLTAGE CONTROL (1932–37)

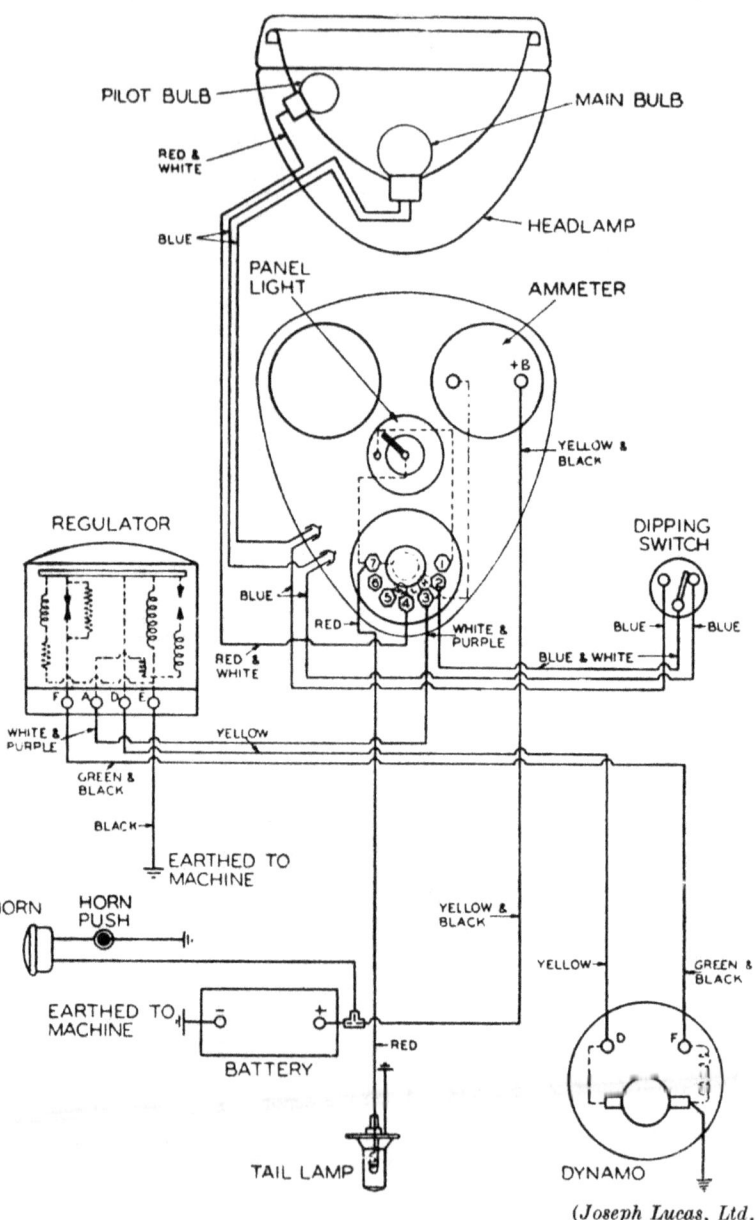

Fig. 54. Wiring Diagram for Lucas Lighting Equipment with Compensated Voltage Control (1937–39)

This W.D. applies to pre-war A.J.S. machines with ammeter and lighting switch mounted on a tank panel instead of the headlamp panel used on post-war models. (See Fig. 50.)

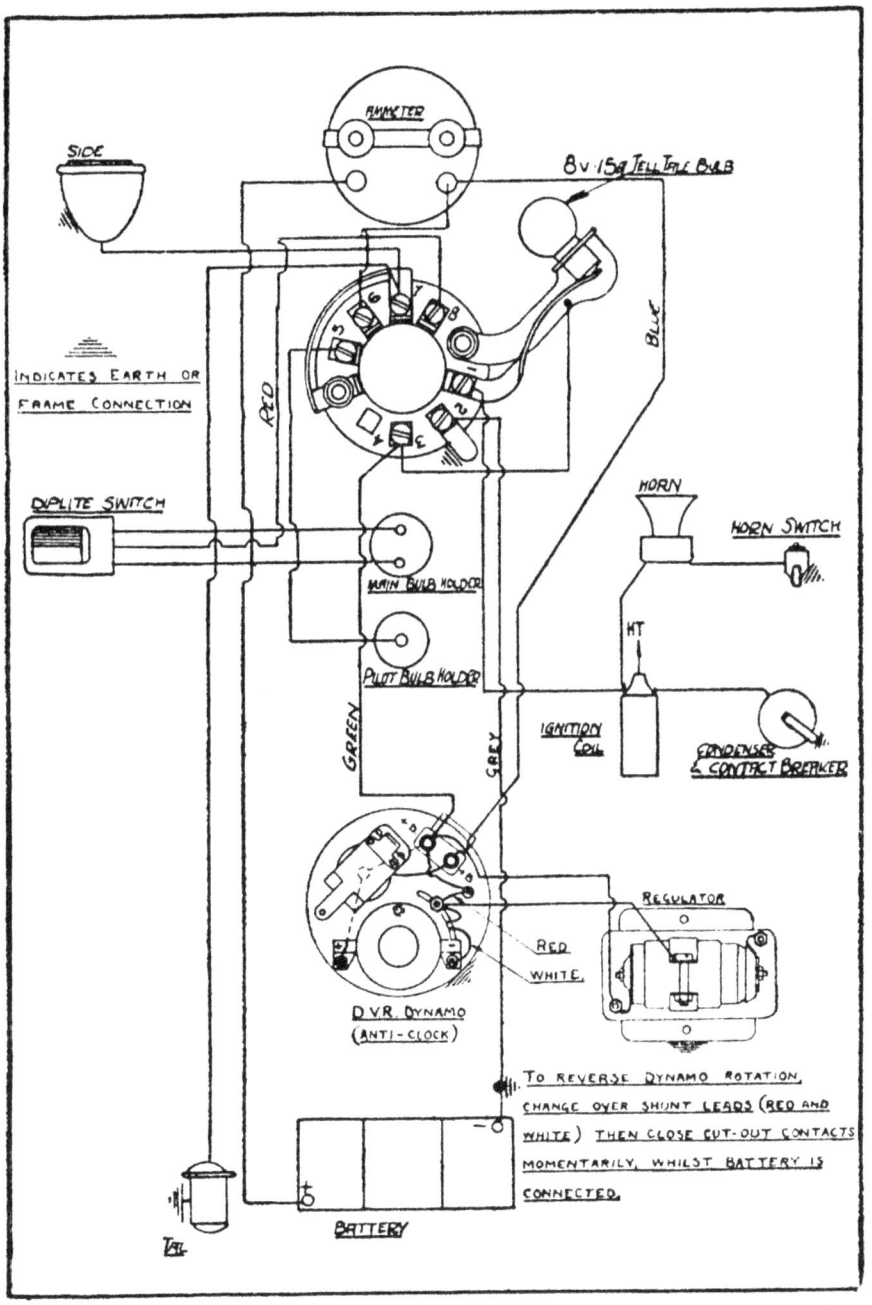

FIG. 55. WIRING DIAGRAM FOR MILLER LIGHTING AND COIL IGNITION EQUIPMENT WITH COMPENSATED VOLTAGE CONTROL (1937–9)

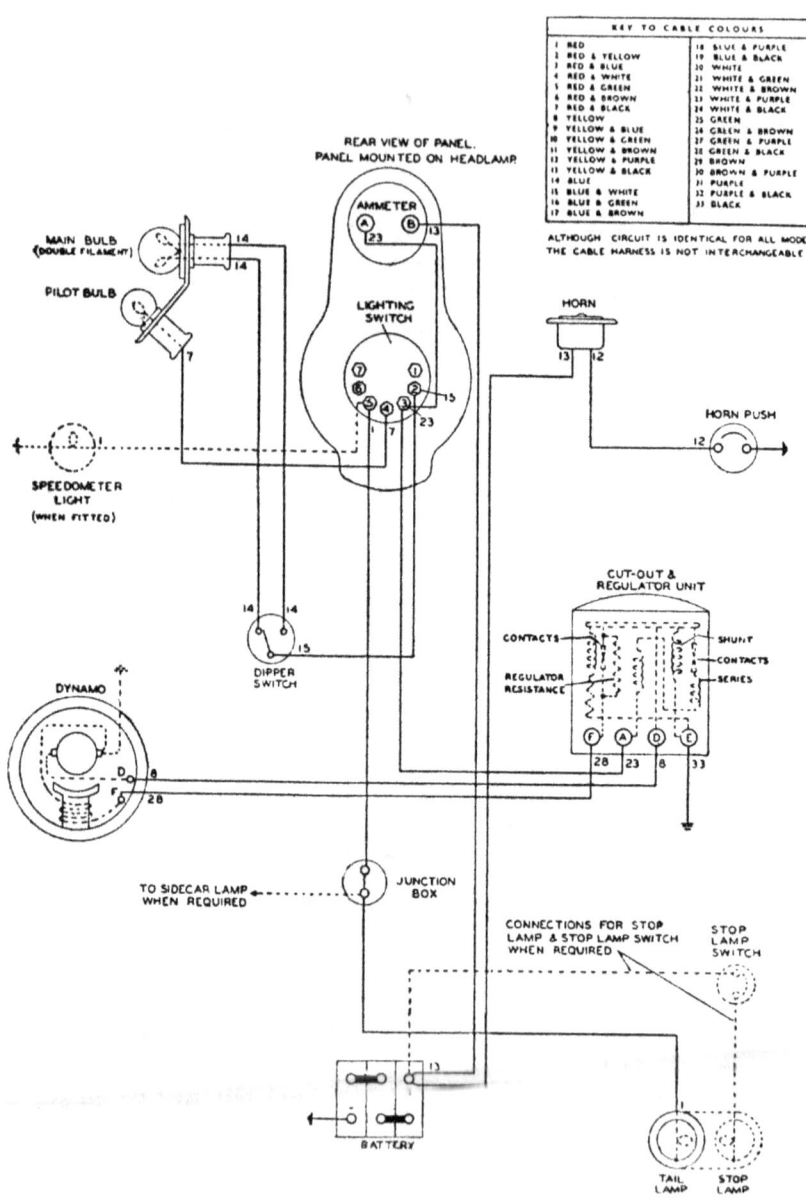

Fig. 56. Wiring Diagram for Lucas Lighting Equipment with Compensated Voltage Control (1945 Onwards)
(*Joseph Lucas, Ltd.*)

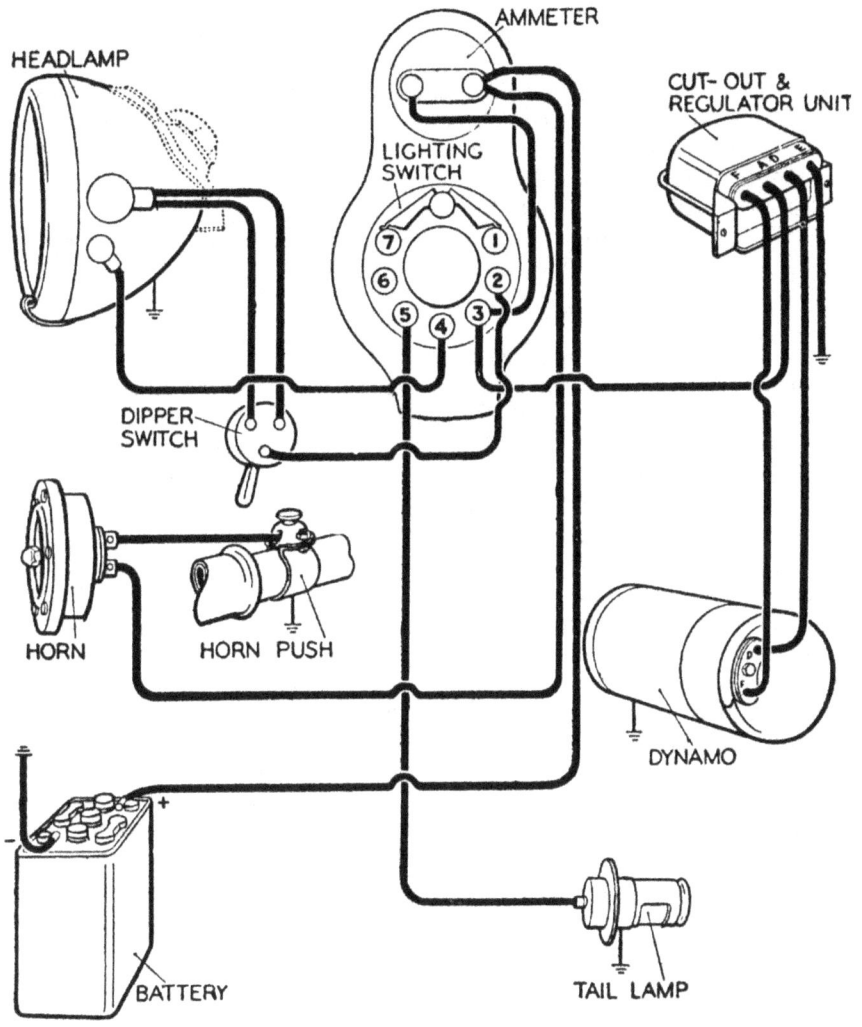

(*A.J.S. Motor Cycles*)

Fig. 57. Pictorial Wiring Diagram of Lucas Lighting Equipment with Compensated Voltage Control (1945 Onwards)

This W.D. applies to all post-war A.J.S. models and should be studied in conjunction with the W.D. opposite.

CHAPTER VI
ALL ABOUT LUBRICATION (1945-8)

THE lubrication system provided on the post-war A.J.S. single-cylinder Models 16M and 18 is a still further improved version of the very efficient dry sump system used on the 1938-9 single-cylinder O.H.V. models. It functions automatically and very little attention is needed, but that little attention must never be disregarded by the rider, remembering the vital importance of engine lubrication. (See notes on page 21.)

ENGINE LUBRICATION

Outline of Dry Sump System. The system is of the full dry sump type. Engine oil is gravity fed from an oil tank (capacity 3 pt.) beneath the saddle to a duplex horizontal reciprocating and rotary plunger pump situated in the crankcase. This double-acting pump is of similar design to the pump used on pre-war engines (described on page 24) and is driven by a worm on the timing side main shaft. The plunger is the only moving pump part, and reciprocating movement is imparted to it by a fixed guide screw engaging a profiled cam groove cut on the (larger) return end of the plunger. This end of the plunger has a greater capacity than the delivery end, which is responsible for pressure feeding oil to various parts of the engine, and the crankcase sump is therefore kept "dry." All oil, after circulation in the engine, drains to the bottom of the crankcase sump, and is returned to the tank by the pump via the upper of the two external pipes to be re-circulated.

How the Oil Circulates. The circulation of oil throughout the single-cylinder O.H.V. engine is shown diagrammatically in Fig. 58. Reference should also be made to Fig. 12, which shows a 1938 engine having a similar type lubrication system.

Oil is pressure-fed by the delivery end of the pump to the big-end bearing through a passage cut in the timing side main shaft, flywheel, and crankpin. Surplus oil from the big-end splash lubricates the piston and cylinder bore. Another pressure feed, however, is the main provision for cylinder lubrication. Oil is forced through a passage (with ball valve control) in the crankcase to an annular channel in the base of the cylinder and reaches the cylinder bore via a number of small holes. All surplus oil falls down into the crankcase sump.

A secondary oil feed is taken to the timing gear and rocker-box. The oil is fed to the timing gear through a passage in the

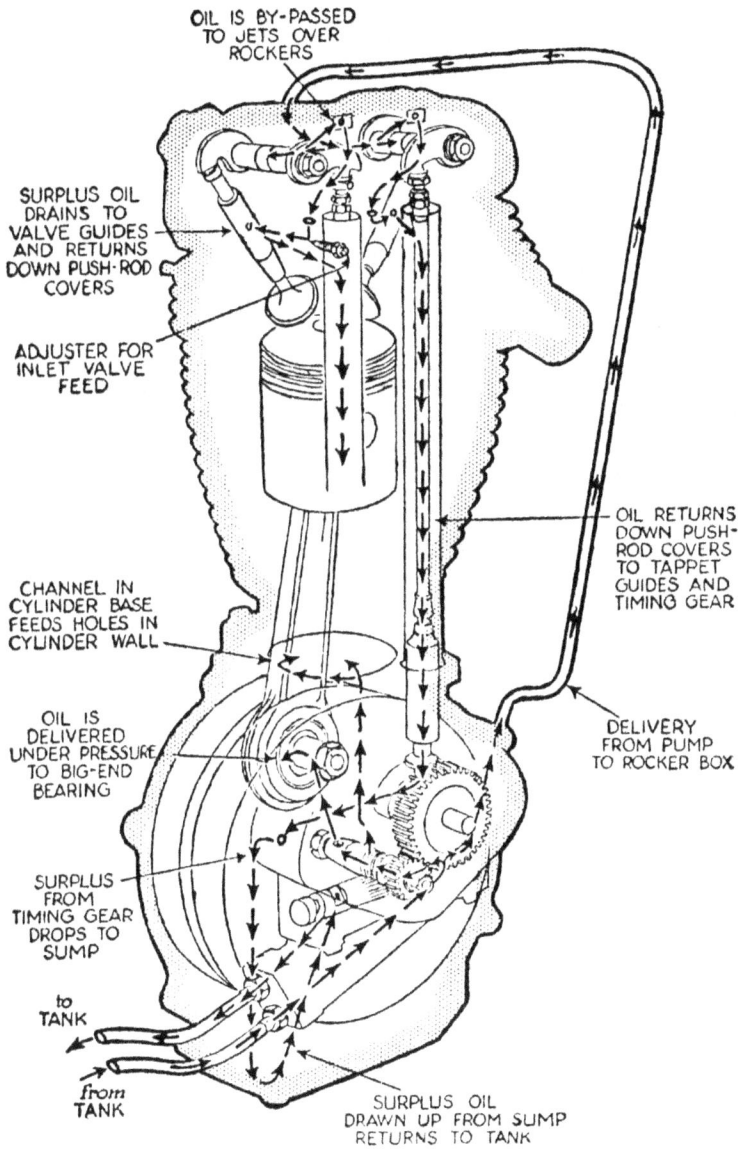

(*From "The Motor Cycle"*)

FIG. 58. OIL CIRCULATION DIAGRAM
This applies to all post-war O.H.V. single-cylinder engines.

timing-case cover and builds up to a predetermined level. The feed to the rocker-box is via an external pipe from the front of the oil pump housing. Oil is by-passed to jets over the inlet and exhaust rockers, and lubricates these thoroughly. Surplus oil drains to the two valve guides. The inlet guide has a needle-pointed screw adjuster by means of which the feed can be regulated. Oil from the valve guides then returns down the push-rod covers and tappet guides to the timing gear case. All lubricant in excess of that required to maintain the predetermined level drains away into the crankcase sump, where it is sucked up by the scavenge end of the pump and returned to the oil tank.

Provision of Filters. Engine oil on its journey back into the tank has to percolate through a cartridge type felt filter contained within a cylindrical housing inside the oil tank. This filter removes all impurities collected by the oil during its circulation throughout the engine, and is readily detachable for cleaning.

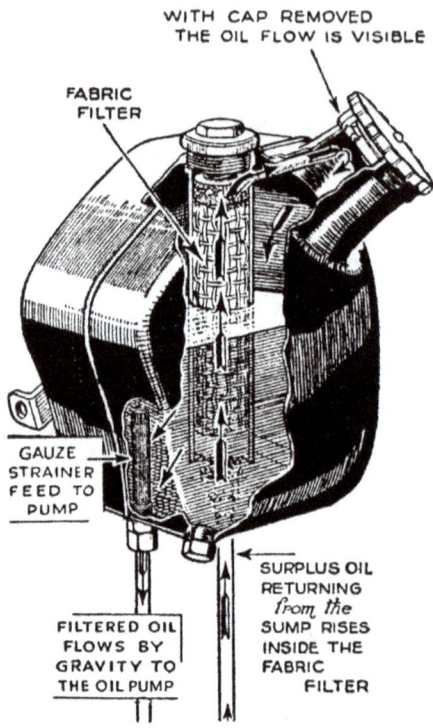

FIG. 59. ARRANGEMENT OF FILTERS IN OIL TANK

This cut-away view of the tank shows how oil returned from the engine sump passes through the fabric filter and enters the tank via a small spout, at whose orifice the flow can be observed with the filler cap removed. Note how the filtered oil has to pass a gauze strainer incorporated in the delivery pipe union.

As may be seen in Fig. 59, a second filter is also incorporated within the oil tank. This comprises a metal gauze strainer mounted on the entry end of the oil-feed pipe union. Its purpose is to trap any pieces of fluff, etc., which may accidentally enter the oil tank during replenishment, and thus prevent their entry into the oil pump.

Use One of These Oils. To maintain high engine performance, easy starting, and to reduce wear to the absolute minimum, every A.J.S. rider should *always* run on a brand and grade of engine oil as recommended by A.J.S. Motor Cycles. If you must economize, cut down on cigarettes, but not on the "life blood" of your engine! You will quickly regret using an inferior or unsuitable engine oil. Use one of these oils: Castrol "Grand Prix" ("XXL" during winter); Triple Shell (Double Shell during winter); Mobiloil "D" ("BB" during winter); Price's Motorine "B" de Luxe ("C" de Luxe during winter); or Essolube "Racer" (summer and winter). Always buy engine oil from branded cabinets or in sealed containers, and specify the brand *and* grade required.

Examine Oil Level in Tank Frequently. To ensure proper cooling and adequate lubrication of the engine, it is essential always to maintain sufficient oil in circulation. If the oil tank is less than about half full, the oil is apt to become dirty, diluted, and hot, and the engine may suffer in consequence. It is advisable to remove the filler cap frequently and inspect the oil level. This inspection should always be made prior to setting forth on a lengthy run. Top up the oil tank with engine oil as required. Suitable brands and grades of engine oil are referred to in the previous paragraph.

Generally speaking, the level of oil in the tank should be kept well above the half-full mark, but it must not be allowed to rise above 1 in. from the filler cap orifice (see Fig. 59). The reason for this is that allowance must be made for the return of accumulated oil in the engine sump, which occurs immediately on starting up. When an engine is suddenly stopped, the pump ceases to function, but oil continues to drain into the sump from various parts of the engine.

Checking Oil Circulation. This precaution should be taken *prior to every run*. Remove the filler cap from the oil tank with the engine running immediately after starting up from cold. A *steady* flow of oil should be observed issuing from the small spout (Fig. 59) inside the filler cap orifice. As surplus oil in the engine sump is disposed of by the scavenge end of the pump, the flow of oil gradually declines and may become spasmodic, possibly accompanied by air bubbles. On suddenly accelerating the engine the flow may temporarily cease, only to resume in greater volume than before on decelerating the engine.

A somewhat erratic flow is normal once the engine has got into its stride, but a poor or erratic flow immediately after starting up from cold is not normal and the cause should be investigated. If no oil return into the tank is visible, stop the engine at once.

Adjustment of Oil Supply. No adjustment is provided for the oil pump and main supply to the engine, as the oil pump is carefully designed to deliver the correct amount of oil to the engine at *all* throttle openings. It is important, however, to keep both end caps on the plunger housing absolutely air-tight. The nuts should periodically be checked for tightness. The only adjustment in the D.S. lubrication system affects the supply to the inlet valve stem.

The adjustment for the supply to the inlet valve stem (see Fig. 58) comprises a needle-pointed screw situated on the right-hand side of the cylinder head. A lock-nut secures the adjuster screw and prevents the adjustment being accidentally upset. Once it has been correctly set, this screw adjustment should require little or no further attention. With an engine in sound condition the normal setting should be *half a complete turn from the fully-closed position.*

If an inlet valve squeak becomes audible, an increase in the oil supply to the inlet valve is called for, and the adjuster screw should be turned very slightly *anti-clockwise* after slackening the lock-nut. Similarly, if blue smoke is noticed at the exhaust, oil consumption is excessive, and the plug oils up or becomes dirty, a reduction in the oil supply is needed, and the adjuster screw should be turned slightly in a *clockwise* direction.

The stem of the exhaust valve is automatically lubricated by oil fed through a duct in the cylinder head and no adjustment of the supply is possible. It should be noted that excess oil from the inlet and exhaust valve stems is by-passed back into the timing case.

Important Note Concerning Oil Pump. Should it be necessary to separate the crankcase halves, the oil pump plunger must first be removed in order to prevent damage. This precaution must never be overlooked.

Removing Oil Pump Plunger. This should not be done unnecessarily. Should removal of the plunger be required for some reason, first drain the oil tank as described in a later paragraph. Also disconnect the lower end of the rocker-box oil feed pipe by unscrewing the union nut. Then remove the hexagon-headed bolts, securing the front and rear end caps of the pump housing to the crankcase. Remove both end caps. Next unscrew the pump plunger guide screw from the oil pump housing (see Fig. 12). It is screwed into the under side of the housing just in front of the rear cap and is located at right angles to the plunger. Now push the pump plunger from the front end and extract it from the rear of its housing.

Replacing Pump Plunger. Check that the pump plunger is clean internally and externally, also that the inside of the housing is clean. Smear some clean engine oil on the plunger and insert its narrow end into the rear of the housing, gently pushing it into position. Replace the guide screw and, while tightening this, oscillate the plunger until the end of the guide screw is felt to engage the profiled cam groove. Then firmly tighten the guide screw. On no account tighten the guide screw firmly until proper engagement has been obtained, otherwise stripping of the teeth on the plunger and timing side main shaft may occur. Replace the front and rear end caps and paper washers. Renew the washers unless the old ones are perfect. When fitting the paper washer to the front end cap, make absolutely sure that it does not obstruct the small oil passage in the cap. To prevent air leaks, it is advisable to smear one side of each paper washer with some liquid-jointing compound and to fit that side so that it is in contact with the cap. Finally, retighten the end-cap, securing screws firmly.

Draining Oil Tank. On a new machine, drain the oil tank completely, and replenish with new oil after the first 500 miles and again at 1000 miles. Subsequently drain the tank and change the oil once every 5000 miles. To drain the oil tank, first see that your A.J.S. is quite level, with both wheels resting on the ground or with the machine jacked up on both stands. Then unscrew the drain plug on the front lower edge of the oil tank, after first placing a suitable receptacle beneath the drain plug orifice. Also remove the crankcase sump drain plug at the bottom of the crankcase on the off-side, and allow any oil accumulated in the sump to drain away.

Cleaning the Filters. Every time the oil is changed (see above), remove and clean the cartridge type felt filter and also the metal gauze filter strainer fitted to the oil feed pipe union inside the oil tank (Fig. 59). Clean both filters thoroughly with petrol, but make no attempt to detach the tubular wire cage from the felt element.

Thorough and regular cleaning of the filters is most important. If the felt element is perforated or the ends are distorted, a new element must be fitted. Inspect the condition of the cork washer beneath the hexagon cap, and renew it if its condition is not satisfactory. Instructions for the removal and fitting of both filters are given in following paragraphs.

It should be noted that a dirty, or clogged, felt filter element obstructs the passage of oil returning from the crankcase sump, and thereby causes oil to accumulate in the sump and cause over-lubrication. A choked gauze strainer can partially or completely starve the engine of oil, as it is on the delivery side; but it should be emphasized that such trouble can only arise through replenishing the oil tank with dirty oil. All oil returned to the tank by the pump is thoroughly cleansed by the felt filter element.

To Remove Felt Element. First remove the two saddle spring securing bolts, and raise rear of the saddle (1945-7). Unscrew the hexagon cap from the top of the oil tank, and withdraw the filter spring and dished cap washer. Now insert the finger inside the filter and withdraw the element towards the rear, taking the utmost care not to allow the filter element to become damaged or kinked. The procedure for assembling is the reverse to that just described. Make sure that the saddle spring securing bolts are very firmly tightened on 1945-7 models.

To Remove Gauze Strainer. To remove the metal gauze strainer after draining the oil tank, first disconnect the oil-feed pipe from the union which is screwed into the base of the oil tank. To do this, unscrew the union nut from the pipe nearest the rear wheel.

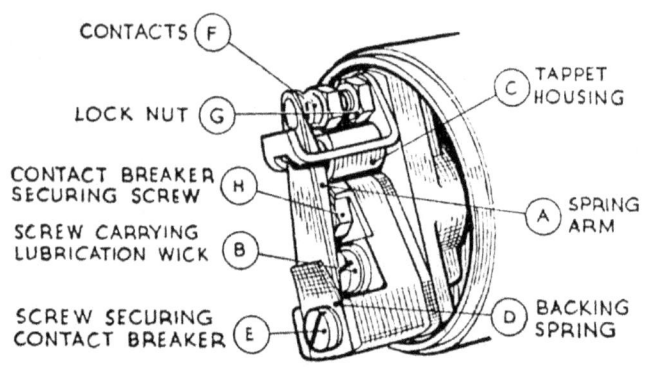

FIG. 60. CONTACT-BREAKER OF LUCAS MAGNETO FITTED TO ALL POST-WAR MODELS

Carefully ease the pipe end away from the union and then proceed to unscrew the union itself and detach this, complete with integral gauze strainer. To replace the strainer, feed pipe and union, proceed in the reverse order of removal.

Lubrication of Lucas Magneto. The bearings of the Lucas type N1/3/AO magneto are packed with grease by the makers, and this should suffice for about 10,000 miles, at which period the magneto should be returned to Joseph Lucas, Ltd., of Birmingham, 19, or to one of their Service Stations for complete servicing. No lubricators are fitted.

About every 5000 miles it is advisable to lubricate the cam and tappet of the face cam type contact-breaker. To do this, the complete contact-breaker must be removed in the following manner. Release the spring blade securing the contact-breaker cover and detach the latter. Then, referring to Figs. 60 and 61, remove the screw E and spring washer which retain the spring arm A to the contact-breaker body L, and detach the curved backing spring D and the spring arm A. Next unscrew the screw B which carries the lubrication wick and remove the fibre insulating bush. Straighten the tab on the locking plate J

behind the contact-breaker securing screw *H*, and remove screw *H* with the spanner provided in the tool kit (Part No. LTK-5). Now lever off the contact-breaker body *L* from the armature shaft.

Having removed the contact-breaker, saturate with a few drops of thin machine oil the wick mounted in the core of the carrying screw *B*. Push the tappet *K* out of the contact-breaker body *L* and wipe it clean with a soft cloth. Then smear it with some thin machine oil and replace it. Assembly should be done

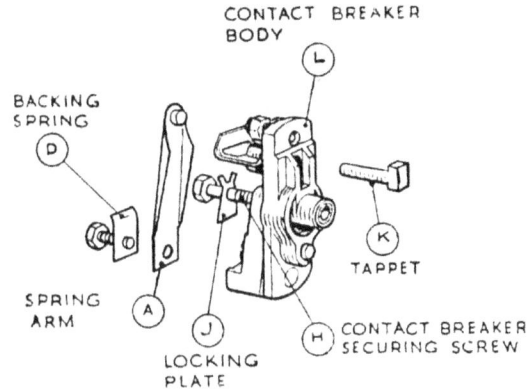

FIG. 61. LUCAS CONTACT-BREAKER SHOWN DISMANTLED

in the reverse order of dismantling, and care must be taken to ensure that the curved backing spring *D* is fitted with the curved portion on the outside.

The Magneto Chain. This runs in a chain case on the off-side of the engine. The case is packed with grease. Every 1000 miles inject a small quantity of grease through the nipple on the chain case cover.

LUBRICATION OF DYNAMO AND THE CYCLE PARTS

Dynamo Lubrication. As with the Lucas magneto, the armature bearings are thoroughly packed with grease by the makers and require no further attention until at least 10,000 miles have been covered. At this period, or when a complete engine overhaul is necessary, return the instrument to a Lucas Service Station for thorough cleaning, overhaul, and lubrication.

The Burman Four-speed Gearbox. On new machines the gearbox is charged with sufficient grease for 1000 miles running. Subsequently every 1000 miles about 2 oz. of grease should be inserted through the grease nipple on the kick-starter case or

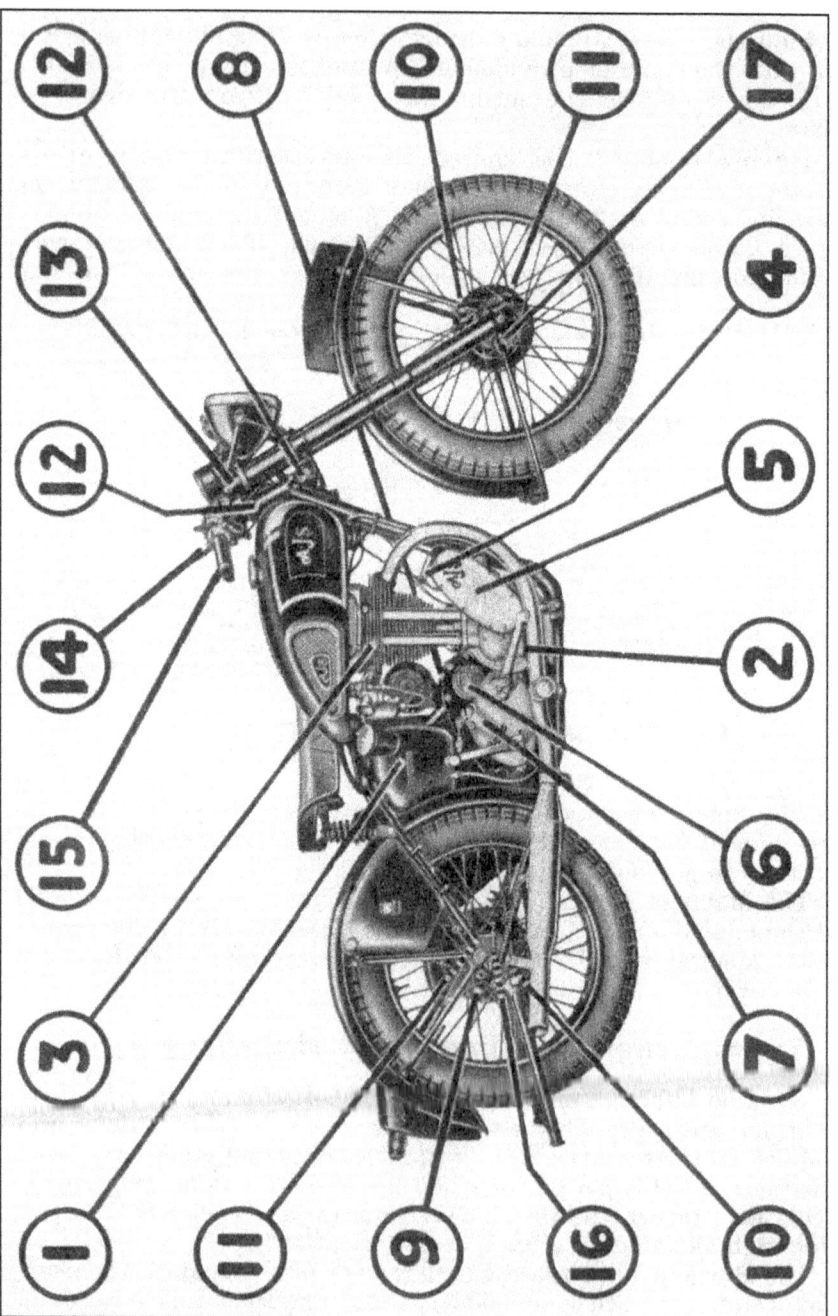

Fig. 62. Lubrication Chart for O.H.V. Models 16M and 18

ALL ABOUT LUBRICATION (1945-8)

through the filler orifice. This should be ample for all normal riding conditions, and it should be noted that the gearbox must not be completely filled. On no account replenish with thick grease. The correct lubricant to use is: Castrolease "Medium," Shell "Retinax" Grease C.D., Mobilgrease No. 2, Esso Grease, or Price's Belmoline "C." 1948 models: *summer grade* engine oil.

KEY TO LUBRICATION CHART (FIG. 62)

(1) *Oil Tank*. Frequently check level of engine oil. Maintain at least half full, but not above 1 in. below filler orifice. Top-up as required. Check oil circulation before each run. Drain every 5000 miles and clean both filters. (See page 109.)

(2) *Oil Pump*. No adjustment is provided, but keep both plunger housing end caps air-tight. (See page 107.)

(3) *Inlet Valve Stem*. If valve squeak develops, regulate needle-pointed adjuster screw on R.H. side of cylinder head. (See page 108.)

(4) *Magneto*. Remove face cam contact-breaker every 5000 miles, and oil cam and tappet. Return magneto for overhaul at 10,000 miles. (See page 110.)

(5) *Magneto Chain*. Inject some grease every 1000 miles. (See page 111.)

(6) *Dynamo*. Return instrument for overhaul at about 10,000 miles, or when a complete engine overhaul is necessary. (See page 111.)

(7) *Gearbox*. Inject about 2 oz. of grease (engine oil, 1948 models) every 1000 miles. Drain, flush out, and replenish every 5000 miles. (See page 111.)

(8) *Oil-bath*. Check level of engine oil every 500 miles and top-up, if necessary, to level of inspection cap orifice. Level not to be below $\frac{3}{16}$ in. from bottom edge of orifice. (See page 114.)

(9) *Secondary Chain*. Inspect and, if necessary, oil every 500 miles. Remove, clean, and immerse in molten tallow every 2000 miles and 1000 miles in summer and winter respectively. (See page 114.)

(10) *Wheel Hubs*. Grease every 1000 miles. (See page 115.)

(11) *Brakes*. Grease nipple in each expander bush every 1000 miles, and pedal every 3000 miles. Oil yoke end pins of rear brake, thread on rod, and front brake cable end monthly. (See page 115.)

(12) *Steering Head*. Grease both nipples every 3000 miles. (See page 115.)

(13) *"Teledraulic" Forks*. Check level of hydraulic fluid every 3000 miles (5000 miles, 1948 forks) and top-up as required. (See page 115.)

(14) *Control Levers*. Oil handlebar levers monthly. (See page 116.)

(15) *Twist-grip*. Occasionally grease handlebars below grip. (See page 116.)

(16) *Speedometer*. Grease speedometer gearbox monthly. (See page 116.)

(17) *Stands*. Oil hinge bolts of both stands monthly. (See page 116.)

After a considerable mileage (say 5000 miles) the gearbox should be drained, flushed out with a suitable flushing oil, and replenished with 1 lb. 14 oz. of grease (1945-7), or with 1½ pints of engine oil (1948). The screwed drain plug is situated low down at the rear of the gearbox. See that the drain plug is firmly tightened after changing the lubricant. It is not easy to drain the gearbox when using the non-fluid lubricant, and it is best to remove the foot-change cover and kick-starter case.

Replenish Oil-bath with Engine Oil. The oil-bath chain case is responsible for lubricating the primary chain, the dynamo-driving chain, and the engine shaft shock-absorber. Harshness arising in the primary transmission is generally a sign that the oil level is too low and, to prevent this, regular inspection should be made. About every 500 miles remove the inspection cap and examine the level of oil in the chain case. This should be maintained level with the inspection cap orifice, and in no circumstances must it be allowed to fall below $\frac{3}{16}$ in. from the bottom edge of the inspection cap orifice, assuming the test is made with the machine jacked up on the rear stand. Top up as required with suitable engine oil, various brands and grades of which are specified on page 107.

To Remove Oil-bath Inspection Cap. Unscrew the knurled retaining screw approximately four turns. Then slide the inspection cap sideways until it is possible to pass the back plate through the orifice and detach the complete cap assembly. It is important when replacing the inspection cap to centralize the cork washer and then firmly tighten the knurled screw. Failure to do this may result in the filler cap being lost while riding.

Lubricating Secondary Chain. Examine the chain about every 500 miles. If it appears dry, apply a little engine oil with a rag or suitable brush. Remove the chain about 2000 miles in summer and every 1000 miles in winter. Clean it thoroughly in paraffin, drain, and allow it to dry. Then immerse the chain in a suitable receptacle containing molten tallow. Allow the chain to remain immersed for about five minutes, then permit excess lubricant to drain off. Afterwards refit the chain to the two sprockets. Engine oil can be used as a substitute for molten tallow, but this is not recommended. If engine oil is used, allow the chain to soak for an hour or two.

The Dynamo Chain. Being enclosed in the oil-bath for the primary chain, this requires no attention other than that given to the oil-bath (see above).

Suitable Greases for Cycle Parts. Greases suitable for lubricating the various cycle parts by means of the grease-gun applied to the appropriate grease nipples are the same as those recommended on page 113 for the Burman four-speed gearbox.

Charging the Grease Gun. The grease gun of the standard type recommended for A.J.S. machines (Part No. LTK20) should be charged so that the grease is on the *top* side of the piston. Grease can be obtained in special canisters having loose collars provided with holes. With this design of canister, to charge the grease gun, place its barrel over the hole in the central floating plate and press firmly downwards. Turn the grease gun and simultaneously remove it from the floating plate. This action will charge the

ALL ABOUT LUBRICATION (1945-8)

gun with grease flush with the top of the barrel. Afterwards replace the screwed top cap.

If no canister of the kind referred to above is available, use a lath or similar implement to charge the barrel of the grease gun by hand.

Lubricating Wheel Hubs. Both wheel hubs are packed with grease on initial assembly. To ensure proper lubrication and prevent the entry of mud and water, inject about every 1000 miles a little grease through the nipple in the centre of each hub. Avoid using excessive grease, otherwise some of it may reach the brake linings and reduce braking efficiency.

The Brakes. Each brake cover plate has a grease nipple provided in the brake expander bush. Inject some grease sparingly about every 1000 miles. The brake pedal also requires greasing slightly about every 3000 miles via the nipple in the heel of the foot pedal.

About once a month smear some engine oil (only a few drops) on the yoke end pins at the front and rear ends of the rear brake rod, also on the threaded rear portion of this rod. In addition, oil the bottom end of the front brake cable.

Lubrication of Steering Head. About every 3000 miles apply the grease gun sparingly to the grease nipple in the head lug of the main frame, and also to the nipple on on the handlebar lug.

Checking Level of Fluid in 1945-7 Front Forks. The A.J.S. "Teledraulic" front forks (see Fig. 72) require no lubrication whatever, but every 3000 miles the level of hydraulic fluid (6 oz. per leg—10 on 1948 forks) should be checked and, if necessary, topped-up with one of the following fluids: Wakefield's "Castrolite," Single Shell, Mobiloil "Arctic," Essolube 20, Price's Motorine "E." The procedure described below should be used for checking the level and topping-up.

Place the A.J.S. so that it is quite vertical and resting on both wheels. To keep the machine in the vertical position, suitably chock up both footrests. Now unscrew the two hexagon plugs which are level with the handlebars at the top of the fork inner tubes. Expose the fork damping rods attached to the under sides of the plugs by pulling upwards each plug to its maximum extent. Eject by pumping action any hydraulic fluid trapped in the tubes above the damper valves. This involves working the plugs and damping rods up and down several times. Take no further action for several minutes and allow any ejected fluid to drain down to the main supply.

Remove the fluid level screws and fibre washers provided on each slider just beneath the securing bolts for the mudguard bridge. If the fluid level is correct, *fluid should just ooze from the fluid level holes*. If no fluid oozes out, topping-up is called for as described on the next page.

Topping-up " Teledraulics " (1945-7). With fluid level screws removed, pour down each fork inner tube about *two tablespoonfuls* of hydraulic fluid. This is equivalent to one fluid ounce. Work the plugs and damping rods up and down several times, and then wait two minutes to permit oil to ooze out of the fluid level holes. If no excess fluid oozes out, pour another two tablespoonfuls of hydraulic fluid down each fork inner tube, and repeat the pumping action by working the plugs and damping rods up and down. If still no fluid oozes, investigate the cause carefully and remedy. Finally replace the fluid level screws, fitting a fibre washer on each screw. Also refit the plug in the top of each fork inner tube.

Do Not Forget the Control Levers. To ensure responsive and quick-acting controls, smear a little engine oil monthly on all the moving components of the levers mounted on the handlebars.

Lubrication of Twist-grip. Stiffness in operation due to insufficient lubrication should be remedied in the following manner. First take out both screws retaining the halves of the twist-grip body. Then slide the entire twist-grip off the end of the handlebars. Lubrication can now be attended to. Smear some grease (high-melting point) around the end of the handlebars. Deal similarly with the friction spring and also the drum in which the inner control wire is wound. Afterwards fit the twist-grip to the end of the handlebars, replace both retaining screws, and tighten the screws firmly.

The Speedometer. The speedometer gearbox requires to be greased about once a month to ensure smooth running. No other part of the speedometer needs attention, and this applies to the driving cable. The appropriate grease nipple for the gearbox (attached to the rear wheel spindle) will be found on top of the box.

Miscellaneous Oiling. Attention to details in connection with lubrication pays good dividends. This applies especially to parts having substantial movement, but parts with small movement should not be forgotten. For instance, the hinge bolts of both stands should occasionally be removed and smeared with engine oil. If a sidecar is attached, do not forget lubrication of the chassis. Grease nipples are provided at various points. A reminder: when attending to lubrication, avoid allowing it to splash or drip on the floor. If this does happen and you have respect for your tyres, clean up the mess before moving the machine over the "lubrication area." Finally, to jog your memory, peruse the lubrication chart on page 112. It shows most essentials at a glance.

Topping-up 1948 " Teledraulics." Instructions for checking the hydraulic fluid content and topping-up are given on page 158.

CHAPTER VII

OVERHAULING (1945-8)

THE instructions in this chapter apply to the 1945-8 Models 16M and 18.

The A.J.S. Tool Kit. As may be seen in Fig. 63, twelve tools are provided in addition to the grease gun and tyre inflator. These should be sufficient for all normal stripping down and assembly. In connection with maintenance, the author would suggest the purchase of the following useful, if not indispensable, items: a

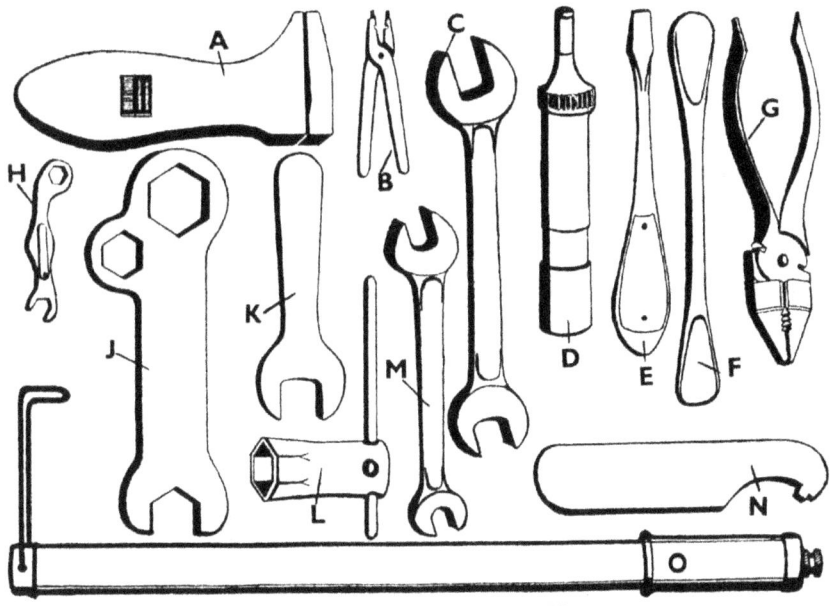

FIG. 63. THE A.J.S. TOOL KIT

The undermentioned items comprise the standard tool kit in the tool bag of each new machine.

A = Adjustable spanner
B = Gudgeon-pin circlip pliers
C = Large double-ended spanner
D = Grease gun
E = Screwdriver
F = Tyre lever
G = Pliers
H = Magneto spanner and feeler
J = Triple spanner
K = Dynamo spanner
L = Box spanner for plug
M = Small double-ended spanner (duplicated)
N = Spanner for hub locking ring
O = Tyre inflator

suitable pressure gauge (such as the Schrader or Dunlop) for checking tyre pressures (see page 42); a hydrometer for testing the specific gravity of the battery electrolyte (see page 93); a chain rivet extractor and box of spare chain links, in case of transmission trouble; a K.L.G. plug detacher for dismantling the plug; a wire-brush type cleaner for the plug; and a feeler gauge for checking the electrode gap.

Desirable Items for the Garage. If you intend to undertake personally as much repair work as possible, in addition to maintenance and routine overhaul, there are a number of items which it is desirable to obtain. If conditions permit, rig up a suitable bench, complete with vice. Purchase a good soldering outfit (for repairing Bowden cables), a hand drill, a set of small files, a hacksaw, a centre-punch, and a medium-size hammer.

Other items which you *must* have include: some emery cloth; tins of valve-grinding paste (coarse and fine), such as Richford's; a good tyre repair outfit containing auto-vulcanizing patches, such as the Dunlop "Vulcafix"; a tin of suitable engine oil (see page 107); a canister of grease for the cycle parts (see page 114); a can of paraffin for cleaning; a stiff brush for scouring dirt off the crankcase; a tin of wax polish for polishing the enamelled parts; two chamois leathers; a sponge and pail (if no hose is available); some soft dusters (preferably of the "Selvyt" type); and a supply of non-fluffy rags. In addition, you will require some enamelled dishes and jars in which to wash various parts, and a receptacle for oil when draining the engine sump and oil tank. Obtain some good hand cleanser.

Illustrated Spares List. It is very convenient to have available an illustrated Spares List. A copy of the A.J.S. List, giving prices for all engine and cycle parts, is obtainable from A.J.S. Motor Cycles for 1s. 6d., post free.

Hints on Cleaning. The advice given on page 38 should be observed. If hose is used to soak the mud off the enamelled parts, be careful not to direct water on to vulnerable and vital items, such as the carburettor, magneto, and dynamo. It is useless having a glittering mount which will not budge.

As has been stated on page 38, it is quite sufficient to use a damp chamois leather to remove tarnish (salt deposits) from the chromium-plated parts. To obtain a good lustre, the chromium should afterwards be polished with a "Selvyt" or similar soft duster. During the damp winter months it is a good plan to smear some rust preventative on all chromium surfaces. "Tekall" (obtainable in ½ and 1 pt. tins) is recommended, and should be applied with a soft rag.

ENGINE OVERHAUL

1. Tappet Adjustment. The tappet adjustment should be checked and, if necessary, adjusted about *once a month*. Adjustment is generally required every 5000 miles, also after decarbonizing and grinding-in the valves. The necessity for tappet adjustment more frequently than about once every 5000 miles is generally due to some fault which should be investigated. It is of vital importance to keep the adjustment correct in order to prevent damage to the valves and to maintain high engine performance.

On Models 16M and 18 the correct tappet clearance is *nil* with both valves closed and the engine *cold*. A clearance of *nil* implies that the push-rods are free to rotate without any appreciable up-and-down play.

Detach the cover from the off-side of the rocker-box after removing the three retaining nuts and fibre washers. This exposes the inlet and exhaust tappet adjustment. As may be seen in Fig. 64, each push-rod has an adjustable head (A) secured by a lock-nut (B) to the top of the push-rod (C).

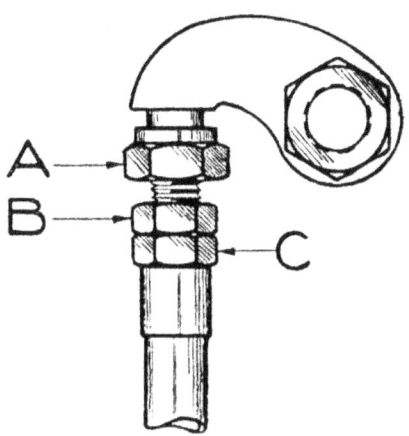

Fig. 64. Tappet Adjustment on Post-war O.H.V. Engines

2. Where No Compression Plate is Fitted. Turn the engine (350 c.c. or 500 c.c.) over slowly until the piston is at T.D.C. on the compression stroke, with both valves closed. See that the exhaust valve lifter is not preventing the exhaust valve from seating fully. Then check the tappet clearance for both tappets (see above). Referring to Fig. 64, if an adjustment of either or both tappets is required, hold the top of the push-rod (C) with one spanner, and with another loosen the lock-nut (B). Then screw the adjustable head (A) up or down until a tappet clearance of *nil* is obtained. Afterwards tighten the lock-nut (B) and again check the clearance.

3. Where a Compression Plate is Fitted. On 500 c.c. O.H.V. engines having a compression plate, to adjust the tappet clearance, first rotate the engine until the exhaust valve lifts off its seat. Referring to Fig. 64, first slacken the lock-nut B on the exhaust push-rod C. Next rotate the engine until the inlet valve is lifed off its seat. Loosen the lock-nut B on the inlet push-rod C. Then screw the adjustable head A of the exhaust push-rod up or down as required to obtain a clearance of *nil*. Further rotate the engine until the exhaust valve is lifted off its seat. Now tighten the lock-nut B on the exhaust push-rod. Afterwards screw up or down as required the adjustable head A on the inlet push-rod C until tappet clearance is *nil*. Again rotate the engine until the inlet valve is raised, and tighten the lock-nut on the inlet push-rod.

4. After Adjusting Tappets. Turn the engine over until both valves are closed. Check that the push-rods are free to rotate without appreciable up-and-down movement. Fit the cover to the off-side of the rocker-box and replace the three retaining nuts. Make sure that the three fibre washers are also replaced beneath the nuts. When tightening the nuts, avoid using excessive pressure on the spanner. Such pressure is quite unnecessary, because a rubber fillet is incorporated at the rocker-box cover joint.

1. Decarbonizing Your A.J.S. Removal of carbon deposits is normally required every 2000 miles, but the exact period when decarbonizing becomes necessary depends to some extent on driving conditions and also on the quality of the fuel used. If the engine tends to knock when hill climbing or suddenly accelerating, and the exhaust loses its crispness, this shows that decarbonizing is overdue and the cylinder head should be removed at the earliest opportunity, and carbon deposits scraped from the head and the crown of the piston. The valves should also be ground-in if necessary.

Every *alternate* decarbonizing, the cylinder barrel and piston should also be removed, and the piston rings and their grooves inspected and cleaned. Stripping down the engine for decarbonizing is dealt with in subsequent paragraphs.

2. Removing Petrol Tank. It is necessary to remove the petrol tank before detaching the rocker-box and cylinder head prior to decarbonizing, also when undertaking any major engine overhaul work. The provision of two petrol taps eliminates the necessity for draining the tank prior to its removal. To remove the petrol tank, turn both petrol taps to the "Off" position. Then sever the locking wires securing the four tank-fixing bolts (see Fig. 67). Now unscrew the four fixing bolts and ease the tank clear of the frame.

3. To Remove Rocker-box. After removing the petrol tank, the next step towards cylinder head removal is to take off the rocker-box and push-rods. First remove the three nuts retaining the cover to the off-side of the rocker-box. Also remove the three fibre washers beneath the nuts. Then take off the rocker-box cover. Disconnect the upper union of the oil-feed pipe from the pump to the rocker-box. Now rotate the engine slowly until both inlet and exhaust valves are closed. On the 500 c.c. engine (Model 18), detach the steady between the engine and frame by removing the nut and washer from the rocker-box bolt extension, and also the bolt from the frame clip.

With a suitable spanner, remove the seven bolts which secure the rocker-box to the cylinder head. Grip the rocker-box, tilt its right-hand side upwards, and withdraw both push-rods. These should not be interchanged, and for this reason should be marked or placed so that they can subsequently be identified. Raise the front end of the rocker-box so as to clear the exhaust valve assembly and swing it round anti-clockwise to clear the frame tube. The rocker-box may now be lifted clear of the inlet valve assembly and removed from the engine. Be careful not to lose the hardened steel caps on the ends of the valve stems. These caps are most important.

4. To Remove Cylinder Head. Having removed the petrol tank and rocker-box as previously described, unscrew the sparking plug. Then proceed to remove, or partially remove, the exhaust system. Before this can be done, however, it is necessary to remove the right-hand side of the footrest rod. Remove the nut and washer on the right-hand side of the footrest rod and partially withdraw the footrest rod from the left-hand side. On Model 16M prise off the right-hand side footrest arm.

To remove the exhaust system, first remove the nuts and washers which secure the exhaust pipe and silencer to their stays. Then pull the exhaust pipe and silencer away from the stays, and pull the pipe downwards from the exhaust port in the cylinder head.

Remove the Amal carburettor by unscrewing the venturi air-intake and the two nuts securing the carburettor flange to the cylinder head. The carburettor may be allowed to rest on the saddle, and it is not necessary to disconnect the throttle and air controls.

Next remove the four bolts which retain the cylinder head to the cylinder barrel. If these are stiff, brush paraffin round their heads and allow to penetrate before again using the spanner. Lift the cylinder head from the cylinder barrel and simultaneously remove the push-rod cover tubes which come away with the cylinder head.

5. Removing the Cylinder Barrel. Rotate the engine so that the piston is near B.D.C. Next remove the four nuts which secure the cylinder barrel to the crankcase, and then gently draw the barrel off the piston. Steady the latter with the left hand as the barrel is withdrawn, and take great care not to allow the piston to fall sharply against the connecting-rod. After removing the cylinder barrel, cover the mouth of the crankcase with a clean rag.

6. Piston Removal. To remove the fully-floating gudgeon-pin, it is only necessary to extract *one* circlip with the special pliers shown at *B* in Fig. 63. Push the gudgeon-pin out from the opposite side and remove the piston. The gudgeon-pin is an easy sliding fit in the piston bosses and the small-end bush. If the piston is not of the split-skirt type, scratch an "F" on the inside to indicate which is the front.

Piston Dimensions. For the benefit of more mechanically-minded readers who perhaps own workshop tools, including a micrometer, and may wish to check piston wear, the various diameters at different piston positions are tabulated below. Normally a piston can be retained in service for very many thousands of miles; but eventually loss of compression and/or piston slap occurs due to wear of the piston, rings, and cylinder

DIAMETERS OF NEW A.J.S. PISTONS (IN INCHES)

Position on Piston	Diameter (350 c.c.)	(Diameter (500 c.c.)
Top Land	2·6872–2·6882	3·2140–3·2150
Second Land	2·6957–2·6967	3·2255–3·2265
Third Land	2·6957–2·6967	3·2185–3·2195
Top of Skirt	2·7127–2·7137	3·2430–3·2440
Bottom of Skirt	2·7138–2·7148	3·2441–3·2451

bore, especially the last-mentioned. Examine the cylinder bore occasionally for longitudinal scores and circumferential ridges. Also inspect the piston for blackening of the skirt, scores, smearing, and other possible damage, particularly in the vicinity of the piston ring lands.

7. Removing and Inspecting Piston Rings. The piston rings should not be disturbed more frequently than once every *alternate* decarbonizing, provided that engine compression remains good. The rings can be removed by "peeling off" with a small knife, but it is preferable to remove them with the aid of three pieces of thin steel in the manner described on page 48, which also deals with the examination of the rings. Renew any rings immediately if their bearing faces are badly discoloured or blackened.

Oversize Piston and Rings Available. The engine manufacturers are able to supply a piston and rings which are ·020 in. oversize in diameter, but their fitting necessitates reboring the cylinder barrel bore to suit. A rebore is generally required when wear at the top of the bore reaches ·008 in. On the 500 c.c. engine the diameter of the standard cylinder bore is 3·250 in. ± ·0005 in. On the 350 c.c. engine it is 2·7187 in. ± ·0005 in. When a rebore becomes necessary it is best to entrust this to the Plumstead factory.

8. Ring Dimensions. The width of the compression rings and the scraper ring (350 c.c. and 500 c.c. engines) are $\frac{1}{16}$ in. and $\frac{1}{8}$ in. respectively. The normal ring gap is ·006 in. to ·008 in. and rings should be renewed when the gap exceeds ·030 in. The normal clearance of each ring in its groove is ·003 in.

After a considerable mileage, or if loss of **compression** occurs with the valves in good condition, check the gap of each piston ring. The best method of checking the gap is to push the ring squarely into the bore of the cylinder barrel with the aid of the piston and then check the gap between the ends of the ring with a feeler gauge, as shown in Fig. 65. If the gap proves excessive, fit new A.J.S. rings (already "gapped"); if the gap is insufficient, remove some metal from one end of the ring to increase the gap to ·006 in.

9. Removing the Valves. The use of a valve extractor is not necessary. Lay the removed cylinder head on the bench or table

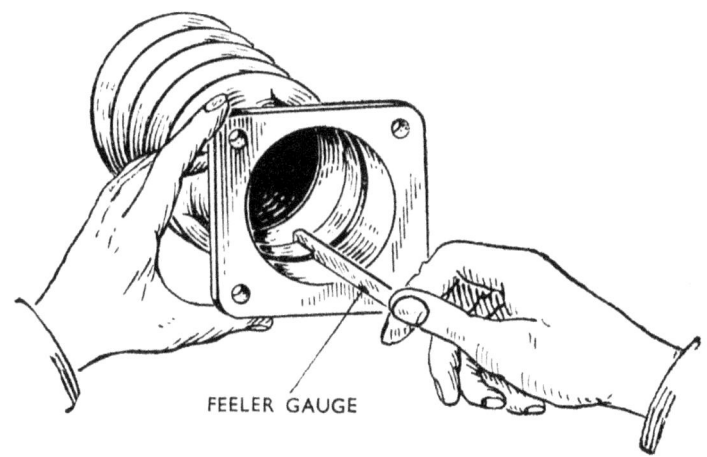

Fig. 65. Checking Piston Ring Gap with Feeler Gauge

and rest each valve head in turn on a small wooden block. Then compress the duplex valve springs by exerting pressure on the outer collar until the split collet can be removed from the valve stem. It may be necessary to tap each collar sharply to free the split collet, as the latter is a taper fit in the collar. On the 500 c.c. engine the inlet and exhaust valves are of identical size, unlike those on the 350 c.c. engine, but they must not be interchanged.

10. Removing Carbon Deposits. With a suitable scraper (see page 45) remove all carbon from the crown of the piston and from the combustion chamber and valve ports. It is inadvisable to use an abrasive, such as emery cloth, on the piston or elsewhere, and the scraper employed should preferably be of soft metal. Leave the skirt and the inside of the piston alone.

If the piston rings have been removed, clean the grooves thoroughly. A suitable scraper can be made by fitting a handle to a broken piece of piston ring. Be very careful not to damage the edges of the grooves or the lands between them. Remove all carbon deposits from the valve heads; and if the valves have been removed for grinding-in, clean both valve stems with some very fine emery cloth, holding the latter between the thumb and forefinger while moving the valve stem up and down. (See also page 46.)

11. Grinding-in the Valves. For general procedure, refer to page 47. Be careful to lift the valve off its seat occasionally and turn it to a new position while grinding-in. Continue grinding-in with the A.J.S. valve grinding tool until a continuous matt ring is observed on both the valve and its seat. If pitting is not appreciable, use a fine grade of grinding paste only. Generally one application of grinding paste is sufficient for the inlet valve, but the exhaust valve may need several applications. If pitting is extensive, use a coarse grade grinding paste first, and then a fine grade. Deep pitting may require re-cutting of the valve seats. The angle of the cutter must be 45 degrees.

After grinding-in the inlet and exhaust valves, make sure that all abrasive is removed by washing the valves and their seats with petrol. Also draw a piece of clean rag through each valve guide.

12. Checking Length of Valve Springs. After considerable use the hard-pressed valve springs may weaken under the influence of heat, and thereby spoil the quick and positive action of the valves, which is so vital to high engine efficiency. The condition of the valve springs is reflected in their free length, which should be checked very occasionally with a small rule. On the 350 c.c. and 500 c.c. O.H.V. engines, the free length of inner and outer valve springs is $1\frac{3}{16}$ in. and $2\frac{1}{16}$ in. respectively. Renew immediately any valve springs whose free length is found to be more than about $\frac{7}{32}$ in. below the free length dimensions quoted above.

13. Replacing the Valves. Having cleaned the insides of both valve guides, smear some engine oil on the valve stems. Then fit the inlet and exhaust valves in their respective guides. On the 350 c.c. engine (Model 16M) the inlet valve can immediately be recognized, as it has a larger diameter head than the exhaust valve. On the 500 c.c. engine (Model 18), however, the dimensions of both valves are identical, though the material differs. In this case, before fitting the valves, note the markings "IN" and "EX" on top of the inlet and exhaust valve stems respectively, above the grooves for the split collets.

Rest each valve head in turn on a small wooden block, and fit the duplex valve springs and collars. Compress the valve springs and then fit the split collet. A distance sleeve must be fitted on the cylinder head under the lower collar for the exhaust valve springs, but this does not apply to the inlet valve. Make quite sure that the split collets are properly located. The two grooves machined in the bore of each split collet must *both* register with the corresponding rings on the valve stem, otherwise damage may result. Finally replace the hardened caps on the ends of the valve stems. Under no circumstances must these be omitted. Failure to replace them will cause wear and possibly actual

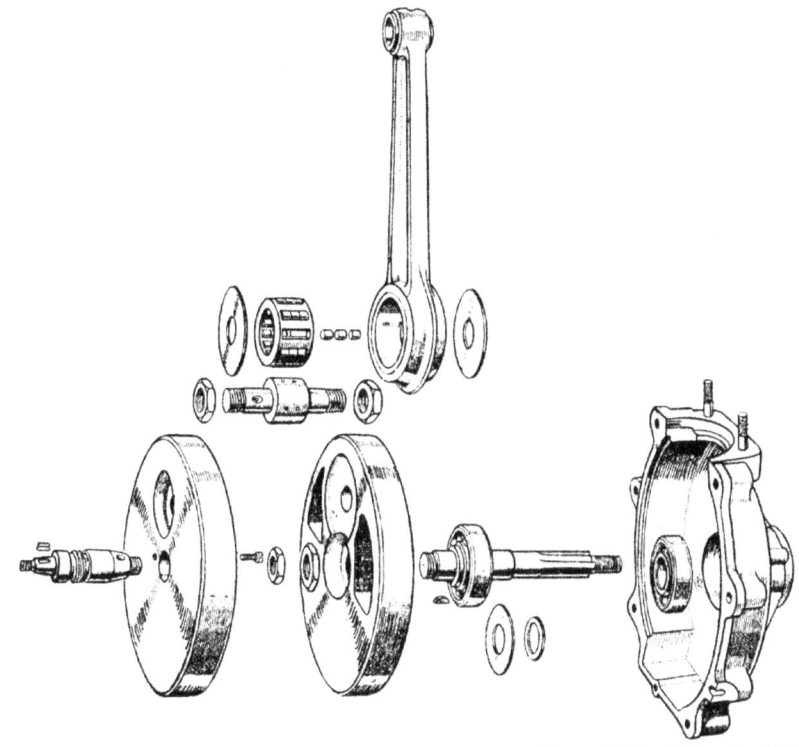

(*From " The Motor Cycle"*)

FIG. 66. EXPLODED VIEW OF A.J.S. CONNECTING-ROD AND FLYWHEEL ASSEMBLY

damage through fouling of the oil lug on the rocker-box by the tappet adjuster head.

14. The Piston Rings. If these have been removed, fit them in their grooves, which should first be oiled. The safest method of fitting the piston rings is to use three pieces of thin steel, as illustrated in Fig. 22. Fit the (bottom) scraper ring first, and then the two compression rings. Space the ring gaps evenly, that is, at 120 degrees to each other. It is assumed that the ring gaps are within the permissible limits (see page 122). If new rings are fitted, these are correctly "gapped" by the makers and ready for immediate use.

15. Fitting Piston to Connecting-rod. It is assumed that all parts are thoroughly clean and that the piston rings have been refitted. Smear some engine oil on the gudgeon-pin and then offer up the piston to the small-end of the connecting-rod. The piston must be replaced in exactly the same position as before. If it is of the split skirt type, the split itself must face to the *front* of the machine. This is important.

Next insert the gudgeon-pin from the side from which the circlip has been removed. Centralize the gudgeon-pin, and with the small pliers, shown at B in Fig. 63, replace the circlip, using a rotary movement to ensure that it beds snugly into its groove. Perfect fitting of the circlip is essential to prevent damage. If the condition of the old circlip is suspect, fit a new circlip immediately.

16. Replacing Cylinder Barrel. A *new* washer must be fitted to the cylinder base,* and its cylinder barrel side should be coated with liquid jointing compound. Make sure that none of the compound chokes any of the oil holes and that the holes register properly. Now smear some engine oil on the piston and cylinder bore, and then turn the engine so that the piston is at or near B.D.C. Verify that the piston ring gaps are spaced at 120 degrees and remove the rag from the mouth of the crankcase.

Ease the cylinder barrel carefully over the piston, pressing each piston ring as required into its groove to enable the barrel to slide over the piston without friction. Finally replace the four cylinder barrel retaining nuts. Tighten the four nuts, first finger-tight, and then firmly in a diagonal order, turning each nut about one-quarter of a turn at a time.

17. Fitting Cylinder Head to Cylinder Barrel. Wipe the bottom face of the cylinder head and the top edge of the cylinder barrel absolutely clean. Then fit the push-rod cover tubes to the cylinder head. See that the rubber gaskets are in good condition, and fitted between the top ends of the cover tubes and the cylinder head. If the push-rod cover tubes were pulled away from the cylinder head during stripping down, it would probably be found that the rubber gaskets have remained located in the cylinder head. Also check that the metal washers are interposed between the top edges of the rubber gaskets and the recesses in the cylinder head.

Fit the cylinder head gasket on the top edge of the cylinder barrel. If the gasket is not in perfect condition, renew it. Also place a rubber gland round the inlet and exhaust tappet guide. Then replace the cylinder head on the barrel, complete with

---

* On the 500 c.c. engine (Model 18) a compression plate is a standard fitment, and in this case a paper washer should be fitted on each side of the compression plate.

push-rod cover tubes, and fit the four head retaining bolts. Each bolt must be fitted with a plain steel washer. Tighten each bolt a few turns and then gradually tighten all four, using a diagonal sequence to ensure an even pressure being exerted on the cylinder head.

18. Fitting the Rocker-box. Wipe the lower face of the rocker-box and the upper face of the cylinder head absolutely clean. Verify that the hardened steel caps are fitted to the ends of the inlet and exhaust valve stems. Then rotate the engine so that the piston is at or near T.D.C. on the compression stroke, with both tappets right down. Place the special composition washer on the cylinder head face for the rocker-box, but before doing this inspect it carefully. Renew this washer if there is the slightest sign of damage. When fitting the composition washer, make sure that its small lip is concentric with the small hole in the cylinder head through which oil is fed to the stem of the inlet valve.

Now place the rear end of the rocker-box over the inlet valve assembly and swing it clockwise over the exhaust valve assembly until it is in the normal position. Next raise the offside of the rocker-box slightly and insert the two push-rods down the push-rod covers, being careful not to interchange the inlet and exhaust rods. Make certain that the push-rod ends engage the tops of the flat base tappets and the overhead rocker arm ends.

Push the rocker-box right home and fit the seven rocker-box retaining bolts and plain steel washers. See that the bolt having a short head is fitted in the centre, right-hand position. On the 500 c.c. engine (Model 18) be careful to replace the bolt with the threaded extension (for the engine steady stay) in its correct position. Tighten all seven bolts lightly and then, using a diagonal sequence starting near the centre, firmly tighten them all, turning each nut a little at a time.

Connect the engine steady stay (500 c.c. only) to the rocker-box bolt with threaded extension, and fit the washer and nut. Bolt the other end of the steady to the clip on the frame down tube. Rotate the engine a few turns to enable all parts to bed home. Then with the appropriate spanner, check that all rocker-box retaining bolts are firmly tightened. Having done this, check the tappet clearances and adjust, if necessary, as described on page 118.

Reconnect the oil-feed pipe from the pump to the rocker-box. Use two spanners when tightening the upper union, so as to prevent the union screwed into the rocker-box from turning. Fit a new rubber fillet to the rocker-box side cover if examination of the fillet shows deterioration. Then fit the rocker-box side cover to the rocker-box, and replace the three fibre washers and securing nuts. Tighten these nuts evenly, but not too tightly.

128   THE BOOK OF THE A.J.S.

The provision of a rubber fillet renders excessive tightening quite unnecessary.

19. Final Reassembly. Final reassembly, after decarbonizing, is completed by replacing the Amal carburettor, the sparking plug, the exhaust system, the footrests, and the petrol tank.

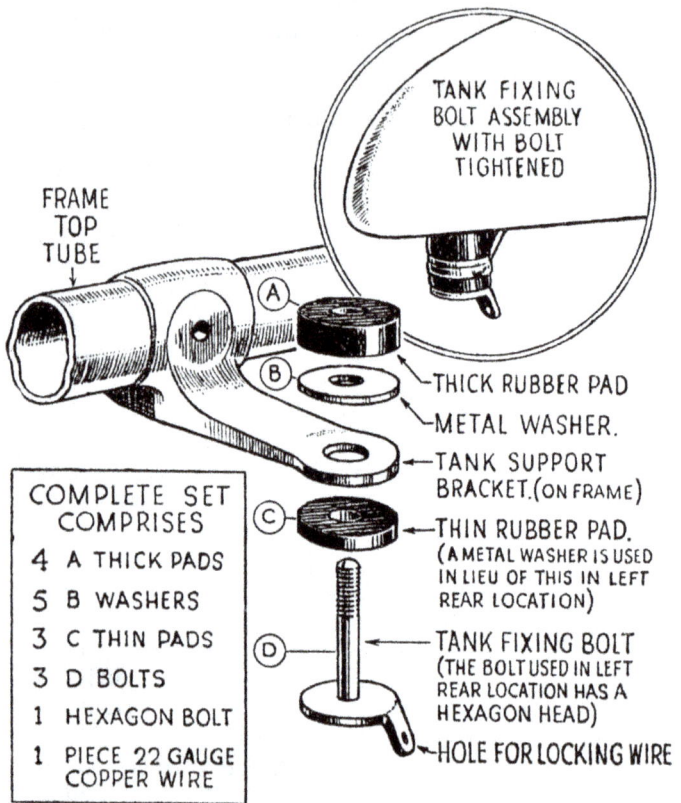

Fig. 67. Details of Petrol Tank Fixing Bolt

The arrangement shown applies to all except the fixing bolt at the rear of the tank on the L.H. side. In this case a hexagon-headed bolt is provided, and a metal washer is used instead of a thin rubber pad.

When fitting the carburettor, it is important to obtain an absolutely air-tight joint at the attachment flange. Renew the washer if not perfect, also the copper washer for the sparking plug.

20. Replacing Petrol Tank. The petrol tank is secured to the frame by four fixing bolts and a number of rubber pads and metal washers. Details of a fixing bolt assembly are shown in Fig. 67, and the correct assembly order should be carefully noted.

To replace the petrol tank, first lay a metal washer on each of the four tank support brackets. Next place a *thick* rubber pad on top of each metal washer and position the petrol tank. It will be noted that one of the four fixing bolts has a hexagon head. Fit a metal washer to this bolt and screw the latter into the rear tank location on the left-hand side. Fit *thin* rubber pads over the other three "D" bolts and fit the bolts.

Having fitted all four fixing bolts, screw the bolts home evenly until the rubber pads are slightly compressed. Do not screw the bolts right home, otherwise the tank will not be effectively insulated. Finally wire-lock the fixing bolts in pairs with 22 gauge wire, and replace the fuel pipe. When tightening the union nuts at the upper end of this pipe, hold the body of each tap with the adjustable spanner provided in the tool kit.

Cleaning Cylinder Fins. Both from the point of view of appearance and in order to assist heat radiation, it is a good plan occasionally to brush some cylinder black on the fins (see page 49).

Engine Lubrication. Full instructions concerning engine lubrication are given in Chapter VI, and a lubrication chart is included on page 112.

The Sparking Plug. It is essential always to run on a good 14 mm. plug. Champion L-10 and Lodge H14 plugs are suitable for Models 16M and 18 respectively.

Other suitable plugs are given on page 50. Keep the plug clean and the gap between the electrodes adjusted to ·020 in. to ·025 in. For advice on plug maintenance, see page 49. When adjusting the gap, always bend the "L"-shaped outer electrode, *never* the centre electrode. For hints on testing a plug, see page 64.

Care of Lucas Magneto. Lubrication of the magneto is dealt with on page 110. Keep the contacts of the face cam type contact-breaker clean and adjusted to give a "break" of ·010 in. to ·012 in. as described on page 51. Use the feeler gauge attached to the magneto spanner (shown at *H* in Fig. 63) to check the gap. Complete removal of the contact-breaker is unnecessary except for lubrication. Occasionally inspect and clean the H.T. pick-up and brush. About every 10,000 miles the instrument should be returned to a Lucas Service Station for dismantling, cleaning, and greasing of the armature bearings.

To Retime Ignition (Models 16M and 18). Your A.J.S. is correctly timed when the contacts of the contact-breaker begin to open with the piston $\frac{7}{16}$ in. before T.D.C. on the compression stroke, with the ignition lever *fully advanced*. An ignition advance greater than the above may cause detonation of fuel and possibly serious damage to the engine. In order to retime the ignition simply and accurately, it is desirable to have available the following: (*a*) A stout screwdriver or an old type tyre lever with turned-up end; and (*b*) a metal rod about $5\frac{1}{2}$ in. long and of $\frac{1}{4}$ in. diameter.

First remove the contact-breaker cover from the Lucas magneto and check the gap between the contacts with the latter fully open. If it is more or less than ·010 in. to ·012 in., adjust the gap as described on page 51. Next disconnect the H.T. lead from the sparking plug terminal and remove the plug from the cylinder head. Also remove the magneto chain case cover and the cover from the offside of the rocker-box.

Slacken off several turns the nut which secures the magneto-driving sprocket to the exhaust camshaft, but do not actually remove the nut. Then with the stout screwdriver or old type tyre lever, referred to above, lever off the driving sprocket until it is freed from the exhaust camshaft taper. Now rotate the engine until the piston is at T.D.C., with the inlet and exhaust valves closed.

Find exact T.D.C. by inserting the $\frac{1}{4}$ in. diameter metal rod through the sparking plug hole. Rotate the engine gently backwards and forwards until the piston is felt to be at the top of its stroke and no motion is imparted to the metal rod. With the piston in this position, mark the rod flush with the top of the sparking plug hole. Withdraw the rod and make another mark on it exactly $\frac{7}{16}$ in. above the first mark. Replace the metal rod and slowly turn the engine *backwards* until the upper mark on the rod is flush with the top face of the sparking plug hole. The best method of turning the engine backwards is to engage top gear and slowly rotate the rear wheel backwards.

At this stage fully advance the ignition lever on the handle-bars by pulling it *inwards* as far as possible. With the piston still exactly at $\frac{7}{16}$ in. before T.D.C., rotate the sprocket (and chain) on the armature of the Lucas magneto *anti-clockwise* (viewed from the sprocket side) until the contact-breaker points are just commencing to separate. The moment when this occurs can be determined by inserting a slip of tissue paper between the contacts and gently pulling on the paper until it is released. Having checked the exact position of "break," tighten the nut securing the exhaust camshaft sprocket, being very careful not to move the camshaft and/or armature shaft.

Finally recheck the ignition timing and replace the cover on the offside of the rocker-box, the contact-breaker cover, and the magneto chain case cover. Before replacing the chain case cover check the tension of the magneto chain as described in the next paragraph. Also fit the sparking plug and the H.T. lead.

Adjusting Magneto Chain. It is advisable occasionally (say, once a month) to remove the magneto chain case cover and inspect the chain for tension. New chains are especially apt to stretch and, in the case of the magneto chain, excessive slackness may spoil the ignition timing. Check the whip of the upper chain run mid-way between the sprockets on the camshaft and magneto armature. Repeat the check with the chain in several different positions. Whip in the tautest position should not exceed ¼ in. on pressing the chain lightly up and down. If chain

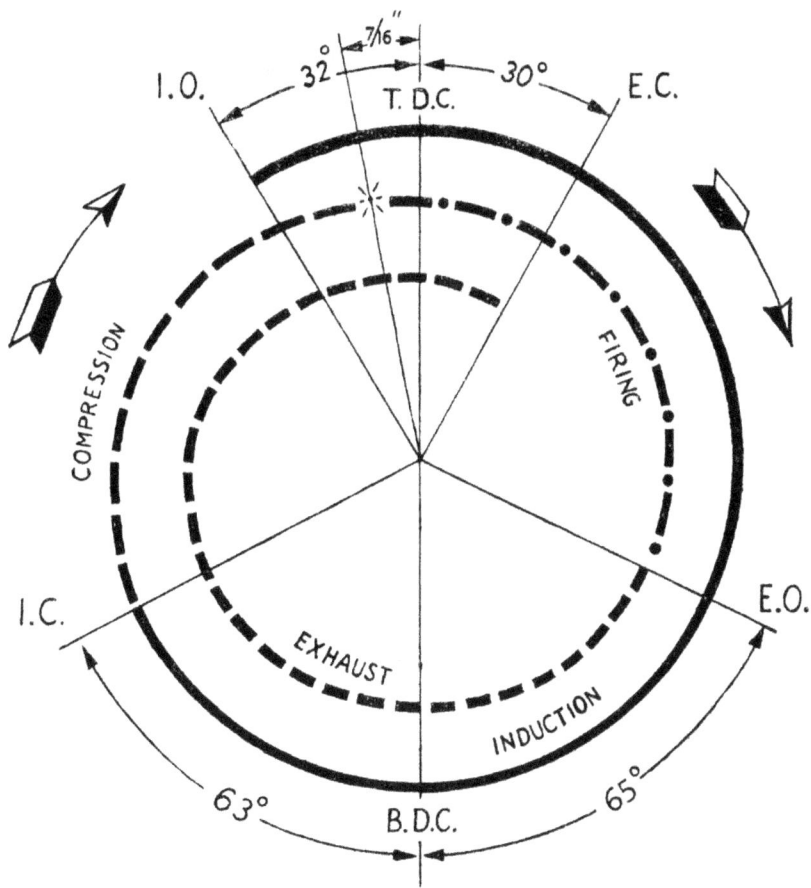

FIG. 68. A.J.S. VALVE-TIMING DIAGRAM
(This applies to all 1945 and later 500 c.c. and 350 c.c. engines.)

adjustment is needed, this can be effected by tilting the magneto platform which hinges on one of its fixing bolts.

To adjust the magneto chain, slacken the nuts on the two bolts which support the magneto platform. Then insert the blade of a screwdriver under the slotted end (the front one) of the magneto platform and lever it upwards until the correct chain tension (see above) is obtained. Afterwards tighten firmly the nuts on the platform supporting bolts, and again check the chain tension.

If it is correct, grease the chain (see page 111) and replace the chain cover. No jointing compound is necessary.

To Retime Valves (Models 16M and 18). If the timing gears have been dismantled (see page 63), it is necessary to retime the valves correctly during reassembly. The correct valve timing is shown in Fig. 68, and the maker's timing should not be interfered with. During assembly of the timing gears it is normally unnecessary to actually check the timing in degrees of crankshaft rotation, as all timing gears are appropriately marked to ensure correct

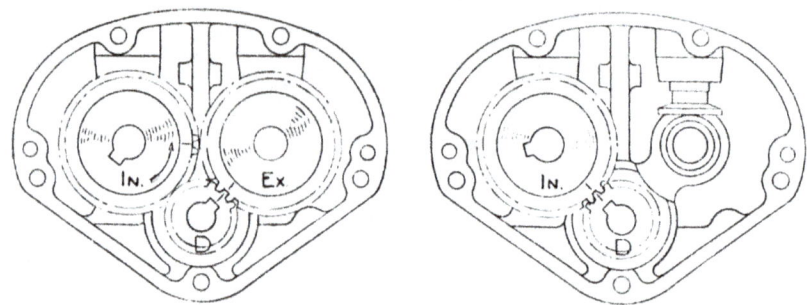

FIG. 69. HOW THE VALVE-TIMING MARKS SHOULD BE ALINED
The right-hand illustration shows correct alinement for the inlet camwheel. In the left-hand sketch the inlet camshaft has been fitted and the engine turned to enable the exhaust camwheel alinement to be obtained as shown

replacement. If the valve timing is checked by attaching a degree disc to the crankshaft, it is essential, first, to adjust the tappet clearances to ·016 in. with the piston at T.D.C. on the compression stroke. Only in these circumstances are the tappets well clear of the cam quietening curves (slight inclines from the base circles to the humps).

To assemble the timing gears correctly, using the maker's system of line markings on the gears, first, rotate the engine until the line mark on the engine pinion, shown at D in Fig. 69, is in line with the centre of the bush for the inlet camshaft (the rear bush). Then replace the inlet camshaft so that the line mark on the camwheel registers with the line mark on the engine pinion, as shown in the right-hand illustration.

Having correctly replaced the inlet camshaft, proceed to fit the exhaust camwheel in the following manner. Turn the engine slowly *forward* until the line mark on the engine pinion, shown at D in Fig. 69, is in line with the centre of the bush for the exhaust camshaft. Then replace the exhaust camshaft so that the line mark on the camwheel registers with the line mark on the engine pinion, as shown in the left-hand illustration. If both camshafts are replaced in accordance with the above instructions, the valve timing *must* be correct, assuming that the timing gear teeth have not become excessively worn after a very big mileage.

Removal of Oil Pump Plunger. Care must be taken in removing and replacing the oil pump plunger, an operation seldom required. The reader is referred to the instructions given on page 108.

Oversize Crankpin Rollers. The author would mention that crankpin rollers, ·001 in. larger in diameter than the standard size rollers are available. These oversize rollers, however, must be fitted by skilled mechanics, because it is generally necessary to "lap" the big-end journals and liners in order to obtain a precision fit.

Overhaul of Flywheel and Connecting-rod Assembly. Unless you are a skilled mechanic and have workshop facilities available, this work is best entrusted to the engine manufacturers (see page 65). The fitting of a new small-end bush, as described on page 65, can perhaps be undertaken; but as the bush contracts slightly during pressing in, it may be necessary to ream its bore to suit the gudgeon-pin, using a suitable reamer.

Concerning Repairs and Spares. Whenever parts are forwarded to the makers for repair or as patterns, it is essential to attach to each part a label giving your full name and address. Clear instructions concerning same should be sent under separate cover. When asking the makers for technical advice or spares, always remember to quote the *complete* engine number or frame number, as the case may be. The engine number (which has a letter prefix) is stamped on the left-hand side of the crankcase. The frame number is stamped on the right-hand side of the seat lug beneath the saddle. Correspondence relating to technical advice and spares should be kept on separate sheets to ensure prompt attention.

Once a Month. Make a practice of checking all nuts and bolts for tightness. This applies to the engine and cycle parts. Also verify that all joints in the fuel system are petrol-tight.

THE CYCLE PARTS

Dynamo Chain Adjustment. The tension of the dynamo chain (which lies behind the primary chain) should be checked monthly, after removing the oil-bath chain case inspection cap (see page 114). Chain whip with the chain in its tautest position, midway between the sprockets, should be approximately $\frac{1}{4}$ in.

To make an eccentric adjustment for chain tension, first slacken the strap bolt clamping the dynamo in its housing. Then apply the spanner, shown at K in Fig. 63, to the flats cast on the dynamo end plate, which is on the left-hand side of the dynamo. Now rotate the dynamo *anti-clockwise* until correct chain tension is obtained. Afterwards retighten the strap bolt and again check the tension of the dynamo chain. If found to be correct, replace the inspection cap on the oil-bath chain case (see page 114).

Adjusting Primary Chain. The tension of the primary chain (which transmits the drive from the engine to the pivot-mounted Burman four-speed gearbox) should be checked about once a month and, if necessary, adjusted. Adjustment of the primary chain must always be effected *before* that of the secondary chain, as it alters the tension of the secondary chain automatically.

To check the primary chain adjustment, place the machine on the rear stand and remove the inspection cap from the oil-bath chain case (see page 114). Then with the fingers check the chain whip (total up-and-down movement) mid-way between the two sprockets, with the chain in its tightest position. The whip should be approximately $\frac{3}{8}$ in.

If an adjustment is needed, slacken: (*a*) the nut on the right-hand side of the gearbox upper fixing bolt; (*b*) the nut on the right-hand side of the gearbox lower fixing bolt. Also loosen a few (2–3) turns the front nut on the gearbox adjuster eye-bolt. Then screw up the rear nut on the adjuster eye-bolt until the chain is felt to be quite taut, as checked with the fingers inserted through the inspection cap orifice. Now loosen the rear nut on the adjuster eye-bolt and carefully tighten the front nut until the chain tension is found to be correct. To obtain the best results, always overtighten first and then slacken back in the manner just described. Afterwards tighten the nuts on both gearbox fixing bolts, replace the inspection cap on the oil-bath chain case, and proceed to check the tension of the secondary chain.

Adjusting Secondary Chain. Check and, if necessary, adjust the tension of the secondary chain (gearbox to rear wheel) about once a month, but, before making an adjustment, attend to the primary chain as previously described. It should be noted that secondary chain adjustment, involving sliding the rear wheel bodily in the slotted fork ends, generally necessitates an adjustment of the rear brake being made, and care must be taken not to upset wheel alinement. Chain adjustment is correct when the chain, in its tautest position, has a whip mid-way between the sprockets of $\frac{3}{8}$ in. to $\frac{1}{2}$ in.

To tighten the secondary chain, first jack up the machine on the rear stand. Then loosen the nuts on the rear wheel spindle. Also slacken 2–3 turns the nuts on the two chain adjuster bolts which are screwed into the front of the fork ends. Then progressively and *uniformly* screw both adjuster bolts further into the fork ends until the tension of the chain is correct. It is vitally important to screw both adjuster bolts into the fork ends exactly the same amount, otherwise wheel alinement (see page 79) will be upset, and this will necessitate a further adjustment being made. Having obtained the correct chain tension without upsetting wheel alinement, tighten the nuts on the rear wheel spindle and again verify the chain tension. Finally tighten the lock-nuts on the chain adjusters and also ascertain whether the rear brake is in need of adjustment (see page 154).

Gear Control Adjustment. With the foot-operated type of gear control (provided on all 1945 and later A.J.S. models) the gear

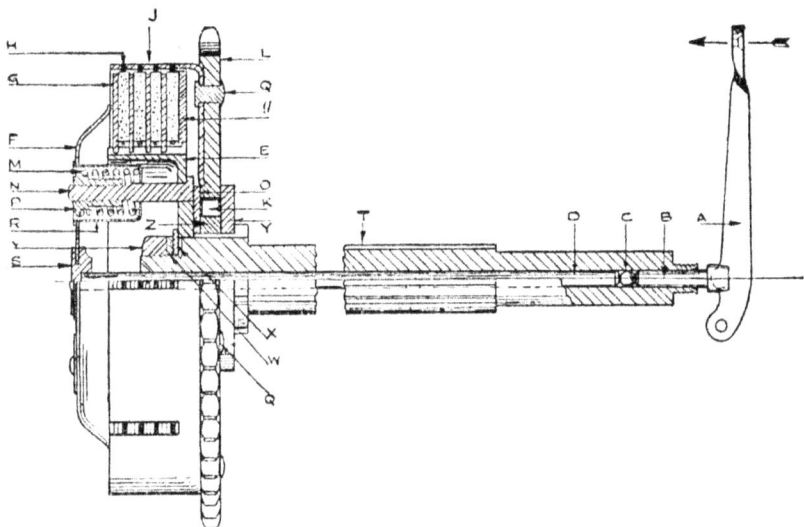

FIG. 70. DETAILS OF CLUTCH ASSEMBLY AND OPERATING MECHANISM

```
A = Clutch operating lever          N = Stud for spring adjustment nut
B = Short steel plunger             O = Washer (thin) retaining roller bearing
C = Steel ball                      P = Spring adjustment nut
D = Long thrust rod                 Q = Rivet
E = Clutch centre                   R = Spring cup (one of four)
F = Spring pressure plate           S = Pressure plate boss
G,g = Steel plain plates            T = Gearbox mainshaft
H = Friction insert plates          V = Nut retaining clutch centre
J = Clutch case                     W = Spring washer
K = Roller bearing rollers (24)     X = Plain washer
L = Clutch sprocket                 Y = Washer (thick) retaining roller bearing
M = Clutch spring (one of four)     Z = Roller bearing ring
```

change lever is mounted direct on the gearbox and no adjustment is necessary or included. An illustration of the gearbox is shown in Fig. 34.

1. Clutch Adjustment. Fig. 70 shows a cut-away sectional view of the assembled clutch and operating mechanism which is completely enclosed in the gearbox casing, as may be seen in Fig. 34. It should be noted that on the 500 c.c. model the clutch has five friction insert plates, whereas on the 350 c.c. model there are only four, as illustrated. Details of the clutch-operating lever and its fulcrum adjustment are clearly shown in Fig. 71.

From a glance at Fig. 70 it will be readily apparent that wear of the fabric inserts in the friction plates gradually causes the clutch plates to close up towards each other, with the result that the effective length of the clutch thrust rod (inside the hollow gearbox mainshaft) is increased. The clutch cable, however, tends to stretch with repeated use of the clutch lever and thereby to some extent neutralizes the effect of clutch insert wear. Clutch slip must be avoided at all costs, as it causes damage and overheating, and spoils performance. Sometimes it is due to incorrect adjustment of the clutch springs (see page 137), but generally it is due to insufficient free movement in the clutch operating mechanism. Referring to Fig. 71, there must always be about $\frac{1}{32}$ in. clearance (with the clutch plates engaged) between the thrust operating plunger (*B*) and the nose of the operating lever (*C*). Periodically inspect and, if necessary, rectify the adjustment. Two means of adjustment are provided, according to whether it is necessary to effect a minor or major adjustment. It is fairly easy to determine by feel the approximate amount of free movement in the clutch control by noting when resistance is met with as the handlebar lever is brought into use.

2. Effecting Minor Adjustment. When wear of the friction inserts is such that only a minor adjustment is called for, loosen the locking nut on the Bowden cable adjuster, which is screwed into the rear of the kick-starter housing (see Fig. 34). Then unscrew or screw up a few turns the cable adjuster, acccording to whether it is desired to decrease or increase the effective length of the control cable respectively. Decreasing the effective length of the cable does, of course, reduce the clearance (see Fig. 71) between the operating plunger (*B*) and the nose of the operating lever (*C*). After making the required adjustment, retighten the locking nut on the cable adjuster.

3. Effecting Major Adjustment. If wear of the friction inserts is such that it is impossible to obtain correct adjustment of the clutch operating mechanism by means of the minor (cable) adjustment just described, a major adjustment is called for. This entails altering the effective position of the fulcrum pin (for the clutch-operating lever) in the kick-starter case.

Referring to Fig. 71, to effect a major adjustment, first remove the two screws (*H*) with a suitable screwdriver, and detach the cap (*G*). Then proceed to adjust the sleeve nut (*F*) with an open-ended spanner until there is a clearance of about $\frac{1}{32}$ in. between the operating plunger (*B*) and the nose of the operating lever (*C*). To increase or decrease the clearance, turn the sleeve nut (*F*) clockwise or anti-clockwise respectively. Normally a sleeve nut adjustment of one or two turns suffices to obtain the correct clearance. Finally, lock the sleeve nut by replacing the cap (*G*) and the two securing screws (*H*.)

4. Adjustment of Clutch Springs. Clutch slip which persists in spite of the operating mechanism and cable being in correct adjustment may take place because the adjustment of the clutch springs requires attention. Before this can be done, it is necessary to remove the outer half of the oil-bath chain case, as described on page 138.

To make an adjustment, screw home *half a complete turn* each of the four adjustment nuts (shown at *P* in Fig. 70). Then make

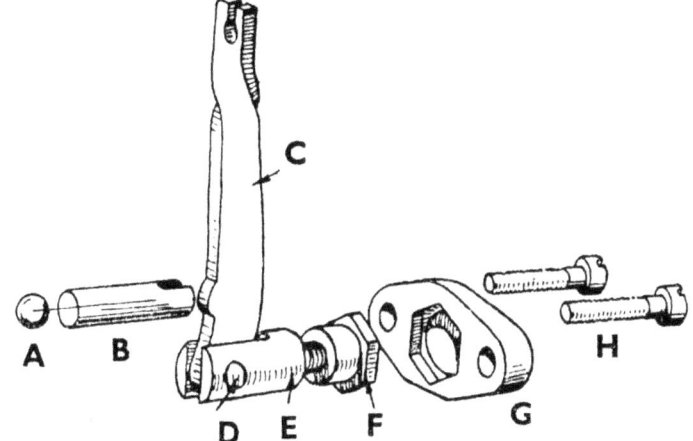

Fig. 71. Fulcrum Adjustment for Clutch-operating Lever

This exploded view of the parts should be studied in conjunction with Figs. 34 and 70. The operating lever fork (*E*) slides in the kick-starter cover case, and its position is determined by the sleeve nut (*F*) locked by the cap (*G*) secured to the outside of the cover by the two screws (*H*).

A = Steel ball
B = Short steel plunger
C = Operating lever
D = Fulcrum pin

E = Fork for operating lever
F = Sleeve nut
G = Cap for sleeve nut
H = Cap securing screws

a careful test to ascertain whether the clutch still slips. If it does, screw home a further half turn each adjustment nut, being most careful to adjust each nut exactly the same amount. It should be noted that the standard adjustment for spring tension is to tighten fully all four adjustment nuts and then to slacken back each nut *four complete turns*. The most suitable tool for tightening the clutch spring adjustment nuts is an old and broad screwdriver, slotted on the engaging edge.

Should it be necessary to screw the four adjustment nuts fully or almost home in order to eliminate clutch slip, this indicates that the clutch springs have weakened and/or the fabric inserts in the friction plates are excessively worn and require to be renewed.

To Remove and Replace Clutch Cable. Should complete removal of the clutch cable be necessary, first remove the oil filler cap from the cover of the kick-starter case. Next screw fully home the Bowden cable adjuster on the back of the case. Now disconnect the clutch cable from the operating lever (shown at *C* in Fig. 71). This can be done through the oil filler cap orifice. Then unscrew completely the clutch cable adjuster and disconnect the cable from the handlebar lever. The cable is now free to be removed from the machine. Pull it away from the lower end and carefully ease it from the various frame attachment clips.

To replace the clutch cable, proceed in the reverse order of removal, and finally check and, if necessary, adjust the clutch operation as described on page 136.

Harshness in Transmission. If harshness in the transmission develops, immediately check the level of oil in the oil-bath chain case. Provided the oil level is maintained correct, proper lubrication of the faces of the two cams of the shock-absorber fitted to the engine shaft is ensured. Top up the oil level, using engine oil, as required (see page 114). If harshness continues, remove the outer half of the oil-bath chain case, and dismantle and lubricate the components of the shock-absorber. (See also page 139.)

When assembling the engine shaft shock-absorber, fit the components in this order: (*a*) the spring collar, which is a sliding fit on the driving side flywheel main shaft and lies between the ball bearing of this shaft and the engine sprocket; (*b*) the engine sprocket, which is integral with the dynamo driving sprocket; (*c*) the shock-absorber cam which overrides the engine sprocket cam under the influence of the engine impulses; (*d*) the shock-absorber spring; (*e*) the cap washer, which retains the shock-absorber spring; (*f*) the sleeve lock-nut, which must be firmly tightened against the driving side flywheel main shaft.

1. Removal of Outer Half of Oil-bath Chain Case. Lay a suitable receptacle beneath the oil-bath to receive the oil as it runs out. Next disconnect the front connection of the rear brake rod. Also unscrew the battery clamping screw and remove the battery from its carrier. Now remove the screw which binds the metal band at the rear of the oil-bath chain case, and detach the band. When doing this it may be necessary to prise up the battery carrier. Take off the rubber oil sealing band, and remove the nut and plain washer from the bolt projecting from the centre of the chain case. Finally withdraw the outer half of the chain case.

2. To Remove Primary Chain and Clutch Assembly. First remove the nut retaining the engine sprocket (and integral dynamo-driving sprocket). This is facilitated by engaging top gear and applying the rear brake. Referring to Fig. 70, remove by unscrewing uniformly the four spring adjustment nuts (P) and withdraw the clutch spring pressure plate (F), complete with the four springs and spring cups (R). Now remove the spring link from the primary chain and take the chain off the sprockets.

With top gear still engaged, again apply the rear brake and, referring to Fig. 70, unscrew the nut (V) retaining the clutch centre (E) to the gearbox mainshaft (T). Remove the spring washer (W) and the plain washer (X) situated on the mainshaft behind the retaining nut. The entire clutch assembly may now be removed.

Withdraw the clutch assembly bodily by pulling it away from the gearbox mainshaft. The use of an extractor is generally quite unnecessary, as the clutch centre is a sliding fit on the mainshaft, but avoid losing any of the twenty-four clutch-bearing rollers which become free to move endwise when the clutch centre and sprocket assembly (including the roller bearing retaining washers) is withdrawn from the mainshaft.

3. Removal of Dynamo Chain and Back Half of Chain Case.
To remove the dynamo chain, first remove the spring locking ring from the nut retaining the sprocket on the dynamo armature. Also detach the locking washer which surrounds the nut. With the spanner, shown at K in Fig. 63, applied to the two flats on the back of the dynamo sprocket, hold the sprocket and unscrew the dynamo sprocket retaining nut. With a suitable extractor tool withdraw the dynamo sprocket from the armature. Now remove in one operation the dynamo sprocket, "endless" dynamo chain, and the engine shaft shock-absorber.

To remove the back half of the oil-bath chain case, straighten the tabs on the locking washers beneath the three bolts which retain the back half of the chain case to the crankcase boss. Then remove the bolts. Also remove the bolt beneath the battery carrier. This bolt has a long head and secures the rear chain guard to the oil-bath chain case. Finally remove the nut from the centre fixing bolt, also the spacer behind it, and take off the back half of the oil-bath chain case.

4. To Replace Back Half of Chain Case.
Smear some liquid jointing compound on the crankcase boss face. Verify that the spacer (between the left-hand engine plate and the oil-bath chain case) is fitted to the centre fixing bolt. On Model 18 the spacer is slightly shorter ($\frac{35}{64}$ in.) than on Model 18. Now replace the back half of the chain case.

Fit beneath the battery carrier the bolt with the long head. Tighten this bolt, which secures the rear chain guard, lightly. Now fit the three locking washers and bolts securing the oil-bath chain case half to the crankcase boss. Tighten these three bolts firmly and lock their tab-washers by turning up the tabs. Next fit the $\frac{7}{8}$ in. long spacer (provided inside the chain case) to the centre fixing bolt and replace the fixing bolt nut. Tighten this nut fully, and also the long-headed bolt which secures the rear chain guard to the oil-bath chain case.

5. Replacing Dynamo Sprocket, Chain, and Clutch Sprocket. Check that the key for the dynamo sprocket is in position on the armature location. Also verify that the spacing collar (between the crankcase ball bearing and the back of the engine sprocket) is replaced on the engine driving side mainshaft. Next engage the dynamo driving chain with the teeth of the dynamo driving sprocket (the smaller sprocket behind, and integral with, the engine sprocket) and the sprocket which fits on the dynamo armature. In one simultaneous operation replace the two sprockets (and chain) on the engine mainshaft and dynamo armature. Then replace the plain washer and sprocket retaining nut on the dynamo armature. Tighten the nut finger-tight only.

While preventing the dynamo armature from turning by applying the spanner, shown at K in Fig. 63, to the flats on the back of the sprocket, tighten the dynamo sprocket retaining nut firmly. Replace the locking washer for the retaining nut, also the locking ring. Make sure that the latter beds down properly in the nut groove. Finally replace the cam of the engine shaft shock-absorber, the spring, cap washer, and retaining nut. At this stage the retaining nut should not be fully tightened (see paragraph 8).

6. Replacing Clutch Centre and Clutch Sprocket. Referring to Fig. 70, fit the roller bearing retaining washer (Y) on the gearbox mainshaft. This is the thicker of the two retaining washers. Next replace the roller bearing ring (Z) on the mainshaft and with thick grease position the twenty-four rollers (K) on the bearing ring. Replace the clutch sprocket (L) over the rollers.

Next fit to the gearbox mainshaft the washer (O) retaining the roller bearing. This is the thinner of the two retaining washers. Then fit the clutch centre (E) to the splined end of the mainshaft and push home. Afterwards replace in this order: the plain washer (X); the spring washer (W), and the nut (V) retaining the clutch centre. This nut should not yet be fully tightened (see paragraph 7).

7. Replacing Primary Chain and Locking Clutch Centre. Replace the primary chain on the two sprockets, being careful that the spring link is correctly fitted (see Fig. 27). Now fit the nut which retains the clutch centre to the mainshaft of the gearbox. When tightening this nut, engage fourth gear and apply the rear brake to prevent the mainshaft turning.

OVERHAULING (1945-8)

8. Fitting Clutch Plates and Springs. Referring to Fig. 70, slide into position in the clutch case (J) attached to the clutch sprocket (L) the thickest of the steel plain plates (g). Make certain that the recessed part of the steel plate faces *towards* the clutch centre (E) and overhangs its flange.

Next slide into position one of the clutch friction insert plates (H). Then fit a steel plain plate, followed by another friction insert plate and so on, alternately, until the complete set of plates has been fitted. It should be noted that Model 16M has five steel plain plates and four friction insert plates, whereas on Model 18 the number is six and five respectively.

Now insert the four spring cups (R) into the spring pressure plate (F) and offer up the pressure plate to the assembly. Fit the four clutch springs (M) and retain the springs in place by screwing the four adjustment nuts (P) on to the studs (N). Tighten each nut a few turns as fitted, and then fully tighten in a uniform manner all four nuts. Afterwards slacken back each adjustment nut *four complete turns*. This is the standard spring adjustment (see page 137).

Fully tighten the engine shaft shock-absorber retaining nut. When doing this, engage top gear and apply the rear brake to prevent the engine from turning. Finally check the adjustment of the primary and dynamo chains as described on pages 133-4.

9. Replacing Outer Half of Oil-bath Chain Case. It is necessary first to make sure that the faces of both halves of the chain case are quite clean and undamaged. The face of the outer half must be smeared with some liquid jointing compound. Remove the knurled adjusting nut from the rear brake rod and depress the pedal to its full extent. Then replace the outer half of the chain case.

Replace the plain washer and nut on the centre fixing bolt and tighten the nut with a suitable spanner. Make quite sure that both halves of the chain case *exactly register* before the nut is firmly tightened. Check that the metal and rubber bands are undamaged and quite clean. Then apply some liquid jointing compound to the edge of the oil-bath chain case.

Press the rubber band in place so that the free ends abut at the rear of the chain case. Now replace the metal band. Begin at the front end of the chain case and draw the two free ends together by hand and replace the binding screw. Tighten this screw firmly, and then replace the brake rod adjusting nut and adjust the rear brake as required (see page 154).

Permit the jointing compound to set properly, and afterwards remove the inspection cap from the chain case and replenish with engine oil (see page 114) to the correct level. Finally replace the inspection cap.

10. Leakage from Oil-bath. Should oil leakage be detected after replacing and replenishing the oil-bath chain case, this may be due to one or both faces of the case being damaged or distorted. Both faces should fit closely to a surface plate and, if there is any suspicion of distortion due to accidental impact prior to assembly, a check with a surface plate should be made. Another possible cause of oil leakage is imperfect registering of the two joint faces during assembly. Great care must be taken to ensure *exact* registering of the halves, without which an oil-tight oil-bath is unobtainable.

Removing Rear Chain Guard. First remove the rear wheel and chain sprocket assembly as described on page 146. Next remove the bolt which secures the front, top end of the rear chain guard to the oil-bath chain case. After this, remove the bolt which secures the front, bottom end of the rear chain guard to the frame, also the bolt securing the rear, top end of the chain guard to the frame. Then withdraw the chain guard.

Chain Repairs. Hints on the repair of chains will be found on page 73.

Handlebar Adjustment. The handlebars on all 1945-8 A.J.S. models are adjustable for angle to suit individual requirements. On 1945-7 models loosen the two nuts which secure the handlebars to the "Teledraulic" front forks and then adjust the handlebars as required. On 1948 models loosen the four nuts on the studs of the box-type clamp provided at the rear of the aluminium alloy head lug, and then adjust the bars for angle. After making the adjustment, be sure to retighten firmly the two or four securing nuts.

Adjusting Steering Head. On a new machine some initial bedding down occurs during the first 100 miles running, and the adjustment of the steering head should be checked when this mileage has been completed. Subsequently it is only necessary to check the steering head adjustment about once a month.

The ball bearing races of the steering head have spherical seats and are of the self-alining type. Thus they are not designed to fit snugly in the handlebar clip and steering head lugs. Both races in the head lug and the race in the handlebar clip lug are of identical type, but the ball race for the fork crown (the lowest of the four races) is not identical to the other three races.

To check the steering head adjustment, jack up the front of the machine by placing a box beneath the engine so as to take the weight off the front wheel. Then exert hand pressure upwards from the extreme ends of the handlebars. There should be no appreciable shake present and the steering head must be quite free to turn. If some shake is detected, adjust the steering head forthwith as described below.

Referring to Fig. 72, the following is the correct procedure for adjusting the steering head. It is assumed that the front wheel is quite clear of the ground. Loosen the two pinch-bolts (41) and (42) in the fork crown. On 1948 models slacken the nuts on the two studs (replacing pinch-bolts). Next slacken the domed lock-nut (4) at the top of the steering column. Having slackened the lock-nut, screw down very gradually the adjusting nut (3) for the steering head stem. This adjusting nut is located immediately below the lock-nut (4) and should be turned with the spanner shown at (J) in Fig. 63. While tightening the adjusting nut, test for steering head slackness by placing the fingers over the gap between the top frame lug and the handlebar lug, while simultaneously exerting upward pressure on the front edge of the front mudguard.

Tighten the adjusting nut (3) until the steering head is free to turn without perceptible up-and-down play. Afterwards tighten the domed lock-nut (4) and the two pinch-bolts (41) and (42) in the fork crown (tighten stud nuts on 1948 models). Finally withdraw the box or other packing from beneath the engine.

Maintenance and Overhaul of "Teledraulic" Front Forks. Apart from checking the level of the hydraulic fluid occasionally (see pages 116, 158) and topping up if necessary, no attention is called for. No adjustment is necessary and all working parts are automatically lubricated by means of the hydraulic damping fluid. Unless damage has been accidentally sustained, the "Teledraulic" front forks (see Fig. 72) should normally not require to be dismantled. However, after a very big mileage (say, 20,000 miles) the oil seal and paper washer in each fork leg, shown at (49) and (21) respectively in Fig. 72, may require attention. The same applies to the leather and fibre washers.

Having regard to the negligible attention normally required in respect of the "Teledraulic" front forks, the author has not included in this handbook detailed instructions for their stripping down and subsequent assembly. Those who on rare occasions require such information should refer to the appropriate instructions given in the instruction book issued with each new A.J.S. machine, or else contact the manufacturers.

To Remove Oil Tank and Battery Carrier. Before removing the oil tank and battery carrier, drain the oil tank and disconnect the positive and negative leads from the battery. Also unscrew the battery clamping screw and remove the battery from its carrier.

Unscrew and withdraw the countersunk-headed screw holding the bottom of the battery carrier to the stay for the rear chain guard. Next disconnect from the bottom of the oil tank the oil delivery pipe, also the oil return pipe. Take off the venturi

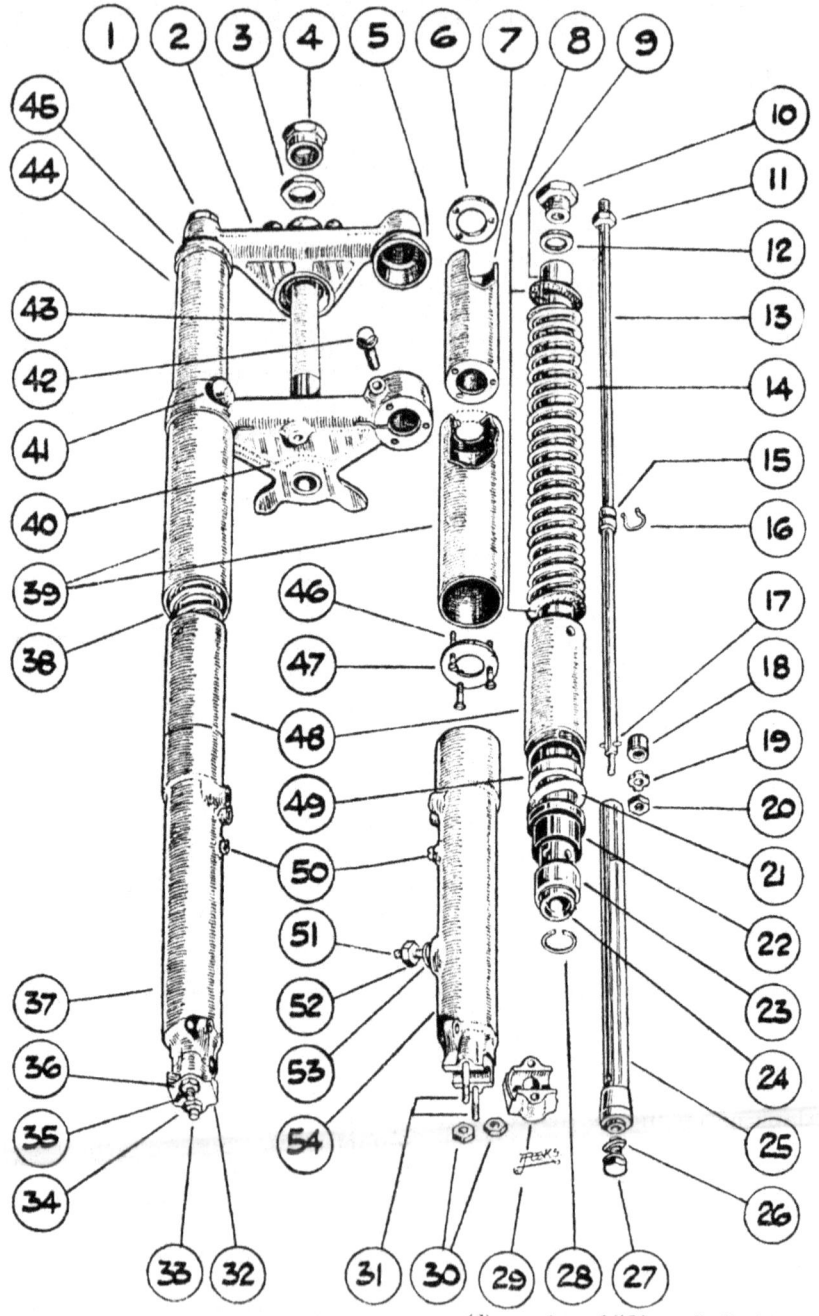

(*By courtesy of "Motor Cycling"*)

FIG. 72. "TELEDRAULIC" FRONT FORKS (1945–7) AND STEERING HEAD ASSEMBLY PARTLY DISMANTLED
(The 1945–7 forks have been simplified internally for 1948.)

OVERHAULING (1945-8)

air-intake from the Amal carburettor. Then remove the securing bolt on the right-hand side of the oil tank.

Remove the bolt which secures the oil tank stay to the rear mudguard. Be careful not to lose the spacer and washer provided on this bolt. Now remove the two nuts and washers which secure the oil tank and battery carrier to the two frame studs. The oil tank and battery carrier should then be detached from the machine. To facilitate their removal, give each a slight circular motion so as to disengage the studs brazed to the frame.

KEY TO FIG. 72

1 = Bolt for top of inner tube
2 = Handlebar lug
3 = Steering head adjusting nut
4 = Domed lock-nut for adjusting nut
5 = Cap for top cover tube
6 = Locating plate for top cover tube
7 = Top cover tube
8 = Leather seating washers for fork spring (14)
9 = Fixed inner tube
10 = Bolt for top of fixed inner tube
11 = Lock-nut for top of damper rod
12 = Steel washer for inner tube top bolt
13 = Rod for damper
14 = Spring in fork leg (L.H.)
15 = Sleeve for damper tube
16 = Clip retaining damper sleeve
17 = Stop pin for damper tube valve
18 = Valve for damper tube
19 = Seat for damper tube valve
20 = Lock-nut for damper tube valve
21 = Paper washer for oil seal
22 = Bakelite bush for fixed inner tube
23 = Steel bush for fixed inner tube
24 = Bottom end of fixed inner tube
25 = Damper tube
26 = Fibre washer for damper tube fixing bolt
27 = Damper tube fixing bolt
28 = Circlip for inner tube steel bush (23)
29 = Cap for L.H. fork slider
30 = Nuts securing fork slider cap (L.H.)
31 = Studs securing L.H. fork slider cap (and front wheel spindle)
32 = Cap for R.H. fork slider
33 = Stud securing R.H. fork slider cap (and front wheel spindle)
34 = Nut securing fork slider cap (R.H.)
35 = Stud securing R.H. fork slider cap (and front wheel spindle)
36 = Nut securing fork slider cap (R.H.)
37 = Fork slider (R.H.)
38 = Spring in fork leg (R.H.)
39 = Bottom cover tube
40 = Fork crown
41 = Pinch-bolt in fork crown
42 = Pinch bolt for fork crown
43 = Steering-head stem
44 = Top cover tube
45 = Cap for top cover tube
46 = Screw retaining locating plates
47 = Locating plate for bottom cover tube (not threaded)
48 = Extension for fork slider
49 = Oil seal for fixed inner tube
50 = Oil level plug for fork slider
51 = Anchorage stud for front brake cover plate
52 = Nut for anchorage stud
53 = Steel washer for anchorage stud
54 = Fork slider (L.H.)

Replacing Oil Tank and Battery Carrier. Position the oil tank and battery carrier on the two fixing studs, and then reconnect the delivery and return oil pipes. Now proceed to complete the assembling in the reverse order of dismantling (previously described). Should the two oil pipes have been completely removed, reconnect the pump ends of the pipes *before* dealing with the unions at the tank end.

Concerning the Stands. Occasionally it may be necessary to remove one or more of the three stands, and a few points concerning their assembly are worth noting. To prevent loss, see that the $\frac{7}{16}$ in. locking nut on the hinge bolt for the prop stand is firmly tightened. The hinge bolt has a slotted head to enable it to be screwed into the stand jaw. Check that all components are quite clean before they are fitted.

As regards the front stand (which should never be used alone), it should be observed that the fixing bolt on the left-hand side is larger than the bolt used on the right-hand side. Split-pin both locking nuts on assembly. Do not drag stand beyond the vertical.

When fitting the rear stand, make sure that the plain steel washer for each of the two fixing bolts is fitted beneath the bolt head, *not below the nut*.

Removing Front Wheel. Referring to Fig. 72, jack the machine up on the front *and* rear stands. Disconnect the yoke end of the front brake cable from the brake expander lever by removing the split pin and retaining pin. Slacken, but do not actually remove, the nut (51) which secures the front brake cover plate to the left-hand fork slider (54). The split pin securing the nut need not be disturbed. On 1948 models, slacken the two anchorage screws instead. Next loosen the nut on the left-hand side of the front wheel spindle.

Remove the four nuts (30), (34), (36) which clamp the fork slider caps (29) to the "Teledraulic" fork sliders. Detach both caps and place them aside separately, so that they may later be replaced exactly as prior to removal. These caps must *not* be interchanged. Then disengage the front brake cover plate from the anchorage stud (51) fitted to the left-hand fork slider (pre-1948) and permit the front wheel to slide out of the fork ends.

Replacing Front Wheel. Referring to Fig. 72, hold the left-hand fork slider cap (29) under the location on the front wheel spindle, and offer up the front wheel assembly and cap so as to engage the cap with its two retaining studs (31). Simultaneously engage the slot in the front brake cover plate with the anchorage stud (51) in the left-hand fork slider (54). On 1948 models engage with two anchorage screws. Fit the two nuts (30) securing the left-hand fork slider cap (and wheel spindle) and tighten the nuts lightly. Then fit the right-hand fork slider cap and tighten lightly the cap securing nuts (34) and (36). Make sure that the caps have not been interchanged and are fitted exactly as before.

Tighten lightly the nut on the left-hand side of the front wheel spindle. Then firmly and evenly tighten the four nuts which secure the two fork slider caps (and wheel spindle). Verify that the gaps, fore and aft, between each cap and the end of the fork slider are *exactly* equal. Ensuring that these gaps are equal is most important. Now firmly tighten the nut on the left-hand side of the front wheel spindle. Finally replace and tighten the nut (52) on the brake anchorage stud (51), and split-pin the nut. On 1948 models tighten firmly the two anchorage screws.

Removing Rear Wheel. Jack the machine up on the rear stand. Disconnect the lead for the rear lamp at the connection (see Fig. 52) provided close to the rear wheel spindle. Next unscrew the gland nut on the speedometer driving cable. Also detach the spring link on the secondary chain, separate the ends, and allow the chain to hang clear of the rear wheel sprocket, but engaging with the small sprocket on the gearbox mainshaft. Remove the knurled adjusting nut from the rear brake rod.

Next detach the rear portion of the rear mudguard. To do this, first remove the two nuts which secure the rear portion to the front portion. Also remove the nut and washer from the bolt securing the mudguard side bridge and tool-box stay to the tubular stay. Next slacken about four turns the two nuts which secure the rear mudguard side stays to their studs. Then remove the rear portion of the rear mudguard, complete with stays. To disengage the top fixing bolt, it is advisable to spring the toolbox outwards as required.

Now slacken the nuts on both sides of the rear wheel solid spindle (see Fig. 73), passing through the hollow spindle, and carefully remove the rear wheel assembly from the fork ends. To enable the assembly to clear the brake cover plate anchor bolt, tilt the wheel slightly, and then withdraw to the rear.

Replacing Rear Wheel. Replace the rear wheel assembly, using the reverse order and procedure employed for removal. Note that it is important, prior to finally tightening the nuts on the ends of the wheel spindle, to position the speedometer gearbox (shown at (32) in Fig. 73) correctly. Positioning must be such as to permit of the gearbox driving cable being properly fitted.

After replacing the rear wheel assembly, it is advisable, especially if the chain adjuster bolts have been disturbed, to check the alinement of the front and rear wheels. This can be done by stretching a piece of string taut across both wheels, about 4 in. from, and parallel with, the ground. The string should contact each tyre on both sides of the wheel hub. A preferable method is to use a straight-edge or else a plain board, as described on page 79.

If the wheels are found not to be in true alinement, or the tension of the secondary chain needs adjusting, or both, rectify matters by means of the adjuster bolts screwed into the fork ends, as instructed on page 124. When making an adjustment, be careful to screw both adjuster bolts into the fork ends *exactly the same amount*. Having obtained correct wheel alinement and secondary chain tension by altering the position of the rear wheel, verify the adjustment of the rear brake which is likely to need attention. Instructions for effecting rear brake adjustment are included on page 154.

To Adjust Wheel Bearings (Front and Rear). About once every three months it is advisable to check the adjustment of the wheel bearings and rectify it if necessary. The roller bearings of both wheels should be adjusted so that a slight amount of end play (approximately ·002 in.) can be felt. Should no end play be pre-

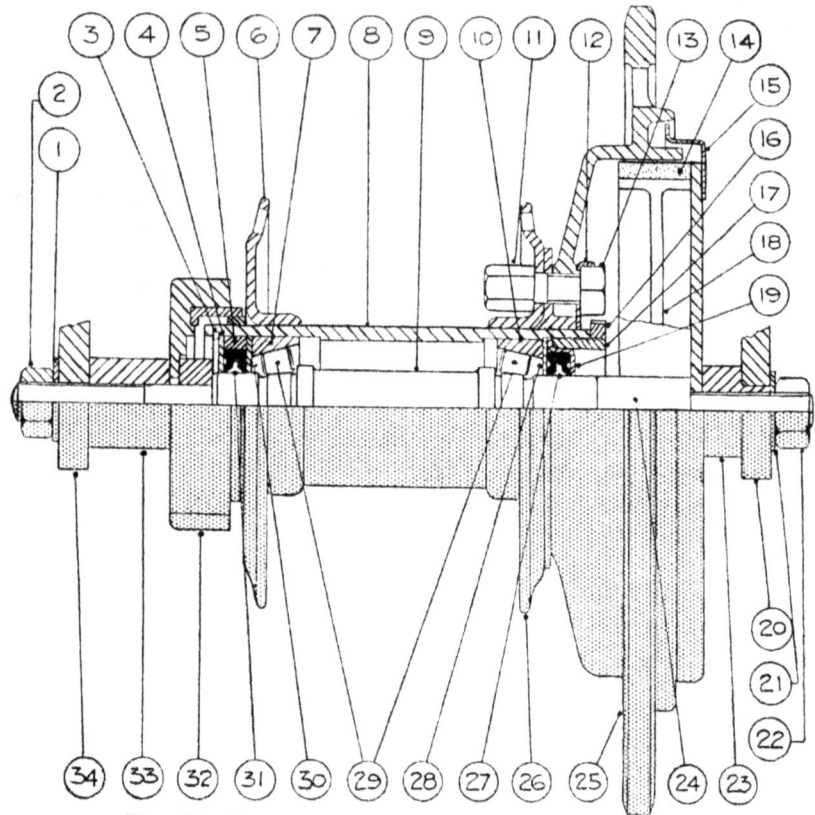

FIG. 73. SECTIONAL VIEW OF REAR HUB ASSEMBLY

The front hub assembly is in all essentials similar, except that instead of having a hollow spindle through which a solid spindle (with two nuts) passes, a single solid spindle (with one nut on the left-hand side) is employed. (See also Fig. 74.)

sent, there is an appreciable risk of the roller bearings becoming damaged during running.

The bearings provided for the front and rear wheels are of the taper roller type, and, as may be seen in Fig. 74, the inner bearing members are integral with the front wheel solid spindle (35) and the rear wheel hollow spindle (9). The hub shells contain the outer cups (7) and (10) for the rollers, these cups being pressed into the shells. Two oil seals (27) and (31) are provided for each hub assembly, one on the outside of each roller bearing outer cup.

As regards bearing adjustment (see Figs. 73 and 74), one of the bearing outer cups (7), pressed into the hub shell, has a fixed location determined by the spring circlip (3). But the other outer cup (10) has a movable location determined by the bearing

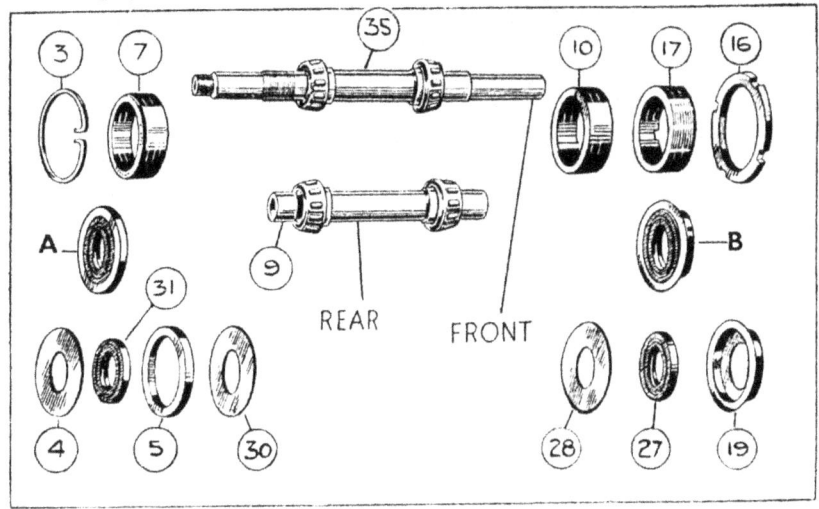

FIG. 74. EXPLODED VIEW OF WHEEL-BEARING COMPONENTS

This sketch (see also Fig. 73) applies to front and rear wheel bearings, the wheel spindles being the only different parts. The solid inner spindle for the rear hub is not shown. The bearing adjusting ring (17) is fitted on the *threaded* side of the hub. At *A* and *B* are shown the felt oil seals, pressed into the spacing collar (5) and the dished cup (19) respectively. The assemblies (*A*) and (*B*) are fitted on the outside of the fixed and movable bearing outer cups (7) and (10) respectively.

KEYS TO FIGS. 73 AND 74

 1 = Washer on solid spindle
 2 = Nut securing solid spindle in rear fork end
 3 = Spring circlip
 4 = Oil seal retaining ring
 5 = Spacing collar round oil seal
 6 = Wheel hub flange (R.H.)
 7 = Roller-bearing outer cup
 8 = Hub shell
 9 = Hollow outer spindle
10 = Roller-bearing outer cup
11 = Sprocket securing bolt
12 = Locking washer for sprocket and brake drum securing nut
13 = Sprocket and brake drum securing nut
14 = Brake lining
15 = Rear brake cover plate
16 = Locking ring for bearing adjusting ring
17 = Bearing adjusting ring
18 = Brake shoe
19 = Dished cup for oil seal
20 = Frame fork end (L.H.)
21 = Washer on solid spindle
22 = Nut securing solid spindle in rear fork end
23 = Spacer between brake cover plate and fork end
24 = Spacer inside brake cover plate
25 = Rear sprocket and brake drum
26 = Wheel hub flange (L.H.)
27 = Oil seal
28 = Oil seal retaining ring
29 = Taper rollers
30 = Oil seal retaining ring
31 = Oil seal
32 = Gearbox for speedometer drive
33 = Spacer between gearbox and fork end
34 = Frame fork end (R.H.)
35 = Front wheel spindle (solid)

adjusting ring (17) on the side opposite the circlip. This adjusting ring abuts the outer cup (10) and enables the end play to be adjusted by moving the outer cup. The adjustment is then secured by the locking ring (16).

To adjust the rear wheel bearings, it is necessary to remove the wheel from the machine (see page 148), but if dealing with a front wheel its removal is not necessary. Bearing adjustment is effected on the left-hand or right-hand side, according to whether the wheel concerned is rear or front respectively.

Referring to Figs. 73 and 74, to adjust the roller bearings of a front or rear wheel, loosen the locking ring (16) for the bearing adjusting ring (17). Next tighten the bearing adjusting ring until *all* play has been eliminated. Then slacken off the adjusting ring exactly *one-half turn*. This should give about ·002 in. end play. Finally retighten the locking ring (16), taking care to see that the adjusting ring does not move in the process.

Dismantling Wheel Bearings (Front or Rear). Having detached the wheel from the machine in accordance with the appropriate instructions given on page 146, remove the brake cover plate, complete with brake shoe assembly. If dealing with a rear wheel, remove the solid inner spindle and also the small gearbox for the speedometer drive.

Now, referring to Figs. 73 and 74, loosen the locking ring (16) for the bearing adjusting ring (17) and completely unscrew the adjusting ring. Remove the adjusting ring together with the locking ring. Then remove in this order: the dished cup (19); the oil seal (27); and the oil seal retaining ring (28). These three members comprise the oil seal assembly shown at (*B*) in Fig. 74, plus the retaining ring.

Reverting to the opposite side of the wheel hub, extract the spring circlip (3) from just inside the hub end, and then proceed to remove in this order: the oil seal retaining ring (4); the oil seal (31); the spacing collar (5) round the seal; and the oil seal retaining ring (30). These four items constitute the oil seal assembly shown at (*A*), plus the two retaining rings.

Complete the dismantling of the wheel bearings by removing the front wheel solid spindle (35), or the hollow outer spindle (9) from the rear wheel hub. Press from the wheel hub shell (do *not* hammer out) the wheel spindle, complete with rollers and cages, and one outer cup (7) or (10). This may be effected from either end, leaving one bearing outer cup (it does not matter which) in position in the hub shell. This remaining cup can be pressed out later if desired.

Assembling Wheel Bearings (Front or Rear). Before commencing to fit the roller bearings and hub spindle, clean all parts thoroughly, including the inside of the wheel hub shell.

Referring to Figs. 73 and 74, press the roller bearing outer cup (7) into the *unthreaded* end of the hub shell. The cups (7) and (10) are interchangeable and are tapered axially. On assembly the *thinner* edge of the cup must always face *inwards*. When pressing the outer cup into the hub shell, check that the cup is absolutely square to the shell, and exert pressure until there is a clearance of not less than $\frac{9}{32}$ in. from its outer edge to the inside edge of the groove cut in the hub for the spring circlip (3).

Now take the oil seal retaining ring (30) and insert this into the *unthreaded* end of the hub so that it abuts the outer edge of the outer cup (7). Press the oil seal (31), interchangeable with the oil seal (27), into the collar (5) and replace assembly (*A*) so that it is in contact with the oil seal retaining ring (30), previously fitted. Now fit the second oil seal retaining ring (4) next to the oil seal assembly (*A*). The oil seal retaining rings (4), (28), (30) are interchangeable and comprise plain steel washers. Secure the oil seal and retaining rings in position by replacing the spring circlip (3) in its groove. Check that it beds down properly. Then from the opposite (threaded) end of the hub shell, force back the bearing outer cup (7) until the oil seal and retaining ring assembly is hard up against the spring circlip (3).

Next insert into the *threaded* end of the hub, the front wheel solid spindle (35) or the hollow outer spindle (9), if dealing with a rear wheel. The spindle concerned must be fitted, complete with rollers and cages. See that none of the rollers is missing, and be most careful to introduce the correct end of the spindle first. With a front wheel, this is the *threaded* end, and with a rear wheel the *shorter* end.

Press into the *threaded* end of the hub shell the roller bearing outer cup (10). This outer cup is, as has previously been stated, interchangeable with the outer cup (7), and care must again be taken to ensure that the thinner edge of the cup is on the inside, so as to provide about $\frac{1}{16}$ in. play in the bearings. Replace the oil seal retaining ring (28) so that it abuts the bearing outer cup (10) already pressed into the threaded end of the hub shell. Fit the oil seal (27) into the dished cup (19) and then insert the oil seal assembly (*B*) so as to contact the oil seal retaining ring (28). The oil seal face must face *inwards*.

Screw the bearing adjusting ring (17) into the *threaded* end of the hub shell and screw the locking ring (16) on to the adjusting ring. Then adjust the roller bearings as described on page 147, to give about ·002 in. play. Afterwards lock the adjusting ring by means of the spanner shown at (*N*) in Fig. 63, applied to the locking ring.

With the grease gun inject two fluid ounces of grease (see page 114) into the hub and finally replace (see below) the brake cover plate, complete with shoes, springs, etc. If assembling a rear wheel hub, replace the gearbox for the speedometer drive, and also the solid inner spindle. The wheel should now be ready for assembly to the motor-cycle, as described on page 147.

Concerning Brake Drums. Removal of the brake drums from

the wheels is seldom called for, but when a wheel is dismantled it is advisable to check the securing screws or nuts for tightness. Harshness in the transmission, and even fracture of wheel spokes, can be caused through slackness of the nuts and bolts which secure the integral brake drum and sprocket to the rear wheel hub.

Referring to Fig. 73, the rear wheel brake drum and sprocket (25) is secured to the hub of the rear wheel by six bolts (11) and nuts (13). Each nut has a locking washer (12) beneath it, and on no account must any of the six locking washers be omitted. The brake drum of the front wheel has no securing bolts and nuts, but instead is screwed to the hub by eight countersunk screws (ten, 1948).

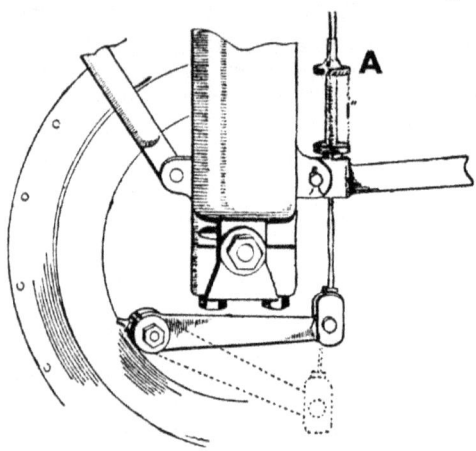

FIG. 75. SHOWING (EXHAUSTED) CABLE ADJUSTMENT ON 1945-7 FRONT BRAKE

The cable adjuster (A) is shown screwed right out, with the result that, besides the brake-operating lever assuming a poor angle, no further adjustment is possible, except by means of brake shoe adjustment. On 1948 models, with a 7-in. diameter chromidium alloy brake drum, the adjuster nut and lock-nut are situated somewhat higher up on the near side fork leg.

The Brake Shoes. The brake shoes and their associated expanders and springs are interchangeable, front and rear, but the two shoes fitted to each individual brake cover plate are not interchangeable. One end of each shoe has a detachable thrust collar (pin, 1948), adjustable to compensate for considerable wear of the brake shoe linings. The other end of each shoe rests against a fulcrum fixed in the brake cover plate. Brake shoe adjustment is dealt with on page 154.

Position Front Brake Cover Plate Correctly. It is most important to position the front brake cover plate correctly, if this has been removed, before replacing the front wheel in the "Teledraulic" front forks, as described on page 146. The cover plate is secured to the solid spindle of the front wheel by means of an internal nut and also an external nut. A locating washer is interposed between the brake cover plate and the internal nut.

The *internal nut* must be positioned so that when the locating washer is fitted adjacent to it, the outer face of the locating washer is $\frac{1}{16}$ in. proud of the brake drum outer edge. To check that this condition prevails, lay a suitable straight-edge across the brake drum outer edge and then make a vertical measurement to verify the relative position of the locating washer outer face.

Adjusting the Front Brake. It is advisable to check the adjustment of the front brake weekly. Unless considerable wear of the brake shoe linings and/or cable stretch has occurred, it is generally sufficient to effect a minor front brake adjustment by means of the knurled cable adjuster shown at (*A*) in Fig. 75.

To effect a minor front brake adjustment, jack the A.J.S. up on the front and rear stands. Then unscrew the lock-nut situated beneath the knurled cable adjuster (*A*) approximately *half a complete turn*. Next take up the slackness in the brake operation by unscrewing the cable adjuster until the brake linings are felt to be just in contact with the brake drum. Spin the front wheel

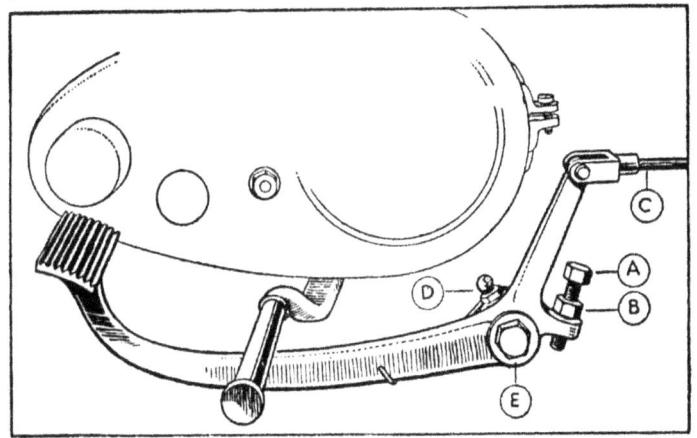

FIG. 76. ADJUSTMENT FOR BRAKE PEDAL POSITION

A = Pedal adjuster bolt
B = Lock-nut for pedal adjuster bolt
C = Rear brake rod
D = Grease nipple for lubricating pedal
E = Pedal-securing nut

to make sure. Then screw down the knurled adjuster (*A*) *two complete turns*, and afterwards tighten the lock-nut firmly.

Should the minor front brake adjustment just described not effect the desired results due to exhaustion of the cable adjustment (see Fig. 75) and the assumption of an ineffective angle by the expander operating lever, a major adjustment is called for. This major adjustment is effected by adjusting the thrust collars or pins on the ends of the brake shoes, as described on page 155.

Adjusting Brake Pedal. Some riders attach considerable importance to the exact position of the rear brake pedal. On the A.J.S. it is possible to alter its position within narrow limits. As may be seen in Fig. 76, an adjuster bolt (*A*) is screwed into the heel of the pedal and secured by a lock-nut (*B*).

To raise the toe end of the pedal permanently, loosen the lock-nut and *unscrew* the adjuster bolt (*A*). For normal purposes it is generally best to effect the adjustment so that, with the foot removed from the brake pedal, the pedal arm just clears the footrest support. Check and, if necessary, rectify (see below) the adjustment of the rear brake itself after altering the position of the brake pedal. Altering the pedal position automatically moves the rear brake rod (*C*).

Adjusting Rear Brake. As in the case of the front brake, it is advisable to check the adjustment weekly. Adjustment, which should never be neglected, is correct when the brake shoes are nearly in contact with the brake drum, with the pedal not depressed.

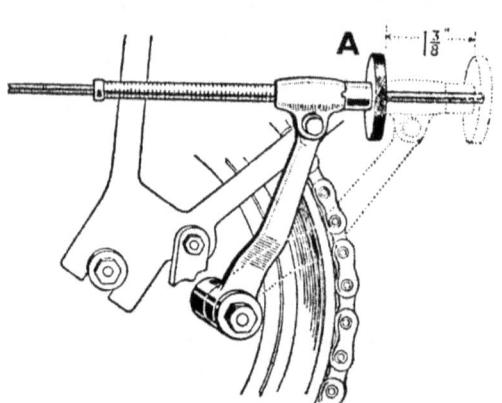

FIG. 77. SHOWING (EXHAUSTED) BRAKE ROD ADJUSTMENT ON 1945–8 MODELS

The brake rod adjuster (*A*) is screwed on the rod to its full extent, and any further adjustment must be made by means of the adjustable collars or pins on the brake shoes.

To effect a minor adjustment of the rear brake to compensate for slight wear of the brake shoe linings, first place the A.J.S. on its rear stand. Then to take up slackness in the operation, screw the knurled adjuster nut shown at (*A*) in Fig. 77 further on the brake rod until it is felt that the brake shoe linings are just contacting the rear brake drum when the wheel is turned. Afterwards unscrew the adjuster nut (*A*) *two complete turns.*

If the minor rear brake adjustment described above does not prove effective due to exhaustion of the brake rod adjustment (see Fig. 77), it is necessary to effect a major adjustment by means of the thrust collars or pins on the ends of the brake shoes, as described below.

Shoe Adjustment (Front and Rear Brakes). Minor brake adjustment to compensate for slight wear of the shoe linings is normally effected for the front and rear brakes by means of the finger-operated adjusters, as described in previous paragraphs. However, after covering a considerable mileage on the road and effecting such minor adjustments as are necessary, it will eventually be found that the effective leverage of the expander operating lever is much reduced (see Figs. 76 and 77), and further minor adjustment becomes wholly ineffective or impossible. To remedy loss in braking efficiency, incurable by making a minor adjustment, proceed to effect a major adjustment by means of the adjustable thrust collars, situated one on the tongue end of each 1945–7 brake shoe, or with the thrust pin on each 1948 shoe.

The Collar. Each thrust collar (7) has machined slots (5), (6), (8) of varying depth (Fig. 78). To make a brake shoe adjustment, it is necessary to remove each collar from its shoe and turn it so that the slot next less in depth engages the brake shoe (3), on replacement of the shoe. The two shallow slots (5) are suitable where the brake linings are badly worn; the two medium depth

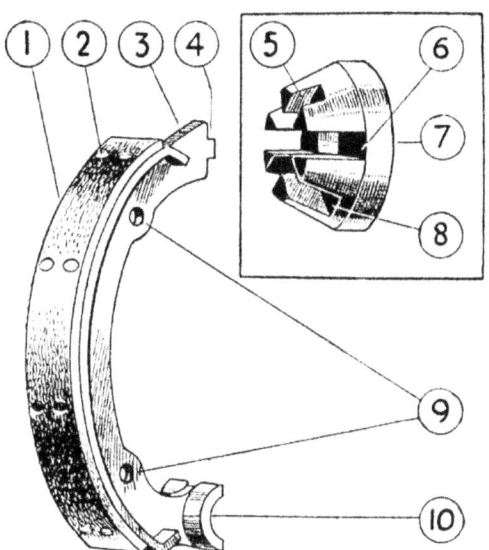

FIG. 78. BRAKE SHOE AND ADJUSTABLE THRUST COLLAR (1945–7)

1 = Brake lining
2 = Brake rivet (8 per set)
3 = Brake shoe
4 = Tongue of brake shoe
5 = One of two shallow slots
6 = One of two deep slots
7 = Adjustable thrust collar
8 = One of two medium depth slots
9 = Holes for brake shoe spring
10 = Brake shoe heel

slots (8) where moderate lining wear has occurred; and the two deep slots (6) where the linings are unworn.

The tongue (4) fits into the centre of the thrust collar (7). It is important to match both shoes belonging to the *same* pair, and whichever slot is used, the same depth slot *must* be employed for both shoes fitted to the same brake cover plate. After adjusting the brake shoes by means of the thrust collars, it is necessary to slacken off the knurled adjuster shown at (*A*) in Figs. 75 and 77, and then to adjust the front and/or rear brake, as described on pages 153–154.

The Thrust Pin (1948). Referring to Fig. 79, to effect a major brake adjustment on a 1948 A.J.S. it is necessary to fit a shim washer (4) beneath the hardened head of the thrust pin (3). The tool-kit of each new machine contains two shim washers (Part No. STD-174) for making an adjustment if necessary. Having made an adjustment, slacken off the adjuster shown at *A* in Figs. 75 and 77. Then adjust (see pages 153-154) the front and/or rear brake in the normal manner.

Centralizing Brake Shoes. If a front or rear brake cover plate has been removed from the wheel and the brake shoe assembly dismantled or disturbed, it is advisable to centralize both brake shoes in the brake drum during subsequent assembly. This ensures equal pressure being exerted by the lining (indicated at (1) in Figs. 78 and 79). A most annoying squeak occurring when

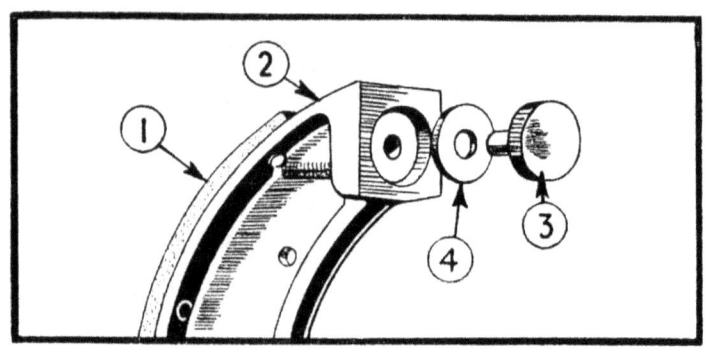

Fig. 79. 1948 Brake Shoe Thrust-pin Adjustment

1 = Brake lining   3 = Thrust pin
2 = Brake shoe   4 = Shim washer

the brake is applied can usually be traced to the brake shoes not being centralized in the brake drum.

Centralizing of the shoes should be undertaken prior to replacing the front wheel or, in the case of the rear wheel, before firmly tightening the nut which secures the brake cover plate (*in situ*) to the wheel spindle.

To centralize the brake shoes, first slacken the nut which secures the brake cover plate to the wheel spindle. Next place a box spanner over the brake expander operating lever so as to increase its leverage. Then expand the brake shoes fully by applying pressure on the spanner, and at the same time tighten the spindle nut securing the brake cover plate.

Loose Wheel Spokes. Keep an occasional eye on the wheel spokes, especially if much riding over rough roads has been undertaken. A.J.S. wheels are of robust design, but should any spokes loosen, they should be tightened immediately (see page 79).

Care of Tyres. To obtain maximum life from the covers and tubes, it is desirable to exercise care in driving and pay regular

OVERHAULING (1945-8)

attention to the tyres. Avoid unduly fierce acceleration, crash braking, and cornering at an unnecessarily sharp angle. Inspect the threads frequently and remove flints and small stones which may have become embedded in the rubber. Be careful not to permit the tyres to stand in oil and, if oil does get on them, clean it off with petrol. Above all, keep the tyres properly alined and correctly inflated. Do not throw away the valve caps!

Correct Tyre Pressures. Where a solo machine is concerned and the rider is of normal weight, the correct inflation pressures for

MINIMUM TYRE INFLATION PRESSURES*
FOR 1945-8 MODELS
(SHOWING LOAD PER TYRE AND RECOMMENDED PRESSURE IN LB. PER SQ. IN.)

Load	Pressure	Load	Pressure
200 lb.	16 lb.	350 lb.	24 lb.
240 lb.	18 lb.	400 lb.	28 lb.
280 lb.	20 lb.	440 lb.	32 lb.

the front and rear tyres are 17 lb. per sq. in. and 20 lb. per sq. in. respectively. Check the tyre pressures weekly with a suitable pressure gauge (see page 81). If the rider is not of average weight and/or carries heavy equipment, the pressures must be modified accordingly. The same applies where a pillion rider is carried. In these circumstances it is advisable to check separately the fully-laden weight on the front and rear tyre. For this purpose a visit should be made to the nearest weighbridge. One is generally found at a large railway station. The table above shows the recommended minimum inflation pressures for specified loads per tyre. See also pages 79-85.

Checking Hydraulic Fluid Content (1948 " Teledraulics ").
Every 5000 miles it is advisable to ascertain exactly how much hydraulic fluid (see page 115) is contained in each front fork leg. Prior to doing this, first see that your A.J.S. is absolutely *vertical*, with the front wheel jacked up clear of the ground. Also remove both bolts from the tops of the fork leg inner tubes (see Fig. 3).

To measure the amount of hydraulic fluid in each fork leg, remove the drain plug from the bottom of the fork slider (on the side of the tube) and permit the fluid to drain off into a graduated flask or beaker. In normal circumstances it will be found that 8 to 8½ fluid oz. will quickly collect in the flask. When draining

* The inflation pressures quoted apply to 3·25 × 19 wired-on covers, fitted as standard to front and rear wheels of 1945-7 models and to the front wheels of 1948 machines.

ceases, replace the drain plug and work the "Teledraulic" forks up and down several times. Again remove the drain plug and catch further fluid in the graduated flask.

It is not possible to drain off the whole of the hydraulic fluid (10 fluid oz.) from the fork leg, but it should be possible to collect 9½ fluid oz. Repeat the draining procedure described above several times until you are sure no more fluid can be collected in the flask. Then measure the amount of fluid collected, and note whether it is 9½ fluid oz. or less.

Topping-up 1948 " Teledraulic " Fork Leg. Having measured, as described in the previous paragraph, the amount of hydraulic fluid (less about ½ fluid oz. which cannot be drained) in each fork leg, top-up if the amount collected is less than 9½ fluid oz. Add fluid to the flask until it contains exactly 9½ fluid oz.

After topping-up the flask, if necessary, pour its contents into the top of the fork tube. When doing this the drain plug must, of course, be replaced, and the fork leg must be fully extended before fitting the hexagon-headed top bolt and washer and tightening the bolt firmly. Deal with each fork leg similarly.

Should the "Teledraulic" front forks be completely dismantled (see page 143), it is necessary after assembly to replenish each fork leg with its full specified content, i.e. 10 fluid oz. Subsequently it is necessary to drain and replenish with 9½ fluid oz. every 5000 miles. The same fluid can be used many times, as its contamination or dilution is unlikely.

MEMORANDA

A.J.S. Telephone No. .... *Woolwich* 1223 ....
Insurance Phone No. ....
Insurance Co.'s Address ....
Insurance Policy No. ....
Your Registration No. ....
Engine No. .... ⎫
Frame No. .... ⎬ See page 133
Mileage ....
New Tyres fitted ....
Complete Strip ....
Decarbonizing ....

INDEX

AIR leaks, 64
A.J.S. models, 1
Alinement, wheel, 77, 79
Amal carburettor, 10–20
Ammeter, 91
Assembling engine, 50–51, 124–129
—— wheel bearings, 150

BATTERY, care of, 92–94
—— carrier, removing, 143
Bowden cables, lubricating, 34
Brake adjustment, 78
—— drums, 152
—— pedal, adjusting, 153
—— shoe adjustment, 82, 154–156
Brakes, lubricating, 115
Burman gearbox lubrication, 31, 111–113

CARBON, removing, 45–46, 123
Carburettor, fitting, 51
—— "flooding," 19
Centralizing brake shoes, 156
Chain guard, removing, 142
—— repairs, 73
Cleaning exhaust valves, 65
—— machine, 38, 49, 118
Clutch adjustment, 69–72, 135–137
—— cable, removing, 138
—— dismantling, 71
—— springs, 137, 141
Commutator, 87–88
Compensated voltage control, 90
Compression, maintaining, 64
Contact-breaker, Lucas, 51, 54–55, 110, 129
—— Miller, 55
Control lay-out, 3
Controls, lubricating, 116
Crankcase, draining, 29
—— splitting, 66
Crankpin rollers, 133
Cut-out, 88

DECARBONIZING, 41–46, 120–124
Down-draught carburettors, 18
Draining oil tank, 109
Dry sump lubrication system, 23–28, 104–106
Dynamo chain, 34, 60, 114, 133, 139
—— lubrication, 30, 111
—— maintenance, 86–92

ENGINE oils, 28, 106
—— repairs, 133
—— timing, 61–63, 132

FRONT wheel, removing, 146
Filters, 106, 109
Flywheels, assembling, 65
Focusing headlamp, 95
Fork spindle lubrication, 34
Front brake adjustment, 153
—— —— cover plate, 152
—— wheel, removing, 78
Fuel consumption, high, 16

GARAGE, items for, 118
Gauze strainer, removing, 110
Gear changing, 6–8, 67
—— control adjustment, 68, 135
Gearbox lubrication, 31–32, 111–113
Grease for cycle parts, 114
Grease-gun, charging, 114
Grinding-in valves, 47, 124

HANDLEBAR adjustment, 74
Horn, Lucas, 97
H.T. pick-up, cleaning, 53
Hub lubrication, 34, 115
Hydraulic fluid, 115, 157

IGNITION, timing, 56, 58–60, 129–130
—— trouble, 53
Inflation pressures, 81, 157

KICK-STARTER, 6, 77

LAMPS, 94–96
Leakage, oil-bath, 142
Lighting equipment, 86
Lubrication chart, 112
——— object of, 21
Lucas bulbs, 96
——— magneto, 129

"MAGDYNO," care of, 54
——— chain adjustment, 60
——— lubrication, 30, 110
Magneto, care of, 51, 129
——— chain, 34, 36, 61, 111, 130
——— lubrication, 30, 110
Main jet, 13, 14
Mechanical lubrication, 21–23, 28
Miller bulbs, 96

NEEDLE jet, 13, 15, 20

OIL-BATH chain case, 33, 114, 138–141
Oil circulation, checking, 29, 107
——— consumption, high, 36
——— pump on D.S. system, 24–26, 28
——— supply adjustment, 107
——— tank, cleaning, 29, 109
——— ——— removing, 143
Overhead valve gear lubrication, 30, 36, 49

PETROL tank, 5, 120, 128
Pilot air screw adjustment, 13, 15
Piston dimensions, 122
——— removing, 45, 121
——— rings, 48, 122, 125
Primary chain adjustment, 67–68, 134
Pressure gauge, tyre, 81
Push-rod removal (1932–9), 42

REAR brake adjustment, 154
——— wheel, removing, 75, 146
Reflectors, 96
Replenishment, oil tank, 28, 107
Rocker-box, 42–43, 120, 127
Running-in, 8

SECONDARY chain adjustment, 68, 134
——— ——— lubrication, 33, 114
Shock-absorber, fork, 75

Sidecar alinement, 80
Slow-running, bad, 17
Slip-ring, cleaning, 53
Small-end bush, fitting, 65, 133
Sparking plug, 49, 64, 129
Speedometer lubrication, 36, 116
Spokes, loose, 79
Spring fork adjustment, 74
Stands, 116, 145
Starting up, 5
Steering head adjustment, 74, 142
——— ——— lubrication, 34, 115
Stopping, 8
Storage, battery, 94
Sturmey-Archer gearbox lubrication, 32
Synthetic tyres, 83
Switch, lighting, 95

TAIL lamp, 95
Tappet adjustment, 38–41, 118–120
"Teledraulic" front forks, 115–116, 143, 157
Terminals, dynamo, 92
Throttle stop screw, 12
——— valve cut-away, 13, 15
Timing gears, dismantling, 63
Tool kit, 117
Topping-up battery, 92
——— "Teledraulic" front forks, 115–116, 158
Transmission harshness, 138
Tyre pressures, 81, 157
——— repairs, 82–85
Tyres, care of, 156–7
Twist-grip, adjusting, 16

VALVE clearances, 38–41, 118–120
——— springs, 124
——— stem lubrication, 36, 107
——— timing, 61–63, 132
——— ——— diagrams, 63, 131
Valves, removing, 45, 123

WHEEL alinement, 77, 79
——— bearing adjustment, 77–78, 147–151
——— removal and fitting, 146–147
Wire connections, 97–98
Wiring diagrams, 99, 103

AUTOBOOKS WORKSHOP MANUALS

ALFA ROMEO GIULIA 1300, 1600, 1750, 2000 1962-1978 WSM
AUSTIN HEALEY SPRITE, MG MIDGET 1958-1980 WSM
BMW 1600 1966-1973 WSM
BMW 2000 & 2002 1966-1976 WSM
BMW 2500, 2800, 3.0 & 3.3 1968-1977 WSM
BMW 316, 320, 320i 1975-1977 WSM
BMW 518, 520, 520i 1973-1981 WSM
FIAT 1100, 1100D, 1100R & 1200 1957-1969 WSM
FIAT 124 1966-1974 WSM
FIAT 124 SPORT 1966-1975 WSM
FIAT 125 & 125 SPECIAL 1967-1973 WSM
FIAT 126, 126L, 126 DV, 126/650 & 126/650 DV 1972-1982 WSM
FIAT 127 SALOON, SPECIAL & SPORT, 900, 1050 1971-1981 WSM
FIAT 128 1969-1982 WSM
FIAT 1300, 1500 1961-1967 WSM
FIAT 131 MIRAFIORI 1975-1982 WSM
FIAT 132 1972-1982 WSM
FIAT 500 1957-1973 WSM
FIAT 600, 600D & MULTIPLA 1955-1969 WSM
FIAT 850 1964-1972 WSM
JAGUAR E-TYPE 1961-1972 WSM
JAGUAR MK 1, 2 1955-1969 WSM
JAGUAR S TYPE, 420 1963-1968 WSM
JAGUAR XK 120, 140, 150 MK 7, 8, 9 1948-1961 WSM
LAND ROVER 1, 2 1948-1961 WSM
MERCEDES-BENZ 190 1959-1968 WSM
MERCEDES-BENZ 220/8 1968-1973 WSM
MERCEDES-BENZ 220B 1959-1965 WSM
MERCEDES-BENZ 230 1963-1968 WSM
MERCEDES-BENZ 250 1968-1972 WSM
MERCEDES-BENZ 280 1968-1972 WSM
MG MIDGET TA-TF 1936-1955 WSM
MINI 1959-1980 WSM
MORRIS MINOR 1952-1971 WSM
PEUGEOT 404 1960-1975 WSM
PORSCHE 911 1964-1973 WSM
PORSCHE 911 1970-1977 WSM
RENAULT 16 1965-1979 WSM
RENAULT 8, 10, 1100 1962-1971 WSM
ROVER 3500, 3500S 1968-1976 WSM
SUNBEAM RAPIER, ALPINE 1955-1965 WSM
TRIUMPH SPITFIRE, GT6, VITESSE 1962-1968 WSM
TRIUMPH TR2, TR3, TR3A 1952-1962 WSM
TRIUMPH TR4, TR4A 1961-1967 WSM
VOLKSWAGEN BEETLE 1968-1977 WSM

VELOCEPRESS AUTOMOBILE BOOKS & MANUALS

ABARTH BUYERS GUIDE
AUSTIN-HEALEY 6-CYLINDER WSM
BMW 600 LIMOUSINE FACTORY WSM
BMW 600 LIMOUSINE OWNERS HAND BOOK & SERVICE MANUAL
BMW ISETTA FACTORY WSM
BOOK OF THE CARRERA PANAMERICANA - MEXICAN ROAD RACE
COMPLETE CATALOG OF JAPANESE MOTOR VEHICLES
DIALED IN - THE JAN OPPERMAN STORY
FERRARI 250/GT SERVICE AND MAINTENANCE
FERRARI 308 SERIES BUYER'S AND OWNER'S GUIDE
FERRARI BERLINETTA LUSSO
FERRARI BROCHURES AND SALES LITERATURE 1946-1967
FERRARI BROCHURES AND SALES LITERATURE 1968-1989
FERRARI GUIDE TO PERFORMANCE
FERRARI OPP, MAINTENANCE & SERVICE H/BOOKS 1948-1963
FERRARI OWNER'S HANDBOOK
FERRARI SERIAL NUMBERS PART I - ODD NUMBERS TO 21399
FERRARI SERIAL NUMBERS PART II - EVEN NUMBERS TO 1050
FERRARI SPYDER CALIFORNIA
FERRARI TUNING TIPS & MAINTENANCE TECHNIQUES
HENRY'S FABULOUS MODEL "A" FORD
HOW TO BUILD A FIBERGLASS CAR
HOW TO BUILD A RACING CAR
HOW TO RESTORE THE MODEL 'A' FORD
IF HEMINGWAY HAD WRITTEN A RACING NOVEL
JAGUAR E-TYPE 3.8 & 4.2 WSM
LE MANS 24 (THE BOOK THAT THE FILM WAS BASED ON)
MASERATI BROCHURES AND SALES LITERATURE
MASERATI OWNER'S HANDBOOK
METROPOLITAN FACTORY WSM
MGA & MGB OWNERS HANDBOOK & WSM
OBERT'S FIAT GUIDE
PERFORMANCE TUNING THE SUNBEAM TIGER
PORSCHE 356 1948-1965 WSM
PORSCHE 912 WSM
SOUPING THE VOLKSWAGEN
TRIUMPH TR2, TR3, TR4 1953-1965 WSM
VEDA ORR'S NEW REVISED HOT ROD PICTORIAL
VOLKSWAGEN TRANSPORTER, TRUCKS, STATION WAGONS WSM
VOLVO 1944-1968 ALL MODELS WSM

BROOKLANDS BOOKS & ROAD TEST PORTFOLIOS (RTP)

AC CARS 1904-2009
ALFA ROMEO 1920-1933 ROAD TEST PORTFOLIO
ALFA ROMEO 1934-1940 ROAD TEST PORTFOLIO
BRABHAM RALT HONDA THE RON TAURANAC STORY
BUGATTI TYPE 10 TO TYPE 40 ROAD TEST PORTFOLIO
BUGATTI TYPE 10 TO TYPE 251 ROAD TEST PORTFOLIO
BUGATTI TYPE 41 TO TYPE 55 ROAD TEST PORTFOLIO
BUGATTI TYPE 57 TO TYPE 251 ROAD TEST PORTFOLIO
DELAHAYE ROAD TEST PORTFOLIO
FERRARI ROAD CARS 1946-1956 ROAD TEST PORTFOLIO
FIAT 500 1936-1972 ROAD TEST PORTFOLIO
FIAT DINO ROAD TEST PORTFOLIO
HISPANO SUIZA ROAD TEST PORTFOLIO
HONDA ST1100/ST1300 PAN EUROPEAN 1990-2002 RTP
JAGUAR MK1 & MK2 ROAD TEST PORTFOLIO
LOTUS CORTINA ROAD TEST PORTFOLIO
MV AGUSTA F4 750 & 1000 1997-2007 ROAD TEST PORTFOLIO
TATRA CARS ROAD TEST PORTFOLIO

VELOCEPRESS MOTORCYCLE BOOKS & MANUALS

AJS SINGLES & TWINS 250cc THRU 1000cc 1932-1948 (BOOK OF)
AJS SINGLES 1955-65 350cc & 500cc (BOOK OF)
AJS SINGLES 1945-60 350cc & 500cc MODELS 16 & 18 (BOOK OF)
ARIEL 1939-1960 4 STROKE SINGLES (BOOK OF)
ARIEL LEADER & ARROW 1958-1964 (BOOK OF)
ARIEL MOTORCYCLES 1933-1951 WSM
ARIEL PREWAR MODELS 1932-1939 (BOOK OF)
BMW M/CYCLES R26 R27 (1956-1967) FACTORY WSM
BMW M/CYCLES R50 R50S R60 R69S (1955-1969) FACTORY WSM
BSA BANTAM (BOOK OF)
BSA ALL FOUR-STROKE SINGLES & V-TWINS 1936-1952 (BOOK OF)
BSA OHV & SV SINGLES - 250cc 1954-1970 (BOOK OF)
BSA OHV & SV SINGLES 1945-54 250-600cc (BOOK OF)
BSA OHV SINGLES 350 & 500cc 1955-1967 (BOOK OF)
BSA PRE-WAR MODELS TO 1939 (BOOK OF)
BSA TWINS 1948-1962 (BOOK OF)
BSA TWINS 1962-1969 (SECOND BOOK OF)
CATALOG OF BRITISH MOTORCYCLES (1951 MODELS)
DOUGLAS PRE-WAR ALL MODELS 1929-1939 (BOOK OF)
DOUGLAS POST-WAR ALL MODELS 1948-1957 FACTORY WSM
DUCATI 160cc, 250cc & 350cc OHC MODELS FACTORY WSM
HONDA 50 ALL MODELS UP TO 1970 INC MONKEY & TRAIL (BOOK OF)
HONDA 90 ALL MODELS UP TO 1966 (BOOK OF)
HONDA MOTORCYCLES 125-150 TWINS C/CS/CB/CA WSM
HONDA MOTORCYCLES 250-305 TWINS C/CS/CB WSM
HONDA MOTORCYCLES C100 SUPER CUB WSM
HONDA MOTORCYCLES C110 SPORT CUB 1962-1969 WSM
HONDA TWINS & SINGLES 50cc THRU 305cc 1960-1966 (BOOK OF)
HONDA TWINS ALL MODELS 125cc THRU 450cc UP TO 1968 (BOOK OF)
INDIAN PONYBIKE, BOY RACER & PAPOOSE ILL PARTS LIST & SALES LIT
LAMBRETTA ALL 125 & 150cc MODELS 1947-1957 (BOOK OF)
LAMBRETTA LI & TV MODELS 1957-1970 (SECOND BOOK OF)
MATCHLESS 350 & 500cc SINGLES 1945-1956 (BOOK OF)
MATCHLESS 350 & 500cc SINGLES 1955-1966 (BOOK OF)
NORTON 1938-1956 (BOOK OF)
NORTON DOMINATOR TWINS 1955-1965 (BOOK OF)
NORTON MODELS 19, 50 & ES2 1955-1963 (BOOK OF)
NORTON MOTORCYCLES 1957-1970 FACTORY WSM
NORTON PREWAR MODELS 1932-1939 (BOOK OF)
ROYAL ENFIELD SINGLES & V TWINS 1937-1953 (BOOK OF)
ROYAL ENFIELD 736cc INTERCEPTOR FACTORY WSM
ROYAL ENFIELD 250cc & 350cc SINGLES 1958-1966 (SECOND BOOK OF)
SUZUKI 50cc & 80cc UP TO 1966 (BOOK OF)
SUZUKI T10 1963-1967 FACTORY WSM
SUZUKI T20 & T200 1965-1969 FACTORY WSM
TRIUMPH PRE-WAR MOTORCYCLE 1935-1939 (BOOK OF)
TRIUMPH MOTORCYCLES 1937-1951 WSM
TRIUMPH MOTORCYCLES 1945-1955 FACTORY WSM
TRIUMPH TWINS 1956-1969 (BOOK OF)
VELOCETTE ALL SINGLES & TWINS 1925-1970 (BOOK OF)
VESPA 1951-1961 (BOOK OF)
VESPA 125 & 150cc & GS MODELS 1955-1963 (SECOND BOOK OF)
VESPA 90, 125 & 150cc 1963-1972 (THIRD BOOK OF)
VESPA GS & SS 1955-1968 (BOOK OF)
VINCENT MOTORCYCLES 1935-1955 WSM

**PLEASE VISIT OUR WEBSITE
www.VelocePress.com
FOR A DETAILED DESCRIPTION
OF ANY OF THESE TITLES**

Please check our website:

www.VelocePress.com

for a complete up-to-date list of available titles

www.ingramcontent.com/pod-product-compliance
Lightning Source LLC
Chambersburg PA
CBHW070549170426
43201CB00012B/1781